# Preventing War
# in the Nuclear Age

# Preventing War in the Nuclear Age

*Dietrich Fischer*

Rowman & Allanheld
PUBLISHERS

Croom Helm
LONDON & CANBERRA

ROWMAN & ALLANHELD

Published in the United States of America in 1984
by Rowman & Allanheld, Publishers
(A division of Littlefield, Adams & Company)
81 Adams Drive, Totowa, New Jersey 07512

**Library of Congress Cataloging in Publication Data**

Fischer, Dietrich, 1941–
  Preventing war in the nuclear age.

  Bibliography: p.
  Includes index.
  1. Atomic weapons and disarmament.   I. Title.
JX1974.7.F54   1984        327.1′72        83-24435
ISBN 0-8476-7342-1
ISBN 0-8476-7343-X (pbk.)


British Library Cataloguing in Publication Data

Fischer, Dietrich
  Preventing war in the nuclear age.
  1. Peace, Arms and Armor
  I. Title
  327.  1-72     JX1952

ISBN 0–7099–1053–3


84  85  86  /  10  9  8  7  6  5  4  3  2  1
Printed in the United States of America

*This book is dedicated to our children, Albert, Heidi and Max, and to their sisters and brothers around the earth.*

# Contents

# Tables and Figures

*Figures*

# Acknowledgments

I am deeply grateful to Johan Galtung, who introduced me to the field of peace research. Without our many inspiring discussions, this book would not have been written. I also appreciate the insights and encouragement I received from William D. Angel, William J. Baumol, Kenneth E. Boulding, Edna Chun, Gustav Däniker, Faye Duchin, Richard A. Falk, Michael Goldberg, Cathérine Guichert, Harry B. Hollins, Robert Holt, Helge Hveem, Mireille Jacquet, Robert C. Johansen, Donald L. Livingston, Robert H. Manley, Saul Mendlovitz, Jan Øberg, Dorothy Ortner, Hans Ott, Roy Preiswerk, Anatol Rapoport, Jinx Roosevelt, Sherle Schwenninger, Mark Sommer, Jaroslav B. Tušek, Bernard M. Wasow, Maureen Wira, from several additional members of the New York University Seminar on Nuclear War and Its Prevention and of the World Policy Institute, and from many others. Of course, I alone am responsible for the views expressed. It was a great pleasure to cooperate with my editors, Spencer Carr and Janet S. Johnston. I am grateful to Bonnie Behrman, Nancy Fernandez, Mary Mateja, and Brenda Sutton for their excellent help in typing the manuscript. Special thanks go to my wife, Philomena, and our children for their constant, loving support.

# Introduction

Modern science and technology have given us unprecedented power, for good or destructive ends. New means of transportation and communication have made it possible for people around the earth to know each other better. New discoveries in medicine can lead to improved health care. New production technologies could provide us with the technical capability to satisfy everyone's basic human needs, even though we may lack the wisdom how to go about it. We have vastly increased our understanding of nature, from the structure of the universe to the forces inside the atom. But the invention of means of mass destruction, particularly nuclear weapons, has also provided us with the capability to destroy ourselves.

The growing awareness of the dangers of a nuclear holocaust has led to a renewed search for ways to achieve durable peace. This book seeks to outline a path that can lead us from the dangerous situation of the present to a secure world, through a series of specific, feasible measures.

While a number of recently published books have given impressive descriptions of the *danger* of nuclear war, the main emphasis here is on the exploration of *solutions* to the problem. Jonathan Schell (1982, p. 219) points out that he has concentrated on stating the problem, not on describing a solution. He writes, "I have not sought to define a political solution to the nuclear predicament . . . to work out the practical steps by which mankind . . . can reorganize its political life. I have left to others those . . . urgent tasks." The present book seeks to address that challenge.

One of this book's main purposes is to dispel some widespread, long-held misconceptions about peace and security. The quest for security is by no means a "zero-sum game," a situation in which one side's gains are by necessity the other side's losses. To be secure, it is not necessary to make potential opponents less secure. In fact, we cannot be completely secure as long as others feel threatened by us, for they will naturally try to find ways and means to eliminate that threat. It is in our own interest that we recognize and respect the legitimate goals of others to be secure also.

It is not the aim of this book to issue any moral prescriptions. Since the objective interest of the potential victims of war, particularly of nuclear war, is to avoid it, the book simply seeks to explore concrete ways in which this goal can be achieved.

The title needs some explanation. Some have stressed that war is not comparable to a natural disaster, like a flood, which happens spontaneously. Unless people make war, there is no war. So what is there to "prevent"? Why not simply avoid making war? The problem is that those who make war and those who want to prevent it are usually not the same. This book is not addressed to those who initiate war, but to its potential victims, those who are faced with the threat of war, caused by others, and who want to find ways to prevent it. While it would be easier for the initiators of war to prevent it, those who would suffer from aggression have a greater motivation.

I have no illusion that all national leaders want to prevent war. On the contrary, many want to increase their power and influence and are willing to resort to war if that seems to advance their goals. But the use of violence is counterproductive in the long run, because it helps make enemies rather than friends. Also, in the nuclear age where even small wars carry a risk of escalation, it is becoming too dangerous to use war to "pursue politics with other means." Because of the danger that a conventional war could escalate into a nuclear war (and also because of the suffering inflicted on the people involved), this book is also concerned with methods to prevent conventional wars.

This book is not written for specialists, but for the growing number of people who are becoming concerned with the issues of war, peace, and national security, which may have such a fateful impact on all our lives. Many of us, with good reason, are no longer satisfied to leave these issues only to the "experts" who have led us into the present situation. A growing number of citizens have begun to examine critically the defense policies of their governments, to see whether these policies are compatible with the usually stated purposes of keeping peace, or whether they may in fact make war more likely. To these concerned citizens everywhere this book is addressed.

The aim of this book may appear ambitious, yet it is, in a sense, rather limited: it will not focus primarily on justice or even peace, but simply on the prevention of war. Most of the remarks will in fact be limited to international armed conflicts and their prevention, even though in most of the world, through most of history, the domestic role of arms has perhaps been more important. Some governments have used arms to stay in power, or to seize power. While this issue will also be touched upon, the main focus is on the prevention of wars between states.

*Peace* is much more than the mere absence of war: it implies active, mutually beneficial cooperation. I address only the problem of *direct violence* (people being killed in wars), and not the broader issue of *structural violence* (people dying from hunger or preventable diseases, as a consequence of inequality and injustice) (Galtung 1975). In the past, structural violence has taken many more lives than direct violence. For example, Köhler and Alcock (1976) have estimated that if per capita income had been equally distributed across the nations of the world, 14 million deaths could have been avoided in 1965 (a conservative estimate of structural violence). By comparison, about 115,000 people were killed in all international and civil conflicts during the same year, less than 1 percent of those who died from structural violence. Nevertheless, with the possibility of a nuclear holocaust, the prevention of direct violence assumes new urgency.

Even a limited discussion of the prevention of war cannot totally ignore the issue of *justice,* in the absence of which the prevention of war becomes much more difficult. People who feel that they suffer from grave injustices and unbearable conditions are more likely to risk war to seek change than are people satisfied with their current situation.

The absence of war is also a narrower concept than *security*.

Security should be seen as encompassing protection against all threats to human life, not only from war, but also from natural disasters, destruction of the environment, poverty, and so on (Bay 1982). The need for a joint human effort to deal with global problems, such as the transition to renewable resources or the prevention of threats to the earth's climate, can perhaps help states overcome the differences over which they now fight wars. But these broader, though urgent, issues cannot all be addressed adequately in one book.

The absence of war should, however, not be understood too narrowly either. By the absence of war, I also include the absence of coercion. The choice is not only between the two alternatives of having to fight a war or submitting to aggression: life in a concentration camp is not what is meant by absence of war. Peace with freedom is attainable, and ways to achieve it will be explored.

This book will discuss nuclear deterrence and the distinction between first-strike and second-strike weapons, the distinction between conventional offensive and defensive arms, nonmilitary defense strategies, and methods of conflict resolution. Much attention will be devoted to short-term measures that can be taken immediately—i.e., the steps we can take to prevent war while we still live in a state of mutual distrust and fear. Even in our "Machiavellian world" (a term used by Lifton and Falk 1982) we can work toward a future world whose inhabitants, while maintaining their loyalty to their own families, peer groups, and nation-states, will also have gained a sense of identification with humanity as a whole.

To guarantee against a nuclear holocaust, which could lead to human extinction, we must abolish war as a human institution, as slavery in the United States was abolished in the 19th century. Even complete nuclear disarmament would be insufficient for that purpose. If nations continued to settle conflicts through war, the danger would remain that nuclear weapons might again be built in an attempt to defeat an enemy. Having been discovered, the secret of making these weapons cannot be eradicated, as long as humankind exists. Schell (1982, p. 103) notes with irony that "the only means in sight for getting rid of the knowledge of how to destroy ourselves would be to do just that—in effect, to remove the knowledge by removing the knower."

Ultimately, it will be necessary to go beyond the present world system, in which the leaders of sovereign nation-states can use whatever forms of violence they consider expedient, with little effective international control to prevent aggression. Within countries, such a primitive state of anarchy has largely been overcome. Most people have long ago realized that it is in their own interest to rely on a court system, backed up by a police force, to obtain justice, instead of carrying guns and taking justice into their own hands. The nations of the earth need to build a similar legal framework at the global level. This does not require that nation-states be abolished. It only means that it would be in their common interest to develop mechanisms for resolving conflicts in ways other than through war. The United Nations charter formally prohibits the use of armed force except for purposes of legitimate self-defense, but implementation has lagged behind. A more-effective global legal order for the prevention of war is highly desirable. A war between any two nations could then become as unthinkable as a war today between New York and South Carolina, between France and Germany, or between the United States and Japan. These states have achieved lasting good relations today, as have many other countries with a past history of wars between each other. There is no convincing reason why this should not be possible on a global scale, given sustained efforts and sufficient time. But many things can and should be done even before that goal is reached.

If we were to wait for the establishment of a global body with the power to enforce international law in order to prevent a nuclear holocaust, the hopes for human survival might be slim. That would make the task unnecessarily difficult. While not giving up that goal, we must also take many smaller, more easily feasible steps that can buy us time.

To stress this point, I would like to use the following analogy. Suppose there is a leak in a gas pipe, and we see someone lighting a match. The first thing we will want to do is to blow out the match, even though we know full well that this alone cannot give us permanent protection against an explosion. It will also be necessary, as soon as possible, to repair the leak. Even better, in the long run, is to shift to a safer heating source so that a gas leak can never recur. But we would certainly not wait until we have rebuilt the heating system before we seek to prevent an explosion; nor would we think that blowing out the match is all that needs to be done.

With respect to the threat of a nuclear holocaust, we are in a similar situation: the catastrophe has not yet occurred, but the international situation is highly volatile. If precautions are not taken, many local conflicts could potentially escalate into a world war and unleash a nuclear exchange.

A relatively quick and simple measure to reduce the threat of nuclear war is a policy of no first use of nuclear weapons. Nothing puts more pressure on an opponent to use his nuclear arsenal during a grave crisis than the fear that he might suffer a nuclear surprise attack. If we can convince him that we will not use our nuclear weapons first, but that if he did, he would face the prospect of retaliation, this is a strong deterrent against the use of nuclear weapons. But if we threaten to use our nuclear weapons first, deterrence is undermined. Of course, more is needed than a mere verbal promise, or even a signed agreement, to make our intentions credible; we would not want to base our security on an opponent's promise what he would or would not do, but on what he *could* do. For the same reason, in our self-interest, we better prove our intentions not to attack first by adjusting our own capabilities accordingly. Nuclear forces must be restructured so that they can survive a surprise attack, but be incapable of carrying out a disarming first strike. What we *cannot* do, we certainly will not do. Any nuclear nation can shift independently to a policy of no first use, without having to wait for the uncertain outcome of long and difficult negotiations. By adopting such a measure, the nation does not take an increased risk, but reduce the risk of nuclear war for everyone. Although there is no strategy that is entirely free from any risk, we can at least *reduce* the risk of nuclear war.

It is clear that a policy of no first use of nuclear arms gives only tenuous protection against the sudden outbreak of a nuclear holocaust. A breach any place, a sudden spark, could make that policy collapse and bring the whole stockpile of nuclear weapons to explosion. But even though this measure is not sufficient, it should be taken nevertheless. Blowing out the match is not sufficient, but should we therefore not blow it out?

A no-first-use policy that still relies on deterrence cannot prevent nuclear war on a lasting basis. It is, in John F. Kennedy's words, comparable to a Damocles sword hanging constantly over all our heads by the thinnest of threads. But it is less dangerous than threatening a first strike. Even though it represents only a small step away from the brink, it is better than a small step over the brink.

People who strive for social change sometimes argue that it is necessary for the situation to get worse in the short run—to shake people up—so it can improve in the longer run. In other cases, this may be true. But with the threat of nuclear holocaust, we cannot afford to take that risk. Any step to defuse the danger, no matter how modest, should be taken, so that we will have an opportunity to bring about more-fundamental long-term changes that can eliminate war. Otherwise there may be no one left to be shaken up.

There is an intense debate between those who search for *national security* through more armament and those who advocate disarmament, even unilateral, to achieve *peace*. Listening to both sides, one could almost get the impression that a choice must be made between either peace or security. But in the nuclear age, peace and security are inseparable. Neither unilateral armament nor unilateral disarmament can bring security and peace. Increased armament stimulates an arms race, bringing greater insecurity to both sides. Unilateral disarmament, beyond a certain point, makes a country vulnerable and therefore an easy target for aggression.

Advocating more offensive arms for defense is like calling for break-in tools to prevent burglary—through the threat of retaliation. Calling for a reduction in defensive arms to promote peace is like prohibiting locks—to avoid offering provocation to a burglar.

There is a more-promising alternative, *transarmament*, a shift from offensive to defensive arms. Of course, our long-term goal must be complete disarmament. But disarmament is risk-free only if it is *mutual*; therefore, it depends on complicated negotiations that can easily stall over conflicting interests. Trans-armament can be undertaken by any country alone, with no increase in the risk to its security. On the contrary, transarmament can contribute to greater security for all because it reduces the risk of war.

This book will concentrate on measures that any country can undertake on its own, without having to wait for agreement on reciprocal steps from other countries. (As Kenneth Boulding once pointed out, agreement is a scarce resource—whenever we can do without it, this is preferable.) It has been argued that "unilateral" measures are not feasible politically, since the public is not ready to accept them. Yet countries have frequently built up arms unilaterally. No country ever insisted that a potential enemy arm itself first or simultaneously, as a condition for its own arms buildup. It is clear that most people are not willing to accept such measures as unilateral disarmament, which they feel would endanger their own security. But independent measures that *increase* a country's own security, by reducing the danger of war, even if these measures also increase the security of others, should be politically feasible, once fully understood. These are the types of independent measures advocated here.

To prevent war, it is not sufficient to make war unattractive for a potential aggressor. It is equally important to make peace as attractive as possible. If we make the status quo unbearable for a potential opponent, his incentive to keep peace is weakened. A broad range of nonmilitary measures aimed at making peace more attractive and war less rewarding will be discussed. While such measures alone may not constitute a sufficiently strong defense in today's highly militarized world, they can certainly *add* to a country's security without threatening the security of others. We do not feel threatened if other countries try to make peace as attractive for us as possible.

Defense is only a last resort to dissuade war when efforts at reaching agreement have failed. Much greater emphasis should be placed on the early discovery and elimination of potential sources of conflict, before they have reached an acute stage. To use an analogy from medicine, the primary emphasis should be on the *prevention* of disease and cure should become necessary only if prevention has failed. Similarly, it is preferable to seek to resolve potential conflicts peacefully, at an early stage. The more we allow tensions to build up, the more difficult it becomes to take corrective actions.

To conclude negotiations successfully, imaginative compromise solutions that can offer something attractive to *both sides* must be sought. It is unlikely that a negotiating partner would agree to a proposal by which he or she would lose something. If we think *only* of our own interests, we tend to fail to reach agreement and end up hurting ourselves.

As many people as possible should participate actively in the discussion about how to prevent wars in general, and nuclear war in particular. The more minds focus on a problem, the more likely is it that someone will produce some good ideas. The more we discuss with each other, learn from each other, and combine our knowledge, the more effective we can be. But good ideas are useless, unless we act and implement them. The more we work together, the stronger we are.

Even if we are in no way responsible for the danger of nuclear war, we should not remain passive and expect that those we consider "responsible" for our current problems should solve them. As Roger Fisher (1981) has pointed out, the concept of *responsibility* should be broadened to include not only those people who have caused a problem and are to blame for it, but all those who can do something toward its remedy. To illustrate this point, he describes an incident he experienced during World War II. His air force unit was assigned to test a plane with a new engine. The test pilot, to frighten the other crew members, turned off all the engines for a moment, putting the plane into a dive. When he wanted to restart the engines, he realized he needed electricity, which required that at least one engine be running. Although this was "his" problem in a strict sense, it affected everyone on the plane. Fortunately, a technician who was not "responsible" for the problem, in the narrow sense, remembered an emergency generator on board and used it to restart the engines, just in time to prevent a crash. With regard to the threat of nuclear war, we are all "passengers on spaceship earth" (to use Buckminster Fuller's expression), in a similar predicament to the passengers on Fisher's airplane. Like the technician who helped restart the engines, we must try to help, even if we have not caused the problem.

I do not claim to have any final answers to these important

problems, but I hope to add some new viewpoints to the debate. The approaches to the prevention of war that I have listed here are not merely my own invention. What I have attempted is to bring together into a systematic, logical framework ideas that have evolved over a long time, from many sources, through theoretical reasoning and practical experience. Many of my historical examples are from Switzerland, the country with which I am most familiar, since I was born and raised there. I am sure that many equally pertinent examples can be found in other countries. The ideas presented here are not wild imagination or wishful thinking, but have proved successful where they have been applied. Yet we hear far more about cases where these principles have been violated, where wars are being fought, because this is more sensational.

If some progress is to be made in dealing with these emotionally charged issues, it is important not to fall into the trap of employing simplistic slogans or of painting a picture only in black and white. If we want to reach others, we must make an effort to understand their concerns and interests, their assumptions and their way of reasoning. Otherwise we cannot expect them to listen to our views either.

Peace research has been accused of not being entirely value-free. There is no point in denying this; it does have a certain bias in favor of peace. Yet, as Johan Galtung has noted, it does not stand alone in this respect. It shares value-orientation with other normative sciences, for example medicine, which has a certain bias in favor of health.

We all share an enormous responsibility to help avoid human extinction. The evolution of life on earth, from the first simple single-cell organisms to intelligent forms of life, has taken more than 3 billion years. We have no confirmation that intelligent life exists anywhere else in the universe. Some point out that human extinction need not be the end of everything; the dinosaurs died out about 65 million years ago, yet intelligent life developed later in the form of human beings. If we became extinct, some 65 million years later other intelligent beings might emerge on earth, perhaps descendants of certain insects. But I agree with Linus Pauling, who once said that he likes human beings and would not want them to disappear.

# 1  The Danger We Face

The discovery of nuclear arms has given enormous destructive potential to humankind. For the first time we possess, or are approaching, the capability to end all human life.

No attempt is made here to describe adequately the dangers of nuclear war; most of us will have heard about those dangers many times. Nevertheless, it is necessary to be clear about the magnitude of potential destruction. For this reason I will begin by repeating briefly some of the most important figures that are now common knowledge. I will also list a number of possible reasons why a nuclear war might break out.

The world stockpile of nuclear arms today includes about 50,000 warheads with a combined explosive power of roughly 20,000 million tons of TNT, or 1,600,000 times the power of the bomb dropped on Hiroshima. That bomb alone killed an estimated 130,000 people. Yet it was small compared to modern hydrogen bombs. A large hydrogen bomb of 20 megatons has over 1000 times the explosive power of the Hiroshima bomb, which had about 12.5 kilotons. The Hiroshima bomb itself had about 1000 times the explosive power of a large conventional bomb (up to ten tons of TNT). This means that a modern hydrogen bomb compares to the Hiroshima bomb like that bomb to a conventional bomb. A single large hydrogen bomb has more explosive power than all the bombs dropped during World War II, about 2 megatons. A single 20-megaton bomb dropped on New York City could cause more than 20 million deaths, if winds carried the radioactive fallout into populated areas. Three hundred one-megaton bombs, about 3 percent of the Soviet Union's arsenal, would be sufficient to kill the 60 percent of the United States population that live in urban areas, and a similar ratio applies to Soviet cities. Most European countries have a higher population density and could be annihilated by a fraction of 1 percent of the superpowers' arsenals.

The greatest danger to human survival, however, does not stem from direct killing through blast, heat, and radioactive fallout. Potentially even more serious are the threats to the life-sustaining environment. Fred Iklé, now U.S. Under-Secretary of Defense, has stated that severe reduction of the ozone layer through nuclear explosions could "shatter the ecological structure that permits man to remain alive on this planet" (quoted in Schell 1982, p. 79). A group of scientists led by astronomer Carl Sagan have discovered, more or less by coincidence, a phenomenon they call "nuclear winter." When the U.S. spacecraft Mariner 9 orbited Mars in 1971, it observed a global dust storm that had filtered out sunlight and had led to a cooling of the surface of Mars. The scientists developed a computer model of the Martian atmosphere and found that the observed temperatures corresponded to what they expected. They applied a similar model to study the climatic effects of a nuclear war on earth and found devastating results. The dust hurled into the atmosphere by ground explosions and the smoke from burning cities and forests would envelope the earth into a dense, dark cloud for months. It would absorb most sunlight and prevent it from reaching the ground. The earth surface would freeze on all continents. Most plants would no longer receive enough sunlight for photosynthesis, the basis of all life. Any human survivors would probably die from starvation. Such effects were predicted by the model even for relatively "limited" nuclear wars with a total explosive power of 100 megatons, about 1 percent of the superpowers' arsenals (Sagan 1983).

New and ever-more serious effects of nuclear explosions have been discovered gradually over the years, and further consequences may still be unknown. A report by the Office of Technology Assessment (1979) has concluded that the most important thing we know about nuclear war is that we don't know enough to make any confident judgments. Complex systems can be extremely vulnerable. Schell (p. 23) points out that "a machine may break down if one small part is removed, and a person may die if a single artery is blocked." The earth's ecosystem is a complex, interdependent system, about which we know far too little to predict exactly what it would take to make it collapse. Some argue that the danger posed by nuclear weapons to human survival has been exaggerated. Maybe it has—but the only way to find out for certain would be to try it out.

The argument that today's quantity of nuclear weapons is not sufficient to end all human life offers little comfort. If the proliferation of nuclear arms continues at its present rate, we will soon reach the point where extinction is possible. Furthermore, the debate whether a nuclear holocaust would definitely lead to human extinction is really beside the point. If the prospect of hundreds of millions of people killed is not enough to arouse our concern, what will?

Helen Caldicott (1981), pediatrician and cofounder of Physicians for Social Responsibility, has pointed out, like many others, that there could be no meaningful medical response to a nuclear war. Any country's peace-time capacity to treat burns and other injuries would be far exceeded by even a single nuclear explosion. Furthermore, most hospitals, which are concentrated in metropolitan areas, would be destroyed, and most doctors would be killed. Of those who survived the initial blast and fire of a nuclear explosion, many would die slowly from burns or radiation sickness, without medical attention or even pain-killers. Others would die from lack of food and drinking water, or from exposure to cold. Those who survived would suffer the agony of having lost many of their loved ones. Life after a nuclear war has been depicted vividly in the television film "The Day After". Yet, as was explained at the end of the film, the real effects would most likely be far worse than even those shown. The earth's environment might be damaged to such an extent that it could no longer sustain human life. Therefore, as with diseases for which there is no feasible cure, the only possible medical response to nuclear war is its prevention.

If we cannot prevent nuclear war, our other preoccupations with inflation, unemployment, crime, energy, etc., become meaningless. Even the urgent problem of hunger, which is fatal for millions, does not threaten the survival of the human race as such. Some other disasters such as climatic changes due to the accumulation of carbon dioxide in the atmosphere, or a depletion of the ozone layer resulting from certain industrial pollutants, could possibly mean an end to human life, but we have some time to work out their solution—decades, perhaps even a few centuries. A nuclear holocaust, on the other hand, could occur suddenly.

Avoiding nuclear war must become our overriding priority. We must not allow a linkage to other issues let us slide into nuclear war. Andrei Sakharov, the Soviet nuclear physicist and outspoken dissident, warned the West against linking nuclear disarmament negotiations to the Soviet Union's treatment of its dissidents, since—as he put it—a nuclear holocaust would not further the cause of Soviet dissidents.

Since there is no prospect of any gain from unleashing a nuclear war, the question naturally arises why such a war might break out at all. The remainder of this chapter seeks to shed some light on this.

*Potential Causes of Nuclear War*

War has always been a "negative-sum game," in the sense that the losses of the loser always exceeded any possible gains by the victor, because of the overall destruction involved. But in conventional wars, there have often been "winners," who gained some advantage that outweighed their own losses. Bueno de Mesquita has assembled strong empirical evidence to show that a necessary (although not sufficient) condition for a country's leaders to start a war was their expectation of winning it, because the power of their own country and its allies exceeded the power of their opponent and his allies. He analyzed 58 interstate wars since 1816 and found that 42, or nearly three-quarters, were won by the side that had initiated combat (Bueno de Mesquita 1981, p. 22). It is plausible that national decisionmakers would not begin a war if they expected to lose it. The relatively few exceptions where the initiator did lose may be assumed to be cases of miscalculation, where the initiator overestimated his or her own country's offensive power, or counted on allies who failed to provide support, or underestimated the defense capability of the opponent and his allies.

Of course, in the great majority of cases where a country could have expected to win a war, no war took place at all. Not every leader started a war each time he or she expected some gain. Restraint, perhaps through enlightened long-term self-interest (the insight that a war now, even if won, might lead to revenge in the future) has usually prevailed. The expectation of winning was only a necessary, not a sufficient, condition for initiating a war.

In a war between two countries possessing nuclear arms, it is meaningless to speak of a winner. Even if one side suffered greater losses than the other side, both would be so devastated that neither side would gain anything. Some believe that for this reason the invention of nuclear weapons may have improved the chances for world peace. They point out that despite great international tensions, a third world war has been avoided since 1945. But even if the likelihood of a world war may have decreased, if such a war should break out, it would be so much more disastrous than a conventional war that on balance our situation has not improved at all.

Although one of the traditional reasons for starting a war, the expectation of some territorial or political gain, has essentially disappeared for nuclear war, a number of reasons for the possible outbreak of such a war still exist. It could start (a) because of a human or technical error, (b) because of insanity, (c) because of escalation of a conventional war or other forms of miscalculation of an opponent's intentions, or (d) through the launching of a preemptive first strike in the hope of reducing losses from an anticipated nuclear attack by an opponent. (Each of these four possibilities will be discussed here in some more detail.) A number of hypothetical scenarios of how a nuclear war might start have also been described by Ground Zero (1982), a nonpartisan educational organization headed by former U.S. National Security Council member Roger Molander.

*Accident*

False alarms indicating a potential Soviet nuclear attack on the United States have been surprisingly frequent. Over an 18-month period from 1 January 1979 to 30 June 1980, no less

than 3804 such alarms were generated by the NORAD computerized warning system (*New York Times*, 29 October 1980). So
far, all of these alarms could be identified as errors in time. Most
were routinely recognized as false warnings, caused, for example, by missile test firings, forest fires, or even a flock of geese.
But four of them were serious enough that nuclear bomber and
missile units were put on an increased state of alert. One of
these false warnings occured when a technician inadvertently
inserted a training tape, simulating a nuclear attack, into the live
warning system. Other errors resulted from computer malfunctions.

The Reagan administration plans to improve the reliability of
the NORAD system, so that "the President could order a retaliatory nuclear strike against the Soviet Union, without risking an
accidental nuclear war, after ascertaining that Soviet missiles are
definitely heading toward the United States" (*New York Times*,
12 October 1981). The firing of missiles in retaliation when radar
signals indicate that an enemy attack appears to be under way is
called "launch on warning." But how could anyone trust the
absolute reliability of such a complex computerized system that
can never be fully tested in the real world? If that system were to
fail, it would not only threaten the security of the Soviet Union,
but also that of the United States.

In a June 1980 article in the *Washington Post* entitled "The
Growing Risk of War by Accident," Iklé wrote,

> the more we rely on launch on warnings (or, for that matter, the
> more the Soviets do) the greater the risk of accidental nuclear
> war. . . . The crux of the matter is that the more important it
> becomes to launch on warning, the more dangerous it will be.
> The tightening noose around our neck is the requirement for
> speed. The more certain one wants to be that our missile forces
> (or Soviet missile forces) could be launched within minutes and
> under all circumstances, the more one has to practice the system
> and to loosen the safeguards [quoted in Deutsch 1983, p. 18].

So far the flight time of intercontinental missiles has been
about 30 minutes, and the time left to detect an error in the
warning system about 25 minutes. But as McGeorge Bundy
(1981), the National Security Adviser to Presidents Kennedy
and Johnson, has stressed, the American Pershing II missiles,

which are now being stationed in Western Europe after the negotiations in Geneva on theater nuclear forces failed to produce results by fall 1983, will be able to reach Moscow in only about five minutes. Any target these missiles can reach can also be reached by existing intercontinental missiles, except that it takes somewhat longer. But speed is not desirable in this case. The short flight time of the Pershing II will leave the Soviets very little time to identify a potential false alarm as an error. *Because of the possibility of error, these new missiles may actually reduce the security of the West, instead of strengthening it.* Similarly, Soviet medium-range missiles aimed at Western Europe reduce, rather than increase, Soviet security, by making a nuclear war more likely. Robert Johansen of the World Policy Institute has pointed out that since the Pershing II is specifically designed to destroy Warsaw pact command centers during a war, this puts pressure on Moscow to delegate authority over nuclear weapons to lower echelons. But such a move would increase the possibilities for error.

*Insanity*

A nuclear war might also occur if a national decisionmaker temporarily lost his senses. Especially with a further proliferation of nuclear arms, that danger will increase. Insane leaders are not unknown in history. It may not even be necessary that a national leader act irrationally for a nuclear weapon to be fired, possibly leading to further exchanges. Thousands of soldiers in nuclear weapons units have had to be transferred because of drug and family problems. Mentally disturbed individuals have often killed innocent bystanders before taking their own lives or being overwhelmed. In the past, their destructive power has been limited. But a single Polaris submarine, which carries 16 missiles with 10 nuclear warheads each, could destroy 160 cities. Of course, special precautions are taken in the case of nuclear weapons to prevent their unauthorized use. At least two people must press a key simultaneously to fire a missile. But with the large and dispersed stockpile of nuclear warheads, the uneasy question remains as to how long it will take before one of them is fired by accident. Accidents usually occur in ways that have not been foreseen.

It is also conceivable that a group of terrorists could construct or steal a nuclear weapon and use it. A misunderstanding about the origin of the weapon could then lead to misdirected retaliation, followed by further escalation.

## Escalation

A nuclear war could also start out of miscalculation. For example, a conventional war could escalate into a nuclear war because a nation's leaders misjudged the determination of an opponent to resort to nuclear arms rather than to admit defeat. If one side should transgress the limits of tolerance of the other, the opponent might turn to the use of nuclear weapons. An all-out exchange could then easily follow, because it is hard to see how one side would capitulate while still possessing nuclear arms.

## Preemptive Strike

Another great danger is the possibility that one side might feel forced to launch a preemptive first strike, out of fear that otherwise it would itself be victim of a first strike. Colin Gray, an arms control adviser to the Reagan administration, and Keith Payne (1980) argue that "an intelligent U.S. offensive strategy, wedded to homeland defenses, should reduce U.S. casualties to approximately 20 million" and that "a combination of counterforce offensive targeting, civil defense, and ballistic missile and air defense should hold U.S. casualties down to a level compatible with national survival and recovery." They criticize what they call the "Armageddon syndrome" amounting "to the belief that because the United States could lose as many as 20 million people, it should not save the 80 million or more who otherwise would be at risk." A counterforce strategy, however, aimed at destroying the opponent's missiles before they can leave their silos, is very dangerous and actually increases the likelihood of the outbreak of a nuclear war. In a moment of great tension, if the Soviet leaders believed that the United States might launch its missiles first in an offensive counterforce strike, this would tempt them to launch their missiles before they were destroyed.

They might seek to eliminate as many U.S. missiles as possible so as to reduce their own anticipated losses—according to a calculation similar to that proposed by Gray and Payne (1980). Hence the adoption of a counterforce strategy reduces rather than increases one's security.

The temptation to launch a preemptive first strike is not a purely hypothetical possibility. A typical example of such a situation, fortunately involving only conventional arms, was the outbreak of the Middle East war in 1967 (see Quester 1977). Both Israel and Egypt had vulnerable bomber fleets on open desert airfields. Each side knew that whoever initiated the first strike could easily bomb and destroy the hostile planes on the ground, thereby gaining air superiority. Whoever hesitated would lose the battle for the skies. In this situation, Israel felt compelled, when war appeared imminent, to destroy most of the Egyptian air force on the ground before it could be used against Israel. It cannot be entirely excluded that such considerations could also lead to the outbreak of a nuclear war, if one or both sides adopted a counterforce strategy.

The main danger, therefore, is not that a nuclear war might start because either side expects to "win" anything, but the more likely and more serious possibility that, during a crisis, one side might launch a preemptive strike against the other side's nuclear forces in an attempt to reduce losses from an anticipated impending attack. Fallows (1981, p. 147) has raised questions about that danger, by stressing the great uncertainties inherent in carrying out a first strike. "The most important questions about how the weapons work cannot be conclusively answered until they are fired" and "no Soviet or American leader who is thinking 'rationally' . . . is likely to risk firing the weapons, because the costs of miscalculation are so high." The risks involved in any first strike are certainly enormous. But the problem is that a leader might misperceive the risks of *not* firing the weapons as equally grave, if he thought an attack were imminent. Psychologist Morton Deutsch writes:

> The abstract character of nuclear war scenarios appeals to the talented, imaginative gamesmen who are the leading strategic analysts in the national security establishments of the U.S. and the USSR. It is an exciting, competitive game calling for the use of

inventive thought, cool, analytic ability, and emotional tough-
ness. It has little of the messiness of war games involving real soldiers, battlefield commanders, rain, mud, and pestilence. It is
basically an abstract, impersonal, computerized game ivolving
nuclear weapons with strategists on each side trying to outsmart
the other.

To play the game, each side has to make assumptions about
how its own weapons (as well as how its command, control, and
communication systems) will operate in various hypothetical
future nuclear war scenarios as well as how the other side's will
operate. There is, of course, very little basis in actual experience
for making accurate, reliable, or valid assumptions about these
matters, since none of these weapons or systems has been tested
or employed in circumstances even remotely resembling the situation of any imaginable nuclear war. However, for the nuclear
game to be played and for scenarios to be developed, assumptions about these matters have to be made. Once these assumptions have been made and have, by consensus, been accepted
within one side's strategic group, they become psychologically
"real" and are treated as "hard facts" no matter how dubious their
grounding in actual realities [Deutsch 1983, p. 20].

Some voices even advocate fighting a nuclear war "for
identified political purposes" (Gray and Payne 1980). They claim
that "nuclear war is unlikely to be an essentially meaningless,
terminal event. Instead it is likely to be waged to coerce the
Soviet Union to give up some recent gain" (p. 26). "Victory or
defeat in nuclear war is possible, and such a war may have to be
waged to that point" (p. 20). Such statements are frightening.
But it is difficult to believe that any rational leader would deliberately initiate a nuclear war, knowing that his country would
lose tens of millions of lives, only for the sadistic satisfaction that
the "enemy" would lose even more. The terms "victory,"
"gaining an advantage," "prevailing," ending a war on "favorable" terms all lose their meaning for a nuclear holocaust. Both
sides would be far worse off than if no war occurred. As Schell
says (p. 73), "those who speak of 'winning' a nuclear 'war' . . .
are living in a past that has been swept away forever by nuclear
arms."

Unless we can eliminate the risk of nuclear war fairly soon,
our prospects are dim. Kenneth Boulding, economist and peace

researcher, once said that anything that is possible, no matter how unlikely, will happen—if we wait long enough. A probability calculation shows that if we assume a constant 2 percent chance of a nuclear war per year, the probability that there will be a nuclear war within 50 years is 64 percent, within 100 years 87 percent, within 200 years 98 percent, within 500 years 99.99 percent, and within 1000 years a virtual certainty.

There is no defensible purpose for which to wage nuclear war. Any values we may find worth defending, whether they be freedom, justice, or truth, assume the existence of human beings who can appreciate these values. None of our goals justifies risking human extinction in order to achieve it.

Certainly, by far the vast majority of people do not want a nuclear holocaust. Unfortunately, a very small minority can bring it about. In the past, risk-takers endangered mainly themselves. Now, a small group of people determined to take a risk for their own objectives can kill millions of human beings, and possibly all future generations.

# 2 Approaches to the Prevention of War

Practically all people desire peace, or at least claim they do. But opinions diverge as to how peace is best achieved. I will discuss some traditionally practiced or proposed approaches to the prevention of war (seeking military superiority, unilateral disarmament, or disarmament negotiations) and point out some of their inherent difficulties. Then I will briefly outline a number of alternative methods that may hold more promise of success and analyze them in greater detail in the remainder of the book.

## Past Difficulties

Many, in the East as well as in the West, are honestly convinced that the best guarantee for peace is absolute military superiority (of their own side, of course). But unless the other side accepts military inferiority, which is a doubtful assumption, this position inevitably leads to an arms race, which has brought us into the dangerous situation of today.

Some others favor total unilateral disarmament as a first step toward the abolition of war, hoping that other countries would then follow suit. Unfortunately, there is no guarantee that such a gesture would be reciprocated. Unilateral disarmament might make a war more likely, not less. If one compares a number of small neutral European countries at the outset of World War II, one notes that Sweden and Switzerland had made relatively extensive military defense preparations, while others were less well prepared. In Switzerland the defense minister in the 1930s, Rudolf Minger, a simple but wise farmer, realized the danger of the approaching storm brewing in the North and insisted that Switzerland make greater efforts to prepare for its defense. Despite their neutrality, Belgium, the Netherlands, Luxembourg, Denmark, and Norway were occupied by Hitler's armies, while Sweden and Switzerland escaped that fate. Of course, many other factors also played a role, but Switzerland's relatively strong army (together with the assurance to all sides that it would fight only if attacked) may have tipped the balance to keep Switzerland out of the war.

James Fallows (1981, pp. 162–63), writing of a "class of American statesmen who came of age during World War II," states: "As they surveyed a devastated Europe, they knew that the weakness of Hitler's neighbors had enticed him to attack." The desire not to repeat the same mistakes explains an understandable, probably justified reluctance to disarm unilaterally.

In countries that possess nuclear arms, a growing number of people are pressing for nuclear disarmament, even unilateral disarmament, if necessary. This position is not as unrealistic as it may sound at first. Most countries, in fact, do not rely on nuclear arms for their national security, and only a minority are allied with a nuclear superpower that promises to extend its "nuclear umbrella" against nuclear threats directed at these countries.

But it is unrealistic to assume that the government of either the United States or the Soviet Union would accept unilateral nuclear disarmament. It is also doubtful whether this would make a nuclear war less likely. Alternative security measures have to be implemented first, to replace nuclear deterrence. In the past, a perception of weakness has sometimes attracted aggression by an opponent. Until new norms of international behavior have become widely accepted, a certain amount of caution and preparedness is necessary to maintain peace and security. Complete nuclear disarmament will have to be mutual.

A less-drastic step is to undertake a small unilateral reduction of nuclear arms, perhaps 10 percent, and wait to see whether the other side follows suit. If it does, another small unilateral or bilateral reduction could be undertaken, reversing the arms race into a "peace race" (Osgood 1962). Given the enormous amount of nuclear overkill that both superpowers possess, they could take such steps without risk of losing their capacity for deterrence. Even if the other side should fail to respond, little would be lost. There would be ample time to halt the process before the other side achieved any "superiority" it could translate into political leverage. One danger, however, is that if the process were not reciprocated, the resulting public disappointment could help a more-bellicose government win power, which might then pursue a further intensification of the arms race.

The apparent solution to this dilemma is negotiated mutual disarmament. All nations would enjoy greater security and at the same time bear a smaller burden of defense expenditures, if all would take *simultaneous*, balanced steps toward disarmament. This must indeed remain the long-term goal, to be pursued with all efforts. But we may not have time to wait for this goal to be reached. Past experience with disarmament negotiations has not been very encouraging. It is sometimes difficult to monitor such agreements reliably. Also, there is no higher authority that could effectively prevent violations.

The ability to enforce agreements is by no means a sufficient condition for success, but without it the situation is difficult. Laws without the possibility of enforcement are not only useless but are counterproductive, because those who observe the law voluntarily may be penalized, to the advantage of those who disregard it. Even if no one has the deliberate intention to cheat, an agreement that cannot be adequately enforced is fragile. An agreement is stable and solid only if it is in each side's own interest to uphold it. Otherwise, there will be skepticism and mutual distrust, not always without justification.

Some reason for hope stems from technological improvements in verification procedures, such as observation satellites, which can help in monitoring compliance with arms control agreements and eliminate the need for blind trust. Also, some methods of approaching negotiations are more promising than others, as will be discussed in Chapter 15. Every attempt should be made to bring disarmament negotiations to a successful conclusion. But even negotiations among allies, for example concerning the allocation of military expenditures within NATO, are sometimes difficult. To expect that negotiations between adversaries lead to success more easily would be self-delusion.

Does this mean that the situation is hopeless? Fortunately, there are alternatives. The remainder of this book outlines a range of measures that can be taken by any country to strengthen peace, without taking an added risk to its own security. These alternatives improve everyone's security by making war less devastating and less likely. The more countries that adopt such measures, the safer the world will be. But it is not necessary to wait for other countries to cooperate. Many of these measures can be undertaken by any country on its own, independently, without risk.

## Short-Term versus Long-Term Strategies

The approaches toward the prevention of war discussed in this book can be divided into four categories. Some can be taken independently, by any country, while others require mutual cooperation. Some are short-term measures with immediate, but limited, effects. Others are long-term measures that require more-fundamental changes. Table 2.1 shows this classification and some examples for each type of measure.

Among the short-term independent measures are those that strengthen a country's defense without posing any threat to potential adversaries, and even improve the security of others.

---

**Table 2.1    A Classification of Possible Measures for the Prevention of War**

|  | Independent | Cooperative |
|---|---|---|
| Short-term | No-first-use policy; transarmament, shift from offensive to defensive arms | Mutually beneficial trade and other forms of cooperation; verifiable mutual arms reductions |
| Long-term | Nonmilitary defense; disentanglement from conflicts among other states; greater self-reliance; internal unity; usefulness to the rest of the world | Peaceful resolution of conflicts; strengthening just international law and its enforcement |

One such measure is a shift from offensive conventional military capabilities to purely defensive ones (*transarmament*). Other possible independent measures include actions taken to reduce the danger of nuclear war by accident.

Independent measures that may require more time to implement include a greater emphasis on nonmilitary defense and a deemphasis of the role of violence. Defense must serve two purposes: to convince a potential aggressor that it is to his or her advantage not to attack, and to protect a society against the effects of war if it should nevertheless be attacked. Nonmilitary strategies to achieve the first goal include skillful diplomacy to determine the type of incentives to which a potential aggressor might respond. For example, if an aggressor's aim is to gain control of certain resources, it should be made clear to him how the response to his aggression would hurt his access to those resources, not improve it. If prestige is high on his list of values, he must be convinced that aggression would undermine, not strengthen, his prestige. The aim is to prove that mutually beneficial cooperation serves the interests of a potential adversary better than war (in his or her *own* judgment of what those interests may be). The second aim of defense, protection through nonmilitary means, requires the implementation of various measures to reduce a society's vulnerability to war. An example is the stockpiling of vital supplies.

Nonmilitary defense measures, which rely on methods subtler than the use or threat of force, do not necessarily require more time for their implementation than shifts in weaponry from offensive to defensive systems. Nevertheless, public acceptance of nonmilitary measures may be slower, since these measures represent a greater departure from the current policies of many countries.

Among cooperative measures that can be implemented relatively quickly are agreements that bring a clearly visible advantage to all parties in the negotiations. One example is the agreement on the prohibition of bacteriological weapons that was concluded in 1972 (Stockholm International Peace Research Institute—SIPRI 1982, p. 227). Since the spread of biologically active killers cannot be controlled, it is in the obvious interest of all parties to ban such weapons. Other areas where agreement is relatively easy to achieve include the expansion of mutually beneficial trade and scientific and cultural cooperation. Even though such agreements do not prevent war directly, they help to improve relations and contribute to a general reduction of tensions. They also ensure that all participants have higher stakes in preserving peace, because all would have more to lose in the event of war.

More difficult to conclude will be agreements in which the benefits to each party are not as immediately obvious. An example is the creation of a new world order with an enforceable legal framework for the peaceful resolution of international conflicts. This will certainly benefit everyone *on average*, over the long run. However, in any particular situation, conflicting parties tend to invoke international law when it supports their position, and to ignore it in favor of military force if it goes against their interests in that particular instance. But law cannot be applied selectively; otherwise it breaks down. International lawyer Richard Falk (1982) has predicted that significant initiatives toward demilitarization, toward a substantial deemphasis of the role of violence in international relations, are likely to come not from governments or governmental organizations, but from voluntary associations of concerned individuals, such as trade unions, churches, and professional organizations.

The easiest to implement are short-term independent measures, because they do not depend on agreement with potential opponents. Such measures can reduce the threat of war most rapidly, and therefore this book will emphasize them. But clearly, such measures cannot be as effective as the more-fundamental long-term measures, which are more difficult to achieve. Short-term measures provide only temporary solutions, but they should be adopted, nevertheless, to bridge the period until more-fundamental changes can be implemented. The most difficult to achieve, but ultimately the most promising are cooperative long-term measures, such as a fundamental restructuring of the global order and the implementation of an effective and comprehensive legal code at the world level. Between these two extremes in terms of difficulty and effectiveness are deeper-reaching independent measures, and more-superficial cooperative measures. These four types of measures will be discussed in the following chapters, roughly in order of increasing difficulty of implementation.

Which type of measure should we seek to implement first? All these measures are important; all need to be worked on. Each of us must choose according to our strengths and skills, our inclinations, and our own assessment of the relative importance and potential success of each course of action. If anyone attempted to impose his or her own priorities on others, this might well have the opposite effect from that intended, and would only weaken efforts toward peace.

Arguments are often heard that short-term measures are only "patchwork" and distract from the fundamental changes needed to survive. On the other hand, people argue that attempting the impossible wastes precious energy that would be better applied to the implementation of feasible steps. In my view, both aims can and should be pursued simultaneously. The following simple analogy may illustrate this point. Suppose a fisherman, who realizes his old boat is developing leaks, decides to build a new boat. Yet he still has to continue fishing every day. He will immediately start building a new, stronger boat but at the same time will repair the weak spots on the old boat, so he will not drown during the next storm. And he certainly will not destroy the old boat before the new one is ready.

Similarly, we should pursue not only short-term *or* long-term goals, but *both*, in a way that these goals mutually support one another. While we work on the development of a new global security system, we should not neglect to eliminate immediately the most dangerous aspects of the existing situation through a policy that

> seeks to diminish the importance of arms as points of political leverage wherever possible without inviting other actors to engage in aggression. The goal is gradually to increase reliance on nonmilitary defenses, both national and global, while decreasing reliance on military power [Johansen 1982, pp. 56–57].

# 3 The Dual Meaning of "Strength"

In many countries today, popular opinion seems to be polarizing into two opposing camps. Those in one camp (sometimes labeled "hawks") stress national security as the overriding goal and want to achieve it through increased military strength. Those in the other camp (sometimes labeled "doves") stress peace as the most important goal and advocate unilateral disarmament regardless of the state of international hostilities. Some adherents of both camps seem to be victims of the same linguistic confusion. The word "strength" has two rather different meanings that are not always clearly distinguished. Strength can mean the capability to harm others and to threaten them; it can also mean the capability to resist harm intended by others and to be immune against threats. Boulding (1978, p. 33) states that he uses "the word 'strength' not in the frequently accepted sense of the ability to create strain through, for instance, violence but in terms of the ability to resist strain." He mentions that this ambiguity, which can be found in many languages, has hampered clear thinking about these issues.

The same ambiguity is also inherent in the notion of "military strength." On the one hand, it can mean the ability to inflict or threaten harm on other nations; on the other, the ability to resist harm intended by others, to be invulnerable against threats. It is neither true that all weapons improve a nation's security, as some "hawks" appear to believe, nor that all weapons jeopardize international security, as some "doves" claim. Defensive arms can improve a country's security without threatening other nations. Purely offensive arms threaten the security of others, without improving a country's own security. Defensive capabilities strengthen peace; offensive capabilities threaten peace. The solution to the security dilemma is not to be found in *more* arms or *less* arms, but in *different* arms: weapons that can help resist aggression without being useful in carrying out aggression.

Confusion between these two meanings of "military power" can be observed, for example, when military leaders in certain countries, in the name of "defense," call for the acquisition of offensive weapons systems that threaten the security of other nations. They mistakenly believe that it is necessary to threaten others to be invulnerable themselves. But even some members of the peace movement may have fallen victim to the same confusion if they advocate unilateral disarmament as a means of reducing tension in the world. To reason that a country should be weak lest it pose a threat to others is to confuse "posing no threat" with "being vulnerable."

To be secure, it is not only unnecessary to threaten others, it is counterproductive; for if others feel threatened, they feel pressure to eliminate that threat. And to have peace, it is not only unnecessary to make oneself more vulnerable, but it is counterproductive; for a weak nation may tempt an aggressive nation to attack. As long as we have no assurance that other nations are not aggressive, a weakening of defense can do a disservice to peace.

It is often said that a "power vacuum" attracts aggression. A vacuum of *defensive* power may attract aggression, because it may lead a potential opponent to expect an easy gain. But an "excess of military power," seen as an offensive threat by neighboring countries, may provoke aggression just as easily, in the form of a preventive attack to eliminate that threat. "Military power" is an ambiguous expression. What strengthens peace is not power over others, but the ability to resist power.

Hidden behind the phrase "balance of power" is a simple image of strength as a one-dimensional variable, like the strength of a boxer who is either stronger than, weaker than, or equally strong as his opponent. But reality is more complex. "Strength" or "power" must be divided into at least the two components of offensive and defensive power. While offensive power is destabilizing, defensive power is stabilizing. Whoever uses expressions such as "military strength," "military power," "balance of power," "military superiority," "military inferiority," or "relative strength," without specifying whether he or she means offensive or defensive power contributes unwittingly (or deliberately?) to a perpetuation of this unfortunate confusion, which has had dangerous consequences.

## A Classification of Human Characters

To bring clarity into this confusion, a diagram proposed by the Austrian mathematician Karl Menger (1934) may help. Menger categorizes people into those who tend to hurt others (*unhöflich*, meaning, literally, impolite or inconsiderate) and those who don't hurt others (*höflich*, i.e., polite, considerate). He further distinguishes between those who are easily hurt (*empfindlich*, literally "sensitive," in the meaning of being easily offended, intolerant) and those who are not easily hurt (*unempfindlich*, in the sense of being tolerant). These distinctions yield the four categories shown in Table 3.1.

We are all familiar with people who are easily offended and yet rude to others, in a way that they would never tolerate themselves (type 4). Theirs is the most difficult type of personality to get along with. Other people are also highly sensitive, but are careful not to hurt others (type 3). Still others may not be polite

---

**Table 3.1  Menger's Classification of Human Characters**

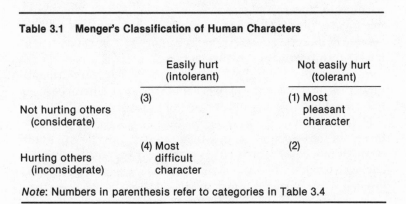

|  | Easily hurt (intolerant) | Not easily hurt (tolerant) |
|---|---|---|
| Not hurting others (considerate) | (3) | (1) Most pleasant character |
| Hurting others (inconsiderate) | (4) Most difficult character | (2) |

*Note*: Numbers in parenthesis refer to categories in Table 3.4

in their relationships, but neither are they easily hurt themselves (type 2). The most agreeable character is kind to others, careful not to hurt them, and at the same time not easily offended (type 1).

Of course, there is no simple and clear-cut dividing line between people who are either considerate or inconsiderate, tolerant or intolerant. People fall into a continuous range from very inconsiderate to extremely considerate, and the same is true of tolerance. Also, people will often show more consideration and/or tolerance toward some individuals than toward others. Nevertheless, Menger's two-by-two classification can help clarify relationships.

Menger then analyzes which of these four types can get along with one another and thus tend to associate, and which cannot stand one another. He observes that intolerant people cannot get along with someone who is inconsiderate, but that the other three combinations (tolerant with someone inconsiderate, intolerant with considerate, tolerant with considerate) are compatible. From this he finds, among other things, that people who are considerate and tolerant (type 1) can get along well with everybody. People who are inconsiderate and intolerant (type 4) cannot even stand others of the same type, but can get along only with people who are both considerate and tolerant.

## A Classification of Nations

An analogous classification, shown in Table 3.2, is applied here to nations and their relations with other nations. By employing

**Table 3.2   A Classification of Nations**

|  | Vulnerable | Invulnerable |
|---|---|---|
| Nonaggressive | (3) "Dovish" posture | (1) Safest posture; greatest contribution to international peace |
| Aggressive | (4) Most-dangerous posture; most likely to become involved in a war | (2) "Hawkish" posture |

this analogy I do not intend to imply that one can "personify" nations as considerate or inconsiderate, but that a structural correspondence exists between aggressivity and the tendency to hurt others, and between invulnerability and the property of not being easily hurt.

Again, in reality the situation is more complex. Aggressivity is a *bilateral* relationship, not a characteristic of one nation alone. A nation may behave aggressively toward some countries, and not toward others. Furthermore, there are degrees of aggressivity and vulnerability. (This problem will be discussed in Chapter 8 in greater detail.) But for the time being we will consider a simple classification into discrete cases.

A nation is invulnerable if it has both the capability *and* the will to defend itself against any potential threat. Neither ingredient alone is sufficient. Similarly, a nation is aggressive only if it possesses offensive arms and also has the intention of using them for aggressive purposes. But since intentions can change relatively quickly, and since verbal proclamations of peaceful intentions are not always believed by an opponent (sometimes with good reason), the only safe way for a nation to show credibly that it is not aggressive may be to refrain from acquiring any offensive arms. (The distinction between offensive and defensive arms will be discussed in Chapter 5.)

The most-desirable characteristic of a country in terms of contributing to international peace is neither to be "militarily superior" over others, nor to be militarily weak, but to be strong in terms of defense and weak in terms of offense (position 1 in Table 3.2). In this way, a country can defend itself and therefore does not attract aggression, while at the same time it has neither the intention nor the capability of attacking others. The most-dangerous position is occupied by a country which threatens others but is unable to defend itself (position 4). Such a country can easily provoke an attack by others, or may feel under pressure to launch a preemptive attack.

Countries which are less vulnerable generally also tend to be less aggressive. Johan Galtung, the renowned Norwegian sociologist and peace researcher, writes:

> A country knowing its own invulnerability to be high may also be less tempted to enter into preemptive military adventures, threat-

ening postures, military encirclement through alliance formation and bases, and "forward defense lines" (in order to have the fighting take place far away from one's own vulnerable homeland) and, consequently, may become a much less aggressive country [1980, p. 409].

A similar tendency can be observed in individuals. People with vulnerable spots tend to be more aggressive and to intimidate others. For example, teachers who are insecure about their knowledge typically tend to criticize students, to give themselves an aura of superiority and to prevent the students from asking questions. People who feel confident about their abilities can afford to be much more tolerant.

### Peacemakers, Warmongers, Hawks and Doves

The four basic defense postures shown in Table 3.2 will be encountered repeatedly throughout this book. For easy reference, I will assign a name to each of them. Those advocating invulnerability without threat (position 1) will be called "peacemakers." Those who adopt a posture of vulnerability with threats (position 4) will be called "warmongers." The more-difficult choice of terms is for positions 2 and 3. Position 2 (invulnerability with threat) is a sort of extreme hardline position. Its advocates claim they want to prevent war through "superior strength" over their opponent. But by failing to accept the legitimate desire of an opponent also to be secure, they are often drawn into conflict. Such a position may come closest to what is popularly called a "hawk," and I will use this label throughout the book. The opposite of a "hawk" is a "dove." Even though most of those who consider themselves to be "doves" would count themselves among the peace forces, (as, by the way, would many "hawks" who claim they seek "peace through strength") "doves" are often accused of not giving enough attention to the need for a strong defense, of being too "soft." A more-accurate description of the position "vulnerability without threat" would be "advocates of unilateral disarmament." But since this is a long and clumsy expression, I have settled for the shorter though more ambiguous designation "dove."

I intend to show that the usual debate between "hawks" (who call for increased armament) and "doves" (who call for unilateral arms reductions) misses the main point. There is an alternative, a strong defense without offense, which truly serves the cause of peace. In terms of Table 3.2, the real issue is not whether to take positions (2) or (3), but (1) or (4). It is not a matter of being a "hawk" or a "dove," but of working for peace or for war.

*Pairs of Nations*

We can now ask which of the four types of nations in Table 3.2 are likely to remain at peace with one another, and which are prone to end up at war. This is analogous to the problem of which types of individuals can get along with each other and which cannot. An aggressive country can generally keep peace only with an invulnerable country, and a vulnerable country only with a nonaggressive country. Any dispute between an aggressive country and a vulnerable one tends to lead to war. Alternatively, a vulnerable country may submit to the aggressor without resistance. The result is then not war, but simply occupation. But this is not a desirable outcome either.

These considerations enable us to construct Table 3.3, which shows which of the 16 possible pairwise combinations of types of countries are likely to stay at peace, and which pairs are in danger of becoming engaged in a war. From this table it is apparent that only countries of type (1), which are both nonaggressive and invulnerable, can maintain peace with every other type of country.

The sharp distinction between war (W) and peace (P) in Table 3.3 should in reality also be replaced by a continuum. Two countries both of which are aggressive and vulnerable are *most* likely to go to war with each other (bottom right entry in Table 3.3). If both countries are nonaggressive and invulnerable (the top left entry in Table 3.3), peace between them is most stable and secure.

If we go beyond pairs of countries and consider groupings of more than two countries, we find that a war may occur in the system if it contains at least one pair of incompatible countries, one of which is aggressive, and the other vulnerable. Obviously,

**Table 3.3   Pairs of Countries Which Are Compatible or Incompatible**

| | | Category of second country | | | |
|---|---|---|---|---|---|
| | | (1) Nonaggressive and invulnerable | (2) Aggressive and invulnerable | (3) Nonaggresssive and vulnerable | (4) Aggressive and vulnerable |
| Category of first country | (1) Nonaggressive and invulnerable | P | P | P | P |
| | (2) Aggressive and invulnerable | P | P | W | W |
| | (3) Nonaggressive and vulnerable | P | W | P | W |
| | (4) Aggressive and vulnerable | P | W | W | W |

*Note:* P = compatible and capable of maintaining peace. W = incompatible and may end in war.

the more countries in the system, the more likely that it contains at least one such incompatible pair. The more countries of type (4) (vulnerable and aggressive) a system contains, the more likely is war. Unless almost all countries are of type (1) (invulnerable and nonaggressive), the danger of war remains. With today's means of transportation, it is no longer necessary that countries at a war with each other have a common border. These considerations once more show how important it is to make an effort to be both *nonaggressive and invulnerable* to contribute toward peace.

*Preemption versus Retaliation*

As we have just seen, the least-dangerous type of country is one that is nonaggressive and invulnerable, because it neither commits aggression nor attracts aggression. But it is less clear whether an aggressive country is more dangerous if it is vulnerable or if invulnerable. Arguments for both views can be made. On the one hand it can be pointed out that if a country is vulnerable, it tends to be more aggressive than an invulnerable one. As an example, let us recall the situation at the outbreak of the 1967 mideast war, which was briefly discussed in Chapter 1. If Israel had been less vulnerable, or if it had had strong, impenetrable air defenses, it might not have found it necessary to carry out a preemptive strike against Egyptian bomber fleets. Instead, Israel could have afforded to wait and see whether an Egyptian attack was indeed going to take place.

On the other hand it can be argued that if an aggressive country is itself vulnerable, its aggressive drive will be restrained by fear of retaliation. Hitler deliberately made Germany less vulnerable and more self-reliant. He actively promoted the development of coal gas as a substitute for gasoline, to make Germany invulnerable to an oil embargo. This also made Germany more dangerous, because there were fewer points at which pressure could be applied against it. Had it been more vulnerable, it would have been less dangerous.

Which view, then, is correct? Is an aggressive country more dangerous if it is vulnerable or invulnerable? The crucial factor is whether a country is vulnerable to a disabling first strike or to retaliation. Vulnerability to retaliation tends to inhibit aggressive behavior, while vulnerability to a first strike precipitates aggression.

To illustrate this point, consider the following story (told originally by the British peace researcher Adam Curle and slightly expanded here). A homeowner hears a suspicious noise at night, takes his gun, steps into the hall, switches on the light, and sees a burglar with a gun. The intruder knows that unless he kills the homeowner, he may be shot dead. Being vulnerable to the homeowner's gun makes him more dangerous. (Similarly, a cornered wild animal with no possibility of escape is more dangerous than otherwise.) If the burglar were less vulnerable (e.g., if he had a bullet-proof vest or the homeowner had no gun), the burglar might be less dangerous, because he would have the option of escaping unharmed. He would therefore be under less pressure to shoot in self-defense. The reverse is true if the guns of the burglar and the homeowner only wound but are not lethal, leaving both the ability to retaliate. In that case, carrying a gun would make the homeowner safer. He could deter the burglar from shooting him by the threat that he would be able to shoot back, and neither would he want to shoot first, because of the fear of retaliation.

Unfortunately, in reality the distinction between the capacity to strike first or to retaliate is not always clear-cut. Weapons that can be used for retaliation can often be used equally well for a preemptive attack. As will be seen in Chapter 7, a nuclear nation's own safety may be best served by its ability to convince a potential opponent that it will never be the first to use nuclear arms, but could retaliate if attacked. To make a no-first-use policy credible, it is best not even to acquire the capacity for a first strike.

Much better than the threat of retaliation is, of course, *defense*, whenever possible. In the above story, the homeowner would have been much safer if he had prevented the break-in in the first place by installing good locks and a burglar alarm system.

From this analogy we can conclude that the least-dangerous type of country is not vulnerable to a first attack, but is vulnerable to retaliation by the opponent if it is the first to attack. (To what extent one can distinguish between vulnerability to a first or second strike will be discussed in later chapters.)

### Dissuasion versus Appeasement

Closely related to the problem just discussed is the question whether threatening one's opponents improves one's security. It is often said about potential opponents that the only language they understand is military strength. This may be true in some cases, but there must be a clear distinction as to *when* that strength should be applied. A potential aggressor should feel afraid if he attacks a country, but *only then*. If an opponent feels threatened even as long as he does not attack, then there is little incentive to dissuade him from an attack. Someone who is being punished even for good behavior has no incentive to show good behavior. (Whether a potential opponent is being threatened intentionally, or whether this is only his subjective impression, makes no difference to the opponent's behavior.)

Four different policies are conceivable regarding threats against a potential opponent. They are summarized in Table 3.4.

The greatest dissuading effect against aggression is obtained if an opponent feels threatened if he should attack, but can be convinced that as long as he does not attack, he has nothing to fear (policy 1). In contrast, there is no dissuasion if the opponent either feels always threatened (policy 2, a sort of "hawkish" posture) or if he feels never threatened (policy 3, a kind of "dovish" posture). The worst policy, which gives the strongest incentive to aggression, is policy (4), which might be called appeasement. It implies that if an opponent takes a threatening posture or commits aggression, one simply yields to his demands. If he takes a conciliatory posture, one interprets this as weakness and threatens him.

The Soviet Union's instant rejection of some American disarmament proposals tended to stiffen the United States' position, instead of helping the search for mutually acceptable

**Table 3.4    Four Ways of Using Threats**

|  |  | Opponent's action | |
|  |  | If opponent attacks | If opponent does not attack |
|---|---|---|---|
|  | (1) Dissuasion (a peace policy) | Opponent is threatened | Opponent is not threatened |
| Own policy | (2) Constant threat (a "hawkish" policy) | Opponent is threatened | Opponent is threatened |
|  | (3) No threat (a "dovish" policy) | Opponent is not threatened | Opponent is not threatened |
|  | (4) Appeasement (a policy that invites war) | Opponent is not threatened | Opponent is threatened |

solutions, and therefore goes against true Soviet security interests. Similarly, the American dismissal of the Soviet Union's unilateral declaration that it would not be the first to use nuclear weapons as "a clever public relations gimmick," as one State Department official called it (*New York Times*, 16 June 1982, p. 9), is the opposite of a prudent policy of dissuasion. Instead of dissuading from war, such a stance dissuades from peace. A better response would have been to indicate that the Soviet declaration was a welcome move, but that words alone were insufficient and had to be backed up by deeds, e.g., steps toward mutual disarmament.

Some people appear to believe that dissuasion consists of exerting a "steady" pressure on a potential opponent, seeking to weaken the opponent by withholding credit and technical know-how, by isolating him diplomatically, by attempting to foment domestic discontent through hostile radio and television broadcasts and, if necessary, by military threats. These people confuse policy (2) in Table 3.4 (a constant threat) with dissuasion. Others go even further and call dissuasion a policy of showing "strength" and "determination" when an opponent makes conciliatory gestures and therefore appears weak to them, and of taking a "prudent" attitude, retracting, when an opponent makes belligerent noises. They confuse dissuasion with policy (4) in Table 3.4 (appeasement). And some people accuse as "appeasers" those who propose to respond to flexibility on the other side with equal flexibility, and to match conciliatory gestures with similar moves. They confuse appeasement with policy (1) in Table 3.4 (true dissuasion). All of these people are dangerously wrong; they advocate policies that increase the likelihood of war. They may, inadvertently, invite aggression.

The widespread notion that if a potential opponent is threatened he will not dare to attack, is too simplistic. How important it is that a country, for its own safety, should not threaten others as long as they don't attack, does not yet appear to be widely understood.

In a simple formula, a prescription for preventing war could be stated in the following two points: (a) do not make war on others, and (b) do not let others make war on you. The following analogy may illustrate this point further. Exploitation is possible only if there are people who do the exploiting *and* others who cooperate by passively allowing themselves to be exploited. In order to prevent exploitation, everyone should refrain from exploiting others, and not permit others to exploit them. In order not to exploit others, do we need to allow others to exploit ourselves? Or in order not to be exploited, do we have to exploit others? Certainly not. Yet many wrongly believe that in order to strengthen one's own security one has to threaten the security of others. To protect oneself against burglary, one does not have to burglarize the homes of others. Yet this perverse view seems to predominate among those who believe that either one defeats others or one is defeated. Richard Barnet (1972) pointed out that

> the national security managers and our governing class are edu- cated and selected in a way that ensures that many will have strong power drives and a conception of human life that leads them to believe that unless one controls and dominates, one will be controlled and dominated [quoted in Deutsch 1983, p. 19].

How false such a view is will be discussed further in Chapter 8.

Some fall into the opposite extreme and assert that to avoid war it is better to offer no resistance and to give up even purely defensive arms. This is like saying that to prevent burglaries, one should prohibit locks and alarm systems.

Extremists in one camp (some "hawks") seem to say that in order to resist threats one must exert threats. Extremists in the other camp (some "doves") seem to say that in order not to exert threats, one should not resist threats. The solution offered is that one should resist threats, but not exert threats. This strengthens both peace *and* security.

Can the two camps form a coalition on this basis?

# 4 What Should a Nation Defend?

In Chapter 5, the distinction between offensive and defensive arms will be discussed. Before that is possible, it is necessary to specify what is to be defended with defensive arms. If the objectives of a nation's military defense are as all-encompassing as to include "interests abroad," then even offensive arms may be claimed to serve the "defense" of such interests. (I have just referred to a "nation's" objectives. In fact, what counts in decisions is not the interests of a nation's population in general, but of its *leaders*, who make the decisions. The leadership's objectives may be quite different from those of ordinary people. Nonetheless, throughout this book I will sometimes refer to nations when in fact I mean those nations' current leadership, to avoid too-clumsy sentences.)

If war is to be avoided, the goals of a nation's defense must not lead to a conflict if other nations seek the same goals for themselves. For example, a nation that defends its internationally recognized territory does not prevent any other nation from defending its own territory. But if it encroaches on territory not internationally recognized as its own, other countries are likely to claim the same right for themselves. Such mutually incompatible claims may lead to war.

The suggestion has been made that in order to reduce the role of borders as a source of conflict, geographical boundaries should be less rigidly defined. But the opposite is true: vaguely defined boundaries are a prime source of dispute and war. There is good reason to deemphasize the *importance* of physical boundaries and to create more institutions and organizations that transcend frontiers. But whatever boundaries remain should be clearly defined.

Some people have suggested that the time has come for the creation of a world without borders. The idea of territorial defense, they argue, has become obsolete in a world where people face so many joint global problems. The abolition of borders is indeed in the long-term interest of the majority of the earth's people, and it is desirable that all countries undertake steps in that direction. But as long as there are countries whose leaders are eager to expand their borders, others cannot simply give up their borders. An equally desirable goal would be that the earth's mineral resources be shared by all, as a common heritage of humankind. Yet if the oil-exporting countries were to declare their oil to be the common property of humanity, some oil-hungry industrialized countries would be only too happy to grab it, giving nothing in return, claiming to put it to "the most productive use." A better idea is mutually beneficial trade. Common property is a nice idea, if *all* share what they have. But as long as some don't share, those who do are the losers. The same applies to national defense. Countries should take joint steps to deemphasize the importance of borders. But as long as some groups are happy to seize undefended territory, defense cannot be abolished unilaterally. Borders should be open to civilians, but not to armies.

Another example of a goal of defense that does not interfere with other nations' aspirations for the same goal is the preservation of national political and cultural institutions. A more-flexible goal does not just seek to maintain the status quo, but allows peaceful change. An example of such a goal is the right to self-determination, which implies the defense not of any particular institution, but of the people's right to choose and develop their institutions according to their own preferences, without the imposition of force from outside. This goal does not prevent any other nation from seeking self-determination.

Defending national borders or national institutions in no way implies hostility against foreign people. We can keep the best of relations with people from other countries, respecting their independence, without trying to impose our own values on them, but neither allowing them to impose their values on us.

*Buying with a Gun*

Is it a legitimate goal to defend sources of raw materials abroad? It has been argued that modern industrialized societies cannot survive without a secure flow of raw materials, such as oil and various metals and minerals, to keep their industries running. Merely defending national borders is said to be insufficient for the society's survival. According to this viewpoint, it is indispensable to guarantee an uninterrupted flow of these vital commodities, if necessary by military force. But if other countries claim the same sources of raw materials for their own use and are ready to "defend" them with military force, this will inevitably lead to war.

Does this mean that to obtain security, nations must give up their interests abroad? This is not necessary. But we will find it to our own advantage to seek to obtain supplies of foreign raw materials through mutually beneficial trade, not through the use or threat of force. To say that certain foreign supplies must be obtained through military force if necessary, because they are vital, would be like saying that since food is vital for our survival, we should—if necessary—point a gun at the grocer in the store to get what we need. If we did so, we might shorten our life. In our own interest, we prefer to pay for what we need.

The same logic applies to foreign sources of raw materials. Some countries have had a near-monopoly on offensive military power in the past and were able to obtain the supplies they needed from around the world, at a price they dictated, through the threat and occasional use of force. Great Britain, for example, surrounded by oceans and possessing a strong navy, was almost invulnerable against an attack from any of its colonies. But in the age of intercontinental nuclear missiles, no country is invulnerable any more. The method of trying to maintain the flow of raw materials by force may sooner or later backfire. In order to defend oneself, it is necessary to prove to a potential adversary that it is in his or her own interest to keep the peace. If peace means being cheated out of one's raw materials, then peace (and with it security) is fragile. (How one can effectively defend oneself against interruptions in the flow of supplies from abroad will be discussed in Chapter 12.)

Another set of goals that will lead to war if several countries pursue them with armed force is the promotion of one's own way of life, ideology, religion, or political and economic institutions abroad. One may well try to attract followers by showing a good example. One can demonstrate that a given economic system works well for oneself and would also work well for others, and hope that others may imitate it voluntarily. For example, a growing number of American and European companies have been impressed by Japan's economic success and are trying to learn from its management system, which gives greater responsibility and participation to employees. But if Japan attempted to impose that system on other countries by military force, this would create resistance and lead to war.

Goals that do not prevent other countries from seeking the same goal for themselves will be called self-compatible. Goals that lead to war if two or more countries pursue them with armed force are self-incompatible. Table 4.1 lists some examples of self-compatible and self-incompatible goals.

*Description, Prescription, and Strategy*

One can distinguish between descriptive theory, prescriptive theory, and theory of strategy. Descriptive theory simply rec-

---

**Table 4.1  Examples of Self-compatible and Self-incompatible National Goals**

| Self-compatible goals (do not prevent others from seeking the same) | Self-incompatible goals (lead to conflict if others pursue the same) |
| --- | --- |
| Defense of internationally recognized territory | "Defense" of foreign raw material sources |
| Preservation of the country's internal political institutions | Extension of one's own political or economic system to other countries |
| Self-determination (= choice of institutions without outside pressure) | Imposition of one's own beliefs on others (religious, ideological) |

ords what can be observed in the world. Prescriptive theory states what should be done. Theory of strategy explains, "If this is your goal, this is how you may achieve it," without telling anyone what their goals *ought* to be.

What I have said here may sound prescriptive. For example, I have indicated that a country "should not" seek to defend interests abroad with military force. But I do not intend to indulge in wishful thinking. National leaders pursue what *they* consider to be their interests and generally ignore well-intended appeals. What has been said is certainly not descriptive of current reality, because many nations today do use armed force to "defend" what they consider to be their national interests abroad. The message of this chapter is meant to be useful for a peace *strategy*. It does not prescribe that a nation should strive for peace, but rather says that *if* a country wants to prevent war, the way to do so is to defend only those goals that do not prevent other countries from pursuing the same goals for themselves. It is unrealistic to expect that in the near future all countries will defend only their own borders, or aim to maintain their own political independence. But those countries which want peace can achieve it by restricting themselves, in their own interest, to goals that are compatible with other nations' search for the same goals.

One of the scenarios for the outbreak of nuclear war offered by Ground Zero (1982) is based on the assumption that during an internal crisis in Iran, both the United States and the Soviet Union come to "defend" it. In Chapter 10 we will see how Iran might dissuade aggression without any such outside "help."

I do not make a distinction here between "good" and "bad" defense objectives in any abstract moral sense. I do not say "thou shalt not covet thy neighbor's territory." My views on this may differ from those of others. But it is a matter of simple logic to explore what goals lead to war and therefore reduce national security, if two or more countries pursue these goals, and what goals strengthen peace and therefore improve national security.

# 5 Defensive versus Offensive Arms

The terms "defensive" and "offensive" have been misused so frequently that this distinction has almost become discredited. For example, Israel has called antiaircraft missiles in Lebanon offensive, but its use of cluster-bombs in Beirut defensive. Is the distinction between offensive and defensive arms arbitrary, having meaning only in the eye of the beholder?

In the following, reasons are given why the distinction between defensive and offensive capabilities is essential for an understanding of the causes of arms races and for the development of strategies to prevent war. It is important to give a clear and precise meaning to these terms.

In this book, the notion of defensive "arms" is used in a somewhat broader sense than usual, for lack of a better word. The category of defensive arms will include such things as bomb shelters and passive obstacles, which are not "weapons" in the strict sense. Mark Sommer (1983) has called such types of "shields" that prevent injury without inflicting injury "protective instruments." Anything that serves to impede the effect of offensive arms will be included here in the category of defensive "arms."

Roughly speaking, one can say that offensive arms are useful for aggression only, but not to prevent aggression. Defensive arms can serve to stop aggression, but not to carry out aggression. For example, an immobile obstacle, e.g., a land mine, can only stop advancing forces, but cannot be used by itself to carry out an invasion. It is therefore a defensive weapon. On the other hand, mechanized forces with long-range mobility are primarily useful for an attack and are therefore offensive.

To develop the concept further, I propose the following definition of defensive and offensive arms: purely defensive arms increase the security of the country acquiring them but do not reduce the security of any other country. Purely offensive arms threaten the security of potential opponents, but do not strengthen the security of the country acquiring them.

### What Is National Security?

These definitions make it necessary, of course, to explain what is meant by national security. It may be difficult to measure the amount of "national security" in precise quantitative terms. Security will be related to a country's ability to avoid war as well as to the probability of its population surviving in case of war. An approximate measure for the opposite of national security could be the average number of war casualties (both military and civilian) per year per million population. National security will also depend on people's ability to maintain their own way of life, free from foreign domination (e.g., living in a concentration camp would not be compatible with national security). But as was discussed in the previous chapter, national security must not include interests abroad, because military "defense" of such interests by two or more parties necessarily leads to war.

In the following, national security will be largely identified with a country's ability to keep its territory free from hostile military force, which also helps to protect the lives of its people and its political independence. Even if the concept of "national security" is not yet as unambiguously defined as, for example, the "gross national product," it is essential to use it, since discussions about national security are central to thinking about defense. The choice of concepts should be made on the basis of their relevance, not their elegance. Intellectuals sometimes yield to the temptation to deal only with concepts for which statistical data are readily available or which permit sophisticated manipulations, but which have little to do with the fundamental problem under discussion. This might be compared to searching for a key in a place where there is light, rather than where it was lost.

*Short-Term Effects of Arms Acquisitions*

The acquisition of additional arms by a country typically has a dual effect: it increases the security of the country acquiring the arms, and it decreases the security of potential opponents. (Of course, this is only the immediate effect, in the absence of any response by other countries, which is not a realistic assumption. It ignores the role of mutual fear in fostering arms races, which will be discussed in the next chapter. But here we shall confine ourselves first to an examination of the immediate effects of an arms buildup.)

Arms that add to one's own security *and* threaten the security of potential opponents are neither purely defensive nor purely offensive, but must be classified somewhere in between. For example, rifles, tanks, and fighter planes can be used to repel an attack on one's own country as well as to launch an attack on another country. But some arms clearly are predominantly offensive and reduce the security of an opponent by more than they add to a country's own security, and other arms are predominantly defensive. Fixed antitank obstacles, for example, cannot be used to attack another country, but can be very helpful in thwarting an attempted tank invasion. They are purely defensive. Antitank and antiaircraft weapons are useful in defending a country, but are not sufficient means to attack another country, even if they are mobile. Other purely defensive installations against bombing attacks are air raid shelters and radar warning systems. (However, true warning systems must be distinguished from radar *guiding* systems that can direct missiles into an opponent's territory, as pointed out by Wilkes and Gleditsch 1979.)

*The Range of Weapons*

Galtung (1984) offers a concrete but more-restrictive definition of defensive and offensive arms: defensive arms are those with short range mobility and limited impact which can be used to fight *only* inside a country's own territory or very close to its borders; anything that can also be used to fight abroad is not purely defensive. As Galtung put it, a good example of defensive installations are the fortresses in man-made caves in the Swiss Alps—since it is not easy to move the Alps into some other country to attack it.

According to Galtung's definition, in general, arms in fixed positions, such as fortresses, fixed shore batteries, minefields, etc., are defensive. Arms with short-range mobility, such as interception aircraft or mobile antiaircraft missiles, are also essentially defensive. Arms with long-range mobility, such as aircraft carriers, long-range bombers, intercontinental missiles, etc., are offensive.

A historical example of a purely defensive installation is the Great Wall of China constructed to help keep our foreign invaders. In principle, even the Chinese wall could have been used in an offensive scheme, as a protection against realiation after an attack abroad. We will return to he question of the possible effects of employing a mixture of defensive and offensive arms at the end of this chapter. For the time being, we simply observe that a fortification like the Chinese wall *in itself* could not be used for aggressive purposes.

There are also arms well suited to aggression, but almost useless for true defense. A historical example is the proverbial gun boat sent by imperial powers to the capital city of a weaker nation to extract concessions. The gun boat clearly reduced the security of the country threatened, but did not contribute to securing the borders of the country from which it originated, since the weaker country was in no position to launch an attack against the country which demanded concessions. The forced opening of Chinese harbors to trade with the West in the 19th century is a typical example of such a situation.

A modern successor to the gun boat is the aircraft carrier, which can be positioned off the coast of a weaker country with no missiles to sink it, and can carry out attacks from there. For the defense of a country's home territory, domestic airfields, which are unsinkable, are equally well or better suited than aircraft carriers.

Another factor that influences the offensive or defensive character of a weapons sytem is also the *logistics of supply*. For example, if tanks depend on fuel depots in fixed positions, they are limited in their mobility and serve essentially defensive functions. If they are accompanied by fuel trucks or pipelines for long-range advances, they can serve offensive purposes.

While offensive arms can also be used for purposes of defense, if this is the intention of the country possessing them, it is not easy to convince a potential opponent that only defensive uses are intended, as long as the objective potential for offense exists. Therefore, the possession of offensive arms may actually lessen one's own national security. On the other hand, defensive arms cannot possibly be used for offensive purposes. While long-range weapons can also be used at short range, short-range weapons *cannot* be used at long range. Here lies a certain asymmetry.

Certain defensive arms can be converted relatively easily into offensive arms. For example, defensive ground-to-air antiaircraft missiles may be converted into offensive ground-to-ground missiles. To make defensive intentions credible, it is important to avoid such convertible or "multi-purpose" weapons having offensive as well as defensive applications.

Some people deny the possibility of drawing a clear distinction between offensive and defensive arms. They argue that almost any country calls its own arms defensive, and those of its adversaries offensive, whatever the arms may be. The point is, however, that what governments may *say* is irrelevant. Switzerland did not ask Hitler whether he would consider its mountain fortresses offensive or defensive. (He probably would have called them offensive.) Rather, in the interest of its own security, each country must seek to convince potential opponents that its armaments serve purely defensive functions. The most effective way to convince others of the defensive nature of one's military posture is *to forego any offensive capabilities*.

Whether the acquisition of certain arms is perceived as defensive or offensive does not depend only on the arms themselves, but also on the past behavior of the country acquiring them. While some countries have not fought outside their own borders for centuries, others keep intervening militarily abroad. Mere declarations of purely defensive intention are often met with skepticism, not always without reason.

To make purely defensive intentions absolutely convincing, it is best to acquire only defensive arms. What determines an opponent's reaction to our acquisition of arms is not our intentions how to use them, but the opponent's *perception* of our intentions. For example, Sweden and Switzerland have deliberately avoided the acquisition of long-range bombers; instead they possess short-range fighter, ground attack, and reconnaissance aircraft (Roberts 1976, p. 98). This choice of aircraft eliminates any suspicion that these planes might be used for bombing missions against an opponent's cities, and will therefore not invite any preemptive strike to eliminate such a potential threat.

Throughout this book, many examples will be drawn from Sweden and Switzerland, because these two countries come very close to a purely defensive military posture. They are also the only two countries in the world to have been free from international war since the end of the Napoleonic period in 1815 (Small and Singer 1982, p. 167ff; several other countries have not experienced war since their founding, but they have not existed as independent countries for as long). In addition to relatively strong defense efforts, both countries have further pursued a policy of neutrality. Of course, a sample of two has no statistical significance, but I will offer reasons other than statistical ones why a purely defensive posture and an attempt to stay out of other countries' quarrels may increase a country's security, rather than reduce it.

## Initiative versus Response

A slightly different definition of what constitutes offensive or defensive arms has been proposed by Quester (1977). He calls those arms offensive which give an advantage to the side which initiates fighting, which strikes first, whereas defensive arms give an advantage to the side which responds to an attack and defends itself. A typical example of an offensive weapon, according to Quester's definition, is (again) the aircraft carrier. If two hostile aircraft carriers face one another, whichever carrier waits may be sunk by the other side. The one that initiates the fighting has a better chance of surviving. A typical example of a defensive weapon in his definition is a machine-gun post inside a bunker. If two hostile posts are facing each other, whoever ventures out first from his safe environment makes himself vulnerable and is likely to lose. Such situations tend to lead to a stalemate (provided no offensive arms are introduced into the battle).

In order not to be under any pressure to launch a preemptive attack, Switzerland emphasizes a strong air defense. It also keeps its fighter planes in bunkers carved under the mountains at the edge of airfields, so that they need not take off before a battle begins, but instead can wait until after an attack has actually taken place. Similarly, Sweden's battleships are hidden in caverns, to make them less vulnerable against a preemptive attack (Roberts 1976, p. 84). Such invulnerability strengthens the defensive value of weapons, because it removes the pressure to use them first in a war to prevent losing them.

The three definitions of defensive and offensive arms listed here are by no means mutually exclusive, but are closely related to one another, and capture various aspects of the offensive/defensive dimension. Table 5.1 summarizes these characteristics and contrasts some conventional offensive and defensive arms. The issue of nuclear weapons and possible defense against them, which raises special problems, will be discussed separately in Chapter 7.

---

**Table 5.1  Main Characteristics and Some Typical Examples of Conventional Offensive and Defensive Weapons**

| Offensive | Defensive |
|---|---|
| (threatens opponent's security, long-range mobility, provides advantage to initiator of combat) | (improves own security, fixed position or short-range mobility, provides advantage to defender) |
| Tanks | Tank barrage, antitank weapons, mine fields |
| Bombers | Antiaircraft weapons, radar warning systems, bomb shelters |
| Landing boats | Coast guard vessels, coastal mines, shore batteries in fixed emplacements |

*Superoffensive versus Superdefensive Measures*

There are even arms that may be called "superoffensive." They not only threaten the security of a potential enemy without adding to a country's own security, but they even reduce directly the security of the country acquiring them. Any weapons that may backfire or fire accidentally are of that nature. An example is an unreliable warning system that could trigger an accidental war. If the United States were to rely totally on the error-prone NORAD warning system and were to launch nuclear missiles on warning, this would reduce not only the security of the Soviet Union, but also that of the United States, as mentioned before. Another class of superoffensive weapons are those that are highly threatening and at the same time vulnerable, so that they may invite a preemptive strike. In Chapter 8 it will be shown that fixed land-based nuclear missiles with multiple warheads are of that nature.

On the other hand, there also exist "superdefensive" measures which *increase* the security of an opponent as well as one's own. For example, stationing a peacekeeping force from a neutral party in a buffer zone along a contested border can increase the security of both sides. Even though it is not always a sufficient solution, it could help in many cases. Far too little is spent for such measures, which truly increase international security. Sivard (1981, p. 5) has calculated that the amount spent worldwide for military purposes exceeded the amount devoted to peacekeeping operations 2300 times. Another superdefensive measure, which France has proposed to the United Nations, would be an international warning satellite. Such a satellite could provide information to all countries on troop movements anywhere in the world, to prevent surprise attacks anywhere. In this way, it could help increase the security of every country.

Among nonmilitary measures, the development of more abundant sources of supply, especially of renewable resources, would be a superdefensive approach aimed at eliminating potential conflicts over scarce resources. A nonthreatening approach to the prevention of war over oil reserves could be research on how to tap safe and abundant energy sources everywhere, and making that technology available worldwide. If it becomes possible to develop cheap solar cells, for instance, this would increase the energy security of all countries.

The entire range from superoffensive to superdefensive measures is represented in Figure 5.1. The diagram indicates what effect the acquisition of certain arms has on a country's own security and on the security of its potential opponents. Superdefensive arms are placed in the top-right corner of the figure, since they increase a country's own security as well as the security of potential opponents. Intermediate arms are placed at the bottom right because they increase a country's own security but reduce the security of opponents. Superoffensive

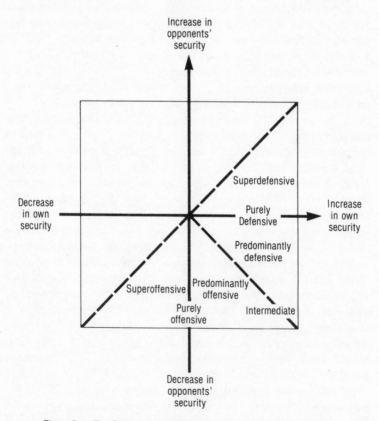

**Figure 5.1** The Spectrum from Superoffensive to Superdefensive Arms

arms, at the bottom left, reduce a country's own security as well as that of its opponents. Figure 5.2 is a replication of Figure 5.1, indicating the positions advocated by "hawks" and "doves."

Much of the current debate between "hawks" and "doves" centers on the wrong issue. "Hawks" want to increase arms, to improve their country's security, while threatening the security of potential opponents, a move to the bottom right in Figure 5.2. "Doves" want to disarm, to reduce the threat to other countries, while possibly increasing the risk to their own country's security (the top left in Figure 5.2). We should break out of this false dilemma and move to the top right: increasing *everyone's* secu-

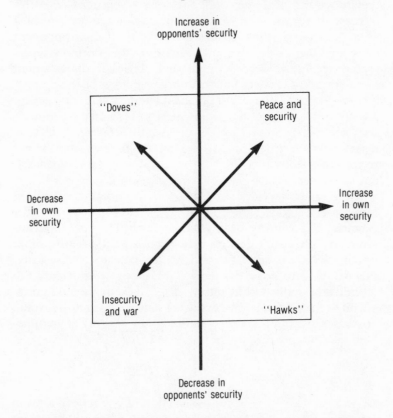

**Figure 5.2** Positions Advocated by "Hawks" and "Doves," and by Promoters of War or Peace

rity by reducing the threat of war by *superdefensive* means. Some perverse individuals are willing to risk their own security in order to threaten other countries, by acquiring superoffensive arms, which make war more likely (a move to the bottom left). The crucial debate should focus on moves along the diagonal from the bottom left to the top right, not the usual debate which concerns positions at the top left versus those at the bottom right. It is not a question of security for "us" versus security for "them," but security for *both* or *neither*.

Let us consider next the effect on the security of two countries if both simultaneously acquire additional arms. For the sake of brevity we will deal with only one case, where both countries increase or reduce their stockpiles of predominantly offensive arms (i.e., those which reduce the security of their opponent more than they add to their own security). The effects are represented in Figure 5.3. As indicated, bilateral disarmament increases the security of both countries, whereas bilateral armament reduces the security of both. Unilateral armament (assuming no response from the other country) increases a country's own security but reduces the opponent's security. Unilateral disarmament is a sort of selfless, heroic measure that, if not reciprocated, increases the opponent's security at the expense of one's own security, as shown at the top left of Figure 5.3.

The diagram developed in Figures 5.1–5.3 could also be used to represent a wide variety of other conceivable measures. For example, if a country destroyed some of its purely offensive arms, an "altruistic" gesture that increased the security of an opponent without adding to or detracting from its own security, this would correspond to a vertical move upward in Figure 5.3. A unilateral reduction in purely defensive arms would correspond to a horizontal move to the left: one's own security would be reduced without any contribution to the security of an opponent. Such a measure might be termed "masochistic."

## A Mixture of Offensive and Defensive Arms

Up to now we have considered the effect of one type of arms in isolation. What happens if offensive and defensive arms are combined? Does the offensive or the defensive element prevail?

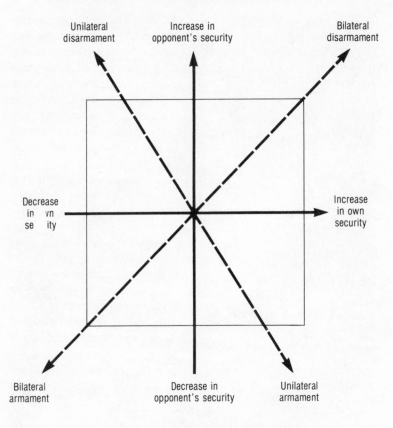

**Figure 5.3** The effects of Unilateral and Bilateral Arms Increases or Reductions (with predominantly offensive arms)

When combined with offensive arms, even apparently purely defensive arms can become highly offensive. The result may be a more-offensive weapons system than either of the two components alone.

For example, shelters alone do not threaten anyone. If, however, a country that possesses nuclear arms begins to build underground shelters for its population and industry, the other side can rightfully consider this as a threatening move, regardless of the first nation's true intentions. Without civil defense shelters, no sane leader would ever use nuclear missiles first (at least as long as they cannot destroy all of the opponent's missiles), since the country's population would be vulnerable to a devastating retaliatory strike. In such a situation, these nuclear missiles may be seen as serving only the function of deterring a nuclear attack. But if the population could be protected to some extent against retaliation, a first strike might become conceivable to some leaders under certain circumstances. Therefore, the addition of shelters to an arsenal of nuclear missiles can convert these missiles from essentially retaliatory, second-strike weapons into highly offensive, first-strike weapons.

In a deterrence situation, a potentially offensive weapons system is used to prevent aggression through the threat of retaliation. If offensive weapons are to serve the function of deterrence (even though not defense in the strict sense), the following conditions must be satisfied: (a) the offensive weapons must *never be used first*, only as a response to their use by an opponent; (b) the response must not exceed the opponent's aggressive action, it must preferably be more limited, otherwise it will lead to escalation; (c) an effort must be made to seek termination of hostilities at the earliest possible moment; and (d) it must be apparent and credible that the threatened response would occur *if and only if* the opponent attacked first. If the opponent fears that we may initiate an attack, the deterrence value is lost. (These four conditions are discussed in more detail from another perspective in the Appendix.)

The 1972 treaty between the United States and the Soviet Union on the limitation of antiballistic missile systems recognizes that a defense of cities against missiles could undermine the precarious stability of the system of mutual assured destruction (MAD). That system is certainly still extremely dangerous, and does not represent a permanent solution to the prevention of nuclear war. We must seek mutual nuclear disarmament. But even worse than MAD is a situation in which one or both sides possesses a first-strike capability.

It is an entirely different issue if a country that does not possess nuclear arms builds nuclear fallout shelters. Since this cannot possibly be seen as preparation for launching a nuclear war, it retains its purely defensive function. Sweden and Switzerland, which like most countries have no nuclear weapons and no plans of acquiring any, have the most-extensive civil defense shelter programs in the world (Roberts 1976, p. 102; General Defense 1979, p. 24). Every new house in Switzerland is required by law to have an underground shelter with heavy concrete walls, filtered ventilated air, and reserves of food and water. Modern shelters for more than 70 percent of the population have been built, and plans are to increase coverage to 100 percent. Of course, even these shelters can offer no protection against a direct nuclear attack. But they could save lives in case of a limited nuclear war in which these countries are not the main targets, by offering some protection against radioactive fallout.

We can have no illusion that building shelters will solve the problem of nuclear war. The main effort must be prevention. Yet, the primary responsibility for avoiding nuclear war rests with the nuclear powers, since countries without nuclear arms have little control over the prevention of nuclear war. Having some limited protection for their population against nuclear blackmail puts these nations into a somewhat better position to forego the possession of nuclear weapons as a deterrent.

Another consideration that has convinced many countries with the technical capability of producing nuclear weapons to forego their development is the awareness that such an initiative on their part would probably induce other countries to do the same. The resulting proliferation of nuclear weapons would make the world a more-dangerous place. This is not to say that the superpowers have shown greater responsibility in their control of nuclear weapons than smaller countries would. Maybe the opposite is true. But it is simply a fact that the more hands there are on a nuclear trigger (whether "big" or "small" matters little), the more likely it is that these weapons will one day be used. For this reason there is a mutual interest in non-proliferation.

Perhaps the greatest danger in the plans of nuclear powers to expand civil defense through civilian shelters, or through the potential evacuation of cities, stems from the resultant false feeling of relative security, which may lead some people to relax their efforts to prevent nuclear war. Even if evacuation plans are unfeasible, as long as some policymakers believe they would work, the false sense of safety created by these plans can increase the danger of war. T. K. Jones, Reagan's Deputy Undersecretary of Defense for Strategic and Theater Nuclear Forces, made an infamous statement concerning makeshift civil defense shelters against nuclear weapons: "If there are enough shovels to go around, everybody's going to make it" (Scheer 1982, p. 23).

Critics of civil defense should be very clear in stating their reasons, to avoid being accused of wanting to make their country vulnerable. Whereas civil defense measures in non-nuclear nations do not increase the danger of nuclear war, the same measures undertaken by a nation possessing nuclear weapons may be perceived by others as a preparation for the use of those weapons.

From the above distinction it follows that it is not very useful to look at individual weapons and to judge whether they are offensive or defensive. The entire combination of weapons and other defense preparations of a country must be considered in order to decide whether the *whole system* is predominantly offensive or defensive. These considerations apply to any defensive weapons, if they are combined with offensive forces.

## Defensive Arms as a Preliminary Step to an Improved World Order

Harry Hollins (1982) proposes that as an intermediate step before the establishment of a global legal order charged with resolving conflicts that could lead to war, all countries limit themselves to purely defensive arms. This would still permit each country to protect its own national security, but would eliminate the possibility of aggression. If this measure were adopted by *all* countries, it would effectively eliminate war. Yet this step is more easily feasible than the establishment of some global authority, because it does not require countries to give up their sovereignty in the area of defense.

It should be clear that a country's ability to defend itself is not the same as its ability to win a "victory" over an opponent. 'Defense means only that a country can protect its territory and retain its freedom. It does not mean the ability to occupy the territory of an aggressor or to impose one's will on another population. But neither does effective defense permit an opponent to win any victory over oneself.

A strategy of limiting oneself to a purely defensive military posture has been criticized by observing that *if* a country with only defensive arms is involved in a war, the fighting will take place on its own territory, whereas a country possessing offensive arms can fight the war on someone else's soil. But such a comparison misses the whole point. As history has shown, the true choice is rather between a concentration on defense, which helps avoid war, and an offensive posture, which is likely to draw a country into war.

There is a widespread and deeply rooted belief, not only among ordinary citizens, but also among many top government officials, that the more a country spends for arms, the safer it is. However, the *type* of arms that is acquired is the crucial factor. As we have seen, certain superoffensive arms directly reduce a country's security, instead of increasing it. In many cases a unilateral acquisition of arms may increase a country's own security and reduce the security of potential opponents. But *arms buildups rarely remain unilateral.* They are likely to lead to increased armament by potential opponents and thus may reduce a country's security in the long run, even if they increase its security over the short run. In the next chapter we will see that offensive arms have a much greater tendency to cause arms races than defensive arms.

# 6 Dynamics of Arms Races

Arms races are not only costly in economic terms, but have a tendency to end in war. The American peace researcher Michael Wallace (quoted in Galtung 1984) found that among 99 cases of "serious dispute or military confrontation" in the period 1820–1964, 23 of the 28 preceded by an arms race ended in war, while 68 of the 71 not preceded by an arms race ended without war. Of course, the arms race need not be the cause of war, but may be a symptom of the intensity of the underlying conflict. Nonetheless, the fact that an intense nuclear arms race is taking place at present is reason for concern, whether the arms race is a cause or consequence of the associated conflict. It seems most likely that the intensity of an arms race and of the corresponding conflict mutually feed on each other.

*Potential Causes of Arms Races*

Many factors are responsible for arms races. They can be divided into the two major categories of "self-stimulation" and "mutual stimulation," or internal and external causes. The following is a partial list.

1. One of the main internal causes of arms races may be the *profitability* of weapons sales to the government. Selling anything to a government can be far more profitable than selling the same goods to private individuals, who are usually more cost-conscious. People who spend public funds tend to be more generous than if they were spending their private fortunes.

"Cost-plus" contracts, which imply that the government pays a fixed percentage of profits on top of actual costs, whatever the costs, are common for military purchases. They have a built-in incentive for waste: the more a firm exceeds the estimated costs on a proposed new weapons system, the higher are its profits. In some instances people have moved back and forth several times between positions in the defense industry and in the government, where they can award defense contracts. Even in a planned economy where private profit is not involved, officials in charge of the defense industry probably have a taste for expanding the operations they control. A military-bureaucratic complex may not be substantially different from a military-industrial complex.

2. Another internal factor responsible for the arms race is the *curiosity of scientists* to develop new and more-sophisticated weapons, and the resulting pressure on the government from research and development establishments. An example is the development of the first atomic bomb, which was initially motivated by fear that Hitler might obtain one first. But, according to Ground Zero (1982, p. 28),

> by early 1945 it was clear that the Germans would not have an atomic bomb. Knowing this, some American scientists sought to shut down or delay the Manhattan Project. But the momentum of the project was now being sustained as much by the desire to know whether or not the bomb could be built as by any clear idea of how and why the bomb would be used.

3. Another factor that has been said to play a role in the United States is that there is not only an external arms race with the Soviet Union, but also an *"internal arms race"* between the Army, Navy and Air Force. If one of the three services gets a new weapons system, the other two want one that is equivalent if not superior.

4. Certain governments may also engage in an arms race or even deliberately seek a confrontation to *rally support* from a dissatisfied population against a supposed "external threat." One example may be the 1982 Argentine/United Kingdom war over the Falkland Islands/Malvinas.

5. In some cases, governments acquire arms allegedly for

their country's defense against outside aggression, but use these arms in fact to *suppress domestic opposition movements*.

6. Despite these possible internal factors, it is hard to believe that an arms race could go on for long without some *external threat*, or at least a perceived threat. To divert large sums year after year from the civilian economy to military purposes, some justification must be offered from time to time. Johan Galtung once said, with slight irony, that the military establishments of the United States and the Soviet Union are each other's best friends—neither can exist without the other.

## Some Models

In the Appendix, a series of simple models of an externally stimulated arms race between two countries are briefly discussed. Various assumptions are examined. The two countries may seek only to defend themselves, as governments typically claim to do; alternatively, they may seek to conquer each other. An asymmetric case is also discussed in which one country desires to attack the other, while the other wishes only to prevent aggression.

I do not claim that any of these models explains "the" arms race. The buildup of arms results from multiple interwoven causes, rather than from a single cause. I only offer reasons why one can expect that the acquisition of offensive arms leads to a much more intensive arms race at higher levels of threats and military expenditures than does the acquisition of defensive arms. (Those interested in mathematical reasoning may wish to read the Appendix at this point, in conjunction with the present chapter.)

Very briefly, the main idea underlying these models is the following: if we acquire *offensive* arms, their main effect is to threaten the security of an opponent. The opponent will want to restore his security by building more arms. If he also uses offensive arms, they contribute little to his own security, and therefore he needs a large quantity to restore his security to an acceptable level. But this in turn reduces our security further, and we will seek even more arms, and so on. The result is a classic arms race. Only the pressure of competing demands from the civilian sectors of the economy will ultimately impose a limit on military expenditures.

If the two countries could reach an agreement on mutual disarmament, both would, of course, be safer, and their economies would be free from the burden of military spending (provided there were no threats from other countries). For this reason, it is important to pursue efforts toward negotiated mutual disarmament. Yet if the prevailing weapons technology is offensive, a situation of complete mutual disarmament may not be stable. If one of the two countries should deviate ever so slightly from total disarmament, the other would find it in its best interest to *overcompensate* with an arms buildup.

With predominantly *defensive* arms, the situation is quite different. If we build defensive arms, their main effect is to add to our security, and they reduce the security of an opponent only slightly. He will want to acquire some additional arms to compensate for that loss of security, but he will add a smaller quantity than we did. The chain of mutual reactions will very soon come to a halt when both sides feel sufficiently protected.

The surprising result, therefore, is that *if the two countries use sufficiently defensive arms to protect themselves, the arms race will eventually stop, even in the absence of any mutual agreement*, provided that each side seeks only to maintain its own security.

It may be difficult to establish precisely how defensive is "sufficiently" defensive. But it is not necessary to know this in order to draw policy conclusions. It is clear that the more defensive the armaments are, the better. In the face of uncertainty as to where the precise borderline between offensive and defensive arms is located, where an arms race would begin to take off, it is preferable to err on the safe side of more highly defensive arms.

The practice of erring on the safe side is a characteristic that also distinguishes engineering from pure science. For example, a physicist may be able to calculate exactly how thick a cable should be to support an elevator. A good engineer will make it perhaps twice as thick, because if the cable were just barely thick enough, elevators would occasionally fall to the ground. We may need a more practical social science that can yield workable prescriptions even when all the underlying assumptions are not completely satisfied, or even if there remains some uncertainty about the true state of the world. Such an applied discipline would relate to political science and economics as engineering does to physics, or medicine to biology (Etzioni 1982).

An analysis of the models in the Appendix shows that the more offensive are the arms used, the lower is both countries' security, the higher is their mutual level of arms expenditures, the greater the burden on the civilian economies, the slower the rates of economic growth, and the lower the living standard of their populations. On the other hand, the more highly defensive are the arms used by both sides, the more secure they are, the less they need to spend for arms, and the more prosperous are their economies.

How do countries choose between using offensive or defensive arms to maintain their security? If there is no mutual agreement, and limited foresight, each country will choose those types of arms that it perceives to provide it with the greatest amount of security per monetary unit spent, regardless of what effect these arms have on the security of the other side. This yields the somewhat paradoxical result that *a breakthrough in weapons technology—namely, the discovery of cheap and effective defensive arms—could bring an end to the arms race*. This may occur even in the absence of any negotiated agreement, as long as the countries involved are interested only in maintaining their own defense, not in aggression. Unfortunately, it also means that the invention of cheap offensive arms will accelerate the arms race, even if neither side has any aggressive intentions.

Even more surprising may be that under certain circumstances it can be in a country's own security interests to make defensive weapons technology available to an opponent. This is the case if a country has no intention of attacking its opponent, but if the opponent is afraid of such an attack and has built threatening offensive arms to defend itself. If the opponent realized that a new type of defensive arms, which pose no threat to others, could be used for cheap and effective protection, the opponent might decide to switch to these new arms. This would considerably improve the security of the country that made available the technology. For example, if we could show to an opponent that she could protect herself more effectively against a feared invasion with antitank weapons than with tanks, she might stop building tanks. Her antitank weapons would pose no threat to us, as long as we do not plan to invade her country.

Arthur Macy Cox (1981), a former CIA official, has stressed that it would be in the United States' own security interest to make its most advanced and reliable computers available to the Soviet Union for its antimissile warning system, so that a nuclear war would not start due to the malfunction of a less-reliable computer. Providing technology to opponents must, nevertheless, be approached with caution. A defensive system can be made available to an opponent only if his knowing it provides no easy way of sabotaging the system. Indeed, there are examples of purely defensive measures that can be disclosed to everyone without risk. For example, the United States, which makes no secret of the fact that it maintains stockpiles of food and strategic raw materials, may well encourage other countries to keep such stockpiles, in order to remove a potential source of conflict that could lead to war. Another example is the "permissive action link" that physically prevents the unauthorized or accidental firing of nuclear missiles unless the secret 12-digit code has been transmitted by the Commander-in-Chief. When the United States developed that technology in the early 1960s, before the Soviet Union, it would have been clearly in the U.S. interest to make that technology available also to the Soviet Union. (It may not even be necessary to make defensive technology officially available to an opponent. It may be sufficient to display it in maneuvers, since there is a natural tendency to imitate the other side.)

The fact that defensive arms tend to lead to an end of arms races has the unfortunate consequence that it is much more profitable to export offensive arms than defensive arms, preferably to both parties in a conflict. Supplying offensive arms to warring factions is like pouring gasoline on a fire. Supplying purely defensive arms is like pouring water on it. The export of offensive arms assures an ever-growing demand. In this respect, it resembles the drug traffic, which is also highly profitable because it creates addiction. If a country were to export purely defensive arms, soon all the arms importers would become secure, and the market would be saturated. The same applies to domestic demand for the defense industry, which is much more profitable when it is an "offense industry."

An analogous problem, which is much less serious than the arms race but which exhibits some similar features, is traffic safety. In a collision, if X has a big, heavy car and Y a small car, X will be safe but Y's car will be crushed. For this reason, people feel safer in a big car. But if *everyone* had a small, light car, then everyone would be safer, at lower costs. Seatbelts, which can protect a driver and his passengers without posing any additional hazard to the occupants of other cars, are a kind of "defensive" technology that can contribute to solving the traffic safety problem.

Despite the obvious advantages of a defensive posture, many countries today favor offensive arms. One reason may be that offensive arms are "cheaper." For example, one missile can threaten thousands of different targets, whereas to seek to protect all those potential targets by building them deep underground would be much more expensive. According to a proverb, "offense is the best defense." The reason is that an attacker has the advantage that he can choose the location and time of attack and concentrate all his forces there, while the defender must seek to protect her territory everywhere and at all times. But if one takes into account the longer-term, indirect effects of an offensive posture in terms of stimulating the arms race and bringing greater insecurity to all, then a true defense still has a great deal in its favor. Figures given in Chapter 14 suggest that an effective defense is not more, but less, expensive than an offensive military posture, contrary to widespread belief.

Let us now briefly compare the model discussed so far to a second model, in which the two countries are not merely interested in protecting their own security, but in conquering each other. In that case, they will prefer offensive arms over defensive ones, even if these arms are more expensive and less effective in maintaining their own security. The nations involved seek deliberately to reduce each other's security, not just to preserve their own. Each country will choose the types of arms that maximize the security differential between itself and its opponent. Under a set of plausible additional assumptions (specified by Fischer 1981), the arms race will proceed at the highest feasible level that the civilian economy can sustain without turning into negative growth, regardless of the arms technologies available. In this case, a technological solution cannot save the situation.

Perhaps of wider concern is the case of mixed objectives, where one country is interested in conquering the other, but the second country is interested only in maintaining its own security. There is a popular saying that no one can live in peace if the wicked neighbor does not want it. Fortunately, the saying turns out not to be true in this case. As long as at least *one* of the two countries is satisfied with defending itself, if it has access to a sufficiently effective defensive technology, it can bring about an end to the arms race, without any agreement from the other side. The Romans used to say, "If you want peace, prepare for war." But a country that wants peace must prepare *against war*, not "for" war—otherwise it will get war.

I will give an illustrative example. Suppose among two countries, which are engaged in a bomber race, one of them is interested only in its own defense and is able to develop a cheap and reliable antiaircraft weapon. This will force the other country to give up the race, even if it has aggressive intentions. For if it continued to build more bombers, it would only ruin its own economy, without any chance of succeeding in its aggressive intentions.

Some recent advances in *precision-guided munitions*, heat-seeking missiles, etc., have improved defensive capabilities. There is some prospect that the days of the battleship and air-craft carrier may be numbered, as the comparatively cheap Exocet missile demonstrated in the war over the Falkland Islands/Malvinas. The tank may also become obsolete, if it becomes possible to build a cheap ray gun. The ray gun accelerates pellets not by chemical explosion, but electromagnetically. The pellets travel at about ten times the speed of a bullet and can pierce even heavy armor. The destructive power of the gun would be highly localized, and would not cause the widespread, indiscriminate destruction of a neutron bomb. (Another improvement on present-day armaments has been proposed by Fallows (1981, p. 181), a nonlethal weapon, a "gas that would temporarily disable people without killing them." He recalls "the scenes from Vietnam in which a patrol would lob grenades into a tunnel, to avoid any risk that the people huddled inside might be 'unfriendlies.' Disabling gas, used by soldiers who were themselves protected against its effects, could eliminate such bloody work." While such a gas could be used in offensive operations as well as for defense, at least it would make warfare less murderous. It could also be used to deal in a more humane way with terrorists or dangerous criminals.)

Without a probing empirical investigation, it is not possible to know which countries seek victory over their opponents, and which simply wish to maintain their own security and seek to prevent war. Practically all countries profess to seek only the latter goal. But it may well be that a number of countries are more interested in winning a war, if a war should arise, than in preventing the outbreak of war. While such a position may have had a certain rationality in the past, when one side could be victorious, with today's growing and spreading arsenal of nuclear arms this view is rapidly becoming obsolete. Any nuclear conflict would not leave any side better off than before, and would bring only destruction to all sides. Therefore, the search for ways to prevent war has become more urgent than ever before.

A widespread belief maintains that technology in itself is neutral in terms of its effect on human welfare. According to this view, whether technology serves good or bad purposes depends entirely on the use made of it. While many examples could be cited to support this position, the argument is not always valid. As we have seen, breakthroughs in defensive technology tend to improve global security, whereas breakthroughs in offensive weapons technology tend to reduce everyone's security, in the long run. Here lies a true challenge for scientists and engineers in weapons research laboratories throughout the world and for the governments who support them: to create cheap and effective defensive arms that can help bring an end to the arms race and put the scientists out of their present jobs—but at least not out of existence.

# 7 Preventing Nuclear War

In this chapter we will examine a number of independent and cooperative measures that nations can take to reduce the threat of nuclear war.

## "Defense" against Nuclear Weapons?

What good are defensive weapons against a possible nuclear attack? Ronald Reagan, in his so-called "star-wars" speech of 23 March 1983, proposed that the United States develop space-based beam weapons that could destroy nuclear missiles in flight. He even offered to share such a defensive technology with the Soviet Union at some future time. He added, "I have become more and more deeply convinced that the human spirit must be capable of rising above dealing with other nations and human beings by threatening their existence. . . . Would it not be better to save lives than to avenge them?"

The underlying idea is praiseworthy, but the proposal has some serious flaws. First, let us try to imagine the United States' reaction if the Soviet Union were to announce that it was going to develop a space-based defense against nuclear missiles (while keeping its missiles). The United States would be terribly frightened, and would have reason to be. Such a technology could theoretically enable the Soviet Union to subject the United States to nuclear blackmail without facing any threat of retaliation. Even if the Soviet Union promised to make that technology available to the United States, the United States would (and should) hesitate to base its security on such a promise. The United States would probably want to increase its nuclear arsenal so it could penetrate any Soviet defense and maintain its potential to deter a Soviet attack. And it must be assumed that exactly the same will also be the Soviet reaction to the proposed U.S. development.

Second, laser or particle beams in space can be effective only against ballistic missiles that leave the atmosphere. The United States has already developed the counterweapon to such a defense, the cruise missile, which follows the ground at low altitude. It must be expected that the Soviet Union will soon possess an equally advanced cruise missile program. This renders space-based beam weapons ineffective against the latest generation of missiles.

Third, the space stations that would be used to emit laser or particle beams to destroy missiles could themselves be destroyed by hostile beams. They would be extremely vulnerable. During a crisis, the first thing each side would want to do would be to destroy the other side's space stations before their own stations were destroyed. Therefore, such a technology would add a new element of instability. This problem would be particularly serious, since one such space station could emit many beams, and could potentially destroy several of the opponent's stations (in the same way as one bomber may be able to destroy several bombers on the ground, a factor contributing to instability).

Therefore, such plans to develop a "nonthreatening" defense against a nuclear attack, as attractive as they may sound, will not work. Worse than that, they would lead to a new and more-dangerous round in the arms race. Instead of eliminating nuclear war, such weapons might be designed to implement a nuclear war–fighting strategy of "damage limitation" and "prevailing" in a nuclear exchange. That could make a nuclear war more "thinkable" to certain people. Such a course is suicidal.

Indeed, no effective military defense against nuclear weapons is known today. Blast and fallout shelters can give only very limited protection and that only at a great distance from a nuclear explosion; they offer no protection against a direct hit. Antiballistic missile systems of any degree of reliability would be extremely difficult to construct, and it would be much cheaper to circumvent them with more ballistic missiles.

Would the discovery of a cheap, automated excavation technology, that would make it possible to build entire cities deep underground, offer any protection against nuclear threats? Unfortunately, the same technology could also be used to construct nuclear "subterrestrials" (analogous to submarines) that would pose a new threat. To build cities in space, as some have proposed as a solution, would be no escape either—it is much easier to transport a nuclear warhead into outer space than an entire city.

### Dissuasion versus Deterrence

The only way to prevent nuclear war on a lasting basis is to transform the international system into a new global order in which disputes between nations can be resolved without resort to violence. As Dwight Eisenhower once pointed out, weapons have reached a stage where there can be no winner or loser, where war means only the destruction of people, and asked, "Won't we have the common sense to sit down at the negotiating table and do away with war as a means of settling our disputes?" Until such a new world order has been established, interim measures are needed for nations to protect themselves against a nuclear attack. Two alternate methods are either deterrence (the threat of retaliation) or "dissuasion"—the ability to convince a potential opponent that it is more attractive for him to maintain mutually beneficial peaceful relations than to destroy you.

The United States, England, and France have nuclear forces with which they could inflict enormous destruction upon one another. But they are not afraid of this, because they maintain friendly relations. They may have some disputes, but they would never think of settling them through war. Even between nations that do not have equally close relations, it is possible to reach accommodation by proving to the other side that more is to be gained for both in the absence of hostility. The dramatic improvement in relations between the United States and China through the opening of trade and diplomatic relations is an example.

An entire range of nonmilitary measures to prove to a potential opponent that leaving you in peace is more attractive for him than waging war against you will be discussed in Chapter 10. Nonmilitary defense has the advantage that it does not cause fear among opponents and thus does not lead to an escalation of threats. The danger of mutual escalation is a problem with deterrence. Yet it is not likely that the major nuclear powers will soon give up reliance on deterrence. And given the amount of fear and suspicion that has accumulated between the superpowers over the years, it is doubtful that anything less than deterrence would work for them in the near future until the international climate has improved considerably.

In this chapter, I will concentrate on a discussion of deterrence and what makes it more or less stable. In doing so I have no illusion that so-called "stable" deterrence can prevent the outbreak of nuclear war on a lasting basis. I intend simply to outline a feasible path away from the danger we are presently caught in to a safer world. The proposed modest steps may enable us to gain enough time to work out the far-reaching changes in the global system that will have to be made.

One may ask what point there is in retaliation, in destroying another nation, and possibly the human race, after one country has already been destroyed in a nuclear attack. Nothing could be gained by such retaliation, no suffering could be undone, and only more suffering would result. But the idea is to *prevent* such an attack in the first place through the threat of retaliation. It is not necessary to threaten retaliation of such enormous proportions that it would risk destruction of the biosphere. Such a threat would indeed be totally senseless, and therefore also hardly credible. But the certain prospect of suffering great damage through retaliation, for example, to a country's seat of government and military industries, may deter a leader from considering a nuclear strike when he or she might otherwise be tempted to do so.

Some ask whether it would not be entirely reasonable for a country to go ahead with unilateral nuclear disarmament and expect that others would then follow. Would any of today's leaders really consider using nuclear arms against a country that had destroyed its nuclear weapons? But the only time nuclear weapons have ever been used, in Hiroshima and Nagasaki, it was against a country possessing no nuclear weapons (even though against a country that had initiated the hostilities). Undoubtedly, *complete* nuclear disarmament will be acceptable only if it is mutual. However, certain steps toward partial nuclear disarmament can be taken unilaterally without risk, as will be shown in the next chapter.

A whole variety of measures can be taken to eliminate or at least reduce the danger of nuclear war. Some are simple short term measures, others are more far-reaching and will take longer. Some can be undertaken independently, others require mutual agreement.

*Cooperative Measures*

I begin by describing some measures that are feasible only if there is negotiated agreement between the superpowers, or even among all countries. Our ultimate goal is, of course, a totally disarmed world, with only some global police forces remaining. In such a world, the construction of instruments of murder with the primary purpose of killing people would no longer be socially acceptable. But this is a long-term goal that cannot be achieved overnight. It is unlikely that the Soviet Union would agree to transfer responsibility for its national security to a supranational body in the near future. Neither would the United States. While we will constantly want to work toward this goal, it would be unwise not to take intermediate steps to reduce the threat of nuclear war now. A somewhat less ambitious but also less difficult goal would be for all countries to agree to limit themselves to conventional defensive arms. These arms could be used only to defend the nation's own territory, not to attack or threaten other countries. This would effectively eliminate war. A still less far-reaching measure would be complete mutual nuclear disarmament, leaving only conventional military forces. More modest is a global agreement to reduce nuclear weapons substantially from today's levels, with each nuclear power keeping only a minimal stock of nuclear weapons considered essential for deterrence.

## A Mutual Verifiable Freeze

The most-modest, but in the short-run perhaps the most-feasible negotiated arms control measure would be an agreement between the United States and the Soviet Union for a verified freeze of nuclear arms at current levels, putting a stop to the testing, production, and deployment of additional nuclear weapons by both sides. Like a train, the arms race must first come to a halt before it can be reversed. Silviu Brucan, the former Romanian ambassador to the United Nations, once said that a nuclear freeze was to the arms race what a cease-fire was to a war. Usually, an agreement on a cease-fire is needed before any meaningful peace negotiations can begin.

A nuclear freeze would prevent the introduction of some destabilizing new weapons systems. For example, once land-based cruise missiles are widely deployed, verified arms control agreements could become virtually impossible, because these missiles are so small that they can easily be concealed (Johansen 1979, p. 3). The U.S. cruise missile Tomahawk is only 18 feet long and 2 feet 3 inches wide (*Newsweek*, 31 January 1983, p. 13). While it is at least possible to count the bombers that carry air-launched cruise missiles, it is practically impossible to count ground-launched cruise missiles. It is much easier to verify a complete ban on a certain type of weapons (such as ground-launched cruise missiles) than it is to verify an agreed-upon numerical ceiling. If there were a total ban, the discovery of a single weapon of this type would reveal a violation of the treaty. But if a certain number of such weapons were permitted, it would be much more difficult to find and count all of them. Cruise missiles are also comparatively cheap and so could introduce the possibility of nuclear weapons proliferation among many countries. It is urgent to agree to a freeze before that happens.

The nuclear freeze proposal enjoys substantial public support in the United States. In a poll published by the *New York Times* (30 May 1982), 72 percent of the American public favored a nuclear freeze, with 21 percent opposed (the remainder were undecided). Under the condition that both the United States and the Soviet Union could catch the other country if it were cheating, 83 percent favored a freeze, with 12 percent opposed. If the freeze would result in approximately equal nuclear strength on both sides, then 87 percent favored it, with only 9 percent opposed. The freeze proposal was approved by voters in eight out of nine states and in 28 out of the 30 cities and counties where it appeared on the November 1982 ballot, in spite of strong opposition from the Reagan administration (*New York Times*, 9 March 1983).

### A Comprehensive Test Ban

Less far-reaching than a freeze but a very useful agreement nevertheless would be a compehensive test ban of all nuclear weapons, whether new or old types. A periodic testing of random samples of existing nuclear weapons is necessary to ascertain that they still work. If they have not been tested for a long time, their "reliability" is diminished. But a high reliability is needed only to carry out a surprise counterforce strike, where the attacker wants to be sure that he can destroy all the opponent's missiles. As a deterrent against a nuclear attack, on the other hand, the prospect that *most* of the weapons would go off if they were used in a retaliatory strike is quite sufficient. In this way, a comprehensive test ban would reduce the instability of nuclear deterrence. It would raise serious doubts about either side's ability to launch a successful first strike, but would not significantly reduce the deterrent effect of a possible retaliatory second strike (Calder 1979, p. 160).

### Independent Measures

In the remainder of this chapter, I will discuss measures to reduce the threat of nuclear war that can be taken independently by either side (or by both). Independent measures are, in a certain sense, easier to take than cooperative measures, because they do not hinge on the outcome of complicated negotiations. And if these measures improve a country's own security, as will be explained, there should not be much difficulty in winning public support for them.

In Chapter 1, four possible causes for the outbreak of a nuclear war were listed: accident, insanity, escalation of a conventional war, or a preemptive first strike. In the following we will examine some independent measures that can be taken by either side to reduce each of these dangers.

### To Prevent Accidents: No Launch-on-Warning

To prevent nuclear war by accident, it is of course, preferable if *all* countries that possess nuclear arms take the utmost care. But there is no need to wait for others before taking the first step. Each country will, in its *own* interest as well as the interests of others, want to do everything it can to reduce the risk of accidental nuclear war, by making all its systems as fail-safe as humanly possible, and by not taking any irreversible steps based on a potentially false warning. There is no need to wait for negotiations to do that.

### To Guard against Insanity: "Multiple Keys"

To prevent the launching of nuclear weapons because someone has temporarily become insane, one precaution is to make it impossible that any single individual, not even a country's leader, can alone authorize the use of nuclear weapons. Instead, at least two or preferably more people should be required to give their consent. The probability that two people will go insane simultaneously is, of course, quite low. The same principle was used in Prague to guard the king's crown, which was kept behind a door with seven locks. One key to each lock was in the possession of one of the seven city fathers, and only if all seven keys were present could the door be opened. This was to prevent loss of the crown in case one key was lost or stolen. Even that system was not perfect—a thief might find another way to break in.

Even the requirement that several individuals approve the launch of nuclear weapons might not protect adequately against catastrophe. All the individuals whose agreement is required could receive the same erroneous information. Some protection against that danger is obtained by not relying on only one source of information, but by consulting several sources that are completely independent of one another.

The most dangerous situation is that in which any one of many individuals has the capability to launch nuclear missiles. In that case, the probability that sooner or later one of them will make an irrational and fatal move is increased greatly. If the decision to use nuclear weapons is delegated to battlefield commanders, the danger is increased enormously that the nuclear threshold will be crossed, with unknown consequences. A great danger lies also in the temptation to "flush" the authorization codes through the whole command system during an acute crisis, for fear that after an attack communications might be disrupted.

### To Prevent Escalation: No First Use

The third danger is that a conventional war may escalate into a nuclear war, if the losing side possesses nuclear arms (or is allied with a nuclear power). It is doubtful that once nuclear weapons are used, the war would remain limited. As long as the losing side possessed still more nuclear arms, it would be tempted to use them. As Schell (1982, p. 191) puts it, "War has never been anything but unilateral disarmament—the disarmament of one side by the other." But with nuclear arms, both sides may be destroyed totally before that happens.

To prevent the escalation of a conventional war into a nuclear war, it is obviously best to prevent a conventional war in the first place. In its own interest, no country should use conventional arms to attack others, or seek more than self-defense in a war started by others, so as not to press others to resort to nuclear arms. Nations should also maintain a sufficiently strong conventional defense, to prevent being faced with the dilemma of choosing between capitulation or using nuclear arms.

Even if the first barrier, prevention of conventional war, is breached, the escalation to a nuclear holocaust should be prevented by a strict policy of no first use of nuclear arms. Such a policy has been unilaterally declared by the Soviet Union (*New*

*York Times,* 16 June 1982) and has been proposed for NATO by four former American officials, McGeorge Bundy, George F. Kennan, Robert S. McNamara, and Gerard Smith (1982). So far, the United States has refused to make such a pledge, citing NATO's numerical inferiority in conventional arms. There is no doubt that the threat of initiating nuclear war in response to a conventional attack in Europe, if that threat is believed, may increase deterrence against such an attack and thus make a war in that region less likely. But it would also make any such war vastly more devastating to both sides, and it would hardly remain limited to Europe.

Deterrence alone is only half the task. An effective defense must serve a dual purpose: (a) it must seek to deter aggression and (b) it must seek to save what it intends to protect, to guarantee, as far as possible, people's survival, and prepare the way for liberation from an occupation force, if deterrence should ever fail (Sharp 1981, p. 6). While nuclear deterrence might contribute to the first of these two objectives (to reduce the likelihood of war), it would fail catastrophically on the second count (to reduce the destructiveness of war).

Adam Roberts (1976, p. 254) says that "NATO's problems in respect of nuclear weapons are expressed in two closely related fears: that these weapons might be used in defense of Western Europe; and that they might not be." He quotes Henry Kissinger, the Secretary of State in the Nixon and Ford administrations: "What our allies understand by nuclear support is less clear. They want the *appearance* of nuclear support so that the Soviets never challenge their vital interests. Whether they are actually prepared to face the consequences of nuclear war is ambiguous." One cannot have it both ways.

Numerous examples from history show that nuclear deterrence occasionally does fail. For example, the Berlin blockade occurred in 1948, when the United States had a monopoly of nuclear weapons; the British navy's nuclear submarines failed to deter Argentina's occupation of the Falkland Islands/Malvinas.

What produces deterrence is not the capability to retaliate, but the credibility of some retaliatory action. If the threat of retaliation is out of proportion with what it seeks to deter, credibility is diminished. A difficult dilemma will then be faced when an opponent considers that threat merely to be a bluff, and calls the bluff. It is far better to have a sufficiently strong conventional defense readiness than to rely on nuclear deterrence against a conventional attack. For example, a potential invasion by a massive tank column is better prevented by a sufficient number of nonoffensive antitank weapons than by the threat of using neutron bombs, which would break the nuclear threshold and possibly lead to all-out nuclear war. Given this prospect, the threat of using neutron bombs might not be believed; instead, a credible conventional defense may well offer a stronger deterrent. Bundy (1979, p. 10) writes, "Those who think that either political will or less-than-nuclear strength is unimportant in such matters will find instruction in considering the record of Yugoslavia under Tito. If Tito could stave off the Soviet Union, must NATO fail?"

Robert S. McNamara (1983), the Secretary of Defense in the Kennedy and Johnson administrations, has pointed to problems with the strategy of "flexible response" (which includes nuclear deterrence against a conventional Soviet attack on NATO): "The ultimate sanction, . . . The launch of strategic nuclear weapons against the Soviet homeland . . . would be an act of suicide. . . . One cannot build a credible deterrent on an incredible action."

Relying on nuclear weapons to deter a conventional attack is a very dubious approach to defense. It is comparable to putting a trip wire around a house, to kill a burglar, and blowing up the trespasser, the house and the people inside. There are less-suicidal and more-effective methods to protect homes against burglary, such as good locks and burglar alarm systems. Similarly, conventional defense against a feared conventional attack is far preferable to reliance on nuclear deterrence, even if the immediate costs should be greater.

It is very important to recognize that what is called for is a strengthening of conventional *defense*, not simply of conventional "forces," as many advocate. Conventional forces that have potential offensive use will accelerate a conventional arms race, and possibly make war more likely. It would also be in the Soviet Union's security interest to recognize this, and to seek to defend itself with antitank and antiaircraft weapons, rather than with more tanks and bombers, or even with nuclear missiles aimed at Western Europe.

A concrete measure that would help reduce the danger of escalation of a conventional war would be the withdrawal of so-called "battlefield" nuclear weapons from the East-West border. This proposal has been stressed by the Independent Commission on Disarmament and Security Issues (1982, p. 146–47) under the chairmanship of Olof Palme, who is now the Swedish prime minister. Many of these short-range nuclear weapons are artillery shells. In a conventional battle, they could fall into enemy hands, which increases the pressure to use them before they are seized by the opponent. It is difficult to maintain centralized control over their use under battle conditions. The presence of such weapons increases the danger that the nuclear threshold may be crossed in case of a war.

Deterrence of a conventional war with a nuclear threat is also very risky because it is sometimes not obvious *who started* the war. It could escalate from a very small incident. There is always *something* that the other side did first. Each side tends not only to claim, but also to *believe* that the other side is responsible for a war. For example, in Vietnam the United States considered North Vietnam to be the aggressor, while North Vietnam considered the United States the aggressor. Unless there is a clear firebreak between conventional and nuclear arms, there may be no limit to escalation.

## To Prevent a Preemptive Attack: No First-Strike Threat

The fourth danger which might lead to the outbreak of nuclear war, a *preemptive first strike* by an opponent, is also best averted by a policy of no first use. Nothing puts as much pressure on a national leader to launch a preemptive first strike as the fear that otherwise *he* might suffer a first strike. His country might then suffer even greater losses from the opponent's full arsenal than from any retaliatory strike after most of the opponent's nuclear weapons have been destroyed in a preemptive strike.

As economist Thomas Schelling has formulated the issue (quoted in Schell 1982, p. 200), once there is the threat of a first strike by either side, both sides may reason as follows: "He, thinking I was about to kill him in self-defense, was about to kill me in self-defense, so I had to kill him in self-defense." For a country's own security, it is important not to threaten a first strike, and not even to allow the misperception to arise on the other side that it might be preparing for a first strike. Deutsch stresses the importance of better communication with an opponent, to

> decrease the risks that conflict would escalate due to poor communication and misunderstandings. As the superpowers are increasingly placing themselves in the position where their leaders and strategic advisors may feel that they have to launch their nuclear-tipped missiles within minutes after being informed that the other side has initiated nuclear attack, the importance of not misinterpreting the other's behaviors and intentions is increasingly urgent [Deutsch 1983, p. 14–15].

A policy of no first use can be adopted unilaterally by any country with nuclear arms, in its own security interest. This will put strong pressure on potential opponents to do likewise, whether they declare such a policy or not. Any opponent will have a strong incentive not to escalate a conflict by using nuclear arms first, because he will know that as long as he refrains from their use, he will not be attacked by nuclear arms, but if he uses them, he faces the prospect of nuclear retaliation. If an opponent is afraid of a first strike, this incentive is removed, and *deterrence against nuclear war is undermined.*

The notion, in this case so erroneous, that the more threatened our opponents feel, the more secure we are, seems to be deeply rooted. For example, during Reagan's presidential campaign in 1980, he said in an interview: "Don't you open up the possibility of being hit by a surprise nuclear attack far more if you assure the rest of the world that under no circumstances would you ever be the first to fire those bombs?" (Robert Scheer 1982, p. 240–41).

James Schlesinger, who was Secretary of Defense in the Nixon and Ford administrations, when asked why the United States did not declare it would not be the first to use nuclear arms, once said that such a promise would in any case not be relied upon by an opponent in a serious conflict situation, so there was no use in making it. It is certainly true that words alone, or even written agreements, will never be trusted fully. But this is no argument against a policy of no first use. It simply means that more is required than words to make the policy credible and thus effective. It is necessary to restructure one's own nuclear forces in such a way that a first strike would never make any strategic sense, but so that a retaliatory strike would always remain an option. This means, for example, that existing nuclear forces are to be made less vulnerable, while at the same time avoiding the possession of missiles that are useful mainly for a surprise attack.

Table 7.1 lists some of the main characteristics of first-strike and second-strike nuclear delivery systems. As with the distinction between offensive and defensive arms, nuclear weapons cannot be sharply classified as *either* first-strike *or* second-strike weapons; rather, there is a continuum of shadings between them.

---

**Table 7.1  Typical Hardware Characteristics of First-Strike and Second-Strike Nuclear Weapons Delivery Systems**

| First-strike system (for a preemptive counterforce strike) | Second-strike system (for a retaliatory countervalue strike) |
|---|---|
| High accuracy necessary, targeted on the opponent's nuclear weapons carriers | High accuracy not necessary; may be targeted at military industries |
| Need not be able to survive an attack (would be used first) | Must be able to survive an attack (e.g., by being mobile, hidden under water, etc.) |
| Number of *warheads* must be large relative to the number of targets (typically multiple warheads on a single missile) | Number of *launchers* (e.g., missile silos) must be sufficient relative to the opponent's warheads (e.g., single-warhead missiles, widely dispersed to survive a surprise attack) |
| Must reach the target rapidly, for an element of surprise | Need not reach the target rapidly (e.g., bombers) |
| Must be highly reliable (requires near *certainty* that it will destroy target) | Need not be highly reliable (*possibility* that it could destroy target is a sufficient deterrent) |

---

First-strike weapons are typically *counterforce* weapons, meaning that they are targeted at nuclear missiles of an opponent. Second-strike weapons are typically *countervalue* weapons, meaning that they are targeted at industries or cities. It may appear that aiming at enemy missiles is less morally objectionable than aiming at industries, which are usually near population centers. But it will be shown that a counterforce strategy is more likely to lead to the outbreak of nuclear war.

If all countries possessing nuclear weapons were to adhere to a policy of no first use, nuclear war would effectively be prevented.

Opponents of a United States declaration of no first use say that even though the Soviet Union has made a no-first-use pledge, it cannot be trusted. But there is no need to trust the other side before adopting such a policy, for it is in each nuclear power's *own* interest to adopt the policy and make it convincing. Confidence-building measures can enhance a country's own security, even in the absence of reciprocity. It is not necessary to reach any mutual agreement. For example, Switzerland increased its own security by reaffirming its policy of neutrality at the beginning of World War II, by declaring, credibly, that it would not participate in the fighting unless attacked, but that it was determined and able to put up heavy resistance if attacked. If Switzerland had first waited for a reciprocal declaration of neutrality from Hitler's Germany, it would have waited in vain.

On the other hand, even a signed mutual agreement can be extremely fragile if it is not backed up by the capability to implement it. For example, Stalin concluded a ten-year mutual nonaggression pact with Hitler in 1939, but two years later Hitler invaded the Soviet Union. When asked about the treaty, Hitler replied that it was "just a shred of paper." For an agreement to be stable, it must be anchored in each side's visible self-interest, not merely based on blind trust.

### The Danger of Multiple Warheads

More effective than a mere "pledge" of no first use is a restructuring of nuclear forces so that a first use would never make any military sense, but so retaliation against a nuclear attack would always remain possible. Unfortunately, the world has been moving in the opposite direction. One of the most dangerous recent developments in nuclear weapons, which has brought the possibility of nuclear war a big step closer, is the increased accuracy of missiles, and especially the technology of multiple independently-targetable reentry vehicles (MIRVs). (This problem is also discussed in Lutz 1981.) As long as each nuclear missile carried a single warhead, it was practically impossible for any side to destroy all the enemy's missiles in a first strike. This was true even if one side had a substantially larger number of missiles than the other, as will be shown in the next chapter. A successful first strike would have required near certainty that every missile would fire and would hit a small target with a reliability very close to 100 percent, which is almost impossible to achieve. The remaining intact missiles of the opponent would have inevitably been used for a devastating retaliatory second strike. This balance of "mutual assured destruction" (MAD), however tenuous, provided at least some deterrence against the initiation of a nuclear war. But now that a typical missile can carry ten or more warheads, as many as ten independent shots can be aimed at the same enemy missile in its reinforced silo, making the probability of destruction almost a certainty. (Some hypothetical calculations will be offered in the next chapter.) If there were no other weapons of significance, a period of high tension would exert an almost irresistible pressure on both sides to attack first, because to wait could be suicidal.

Of course, a country does not want its own missiles to be vulnerable. But many believe it would be to their advantage if they could make an opponent's missiles more vulnerable. Yet the opposite is true. If an opponent knows that his missiles are vulnerable to a potential first strike, he will feel strong temptation, during a crisis, to launch them before they may be destroyed. This is hardly to the advantage of the country facing such an opponent. It is very important that, as long as countries rely on nuclear deterrence, the missiles of *both sides* be invulnerable. If X's missiles are vulnerable, this will tempt Y to destroy them before they may be used; and it will tempt X to use them before they may be destroyed. The same applies to the missiles of country Y.

The principal argument offered in favor of building MIRVs has been that to put ten nuclear warheads on a single missile is "cheaper" than to put them on ten separate missiles. This should be rather obvious. Yet when survival is at stake, cost considerations should become secondary. Have these cost-conscious analysts figured the cost of a nuclear war in their calculations? *Anything that brings us insecurity, even if it is cheap, is not a good buy.* Even if these MIRVs were offered to a country at no cost, it would do better to reject them—like a Trojan horse.

The search for "hard target kill capability," as it is called in military jargon, is suicidal. In its own security interest, a country should rather reduce its number of warheads but increase instead the number of missile launchers, by placing fewer warheads on each missile. As will be shown in the next chapter, this will reduce the vulnerability of its own as well as its opponent's nuclear forces, because, on both sides, there will be fewer warheads to be targeted at each missile. This will enhance stability. There is no use for any overkill capacity. But the certainty of a retaliatory capability that can survive under a surprise attack will act as a deterrent, even if the capacity to retaliate is less enormous. If military budget constraints permit the construction of fewer warheads if MIRV technology is not used, that smaller number will still provide a more-effective deterrent than a larger number of more-vulnerable warheads. For example, 200 warheads on 200 missiles are less vulnerable than 1000 warheads on 100 larger missiles. If warheads are vulnerable, this can easily attract a preemptive first strike.

Henry Kissinger has publicly regretted his earlier role in the decision to build MIRVs. Like many others, he has correctly proposed that the United States, in the interest of its own security, should eliminate its MIRVs and replace them by mobile missiles with a single warhead, even if the Soviet Union should refuse to do the same (*Time*, 21 March 1983). On the other hand, the proposal for strategic arms reductions that Reagan outlined in his Eureka College speech of 9 May 1982 is potentially destabilizing. It would reduce the number of intercontinental nuclear weapons from about 7500 for both the United States and Soviet Union to 5000 for each, but the number of missiles from about 1700 for the United States and more than 2000 for the Soviet

Union to only 850 each. In this way, it would lead to an even higher ratio of warheads to missiles than exists at present. Arms reductions are highly desirable, but they must take a form that increases strategic stability and does not reduce it.

Fallows (1981, pp. 155–56) stresses how uncertain the accuracy of missiles is on untested routes, and argues that the problem of missile vulnerability is therefore less serious than is often portrayed. We can only hope that decisionmakers of the nuclear nations are aware of this.

To claim an imaginary accuracy for one's own missiles is like approaching, without any protection, a gunman, while pointing a toy gun at him. Actually to build such accurate missiles is like confronting a gunman and pointing a real, loaded gun at him. Either strategy is dangerous and unwise. A safer approach to self-protection is not to pose any threat to the other side as long as he does not attack, but to maintain the capacity to retaliate if attacked.

One possible response against a potentially disabling first strike is a policy of "launch on warning." Instead of leaving the missiles in their silos until they are destroyed, they could be launched before they are hit. But given the many past failures of radar warning systems, such a policy would be extremely risky and would raise the specter of an accidental nuclear holocaust. Once missiles are launched, there is no possible way to recall them. For this reason, McNamara has recently called on the United States and its NATO allies to adopt a policy of "no second use—until . . ." He writes, "Under this policy, we would not authorize the launching of nuclear weapons, even in response to an assumed nuclear attack, until we could determine whether a reported attack was real or imagined and, if real, deliberate or accidental" (*New York Times*, 2 February 1983). He emphasizes that "Nuclear weapons serve no military purpose whatsoever. They are totally useless—except only to deter one's opponent from using them" (McNamara 1983).

A certain stabilizing element is provided by manned bombers, which *can* take off on warning and then be recalled if the alarm turns out to be false. It is a question, however, how long the relatively slow-flying bombers can remain invulnerable to antiaircraft weapons, even with "stealth" technology.

Fortunately, the dangerous situation in which both sides possess a first-strike capability has not yet been reached, because the nuclear powers also have missiles on submarines, whose precise location cannot yet be detected with today's technology, and which are thus almost invulnerable. Any attacker would thus have to expect massive retaliation from submarine-launched missiles. This not only deters a first strike, but also removes the pressure either to act first or to be left defenseless. But in an incomprehensible drive toward doom, both East and West are working feverishly on antisubmarine warfare capability and on submarine detection systems, seeking methods to make the oceans "transparent." Once a single nuclear warhead can destroy an enemy submarine with more than 100 warheads, the pressure on both sides to launch their missiles first in a crisis becomes enormous. (For example, a U.S. Polaris submarine can carry 160 nuclear warheads, on 16 missiles with 10 warheads each. The new Trident submarine carries even more.) Once submarines can be detected, submarine-based missiles will be even far more vulnerable than land-based missiles because they are assembled in larger concentrations and are less dispersed.

A reason typically offered for research on antisubmarine warfare is that "we must keep ahead of the other side, to avoid surprises." But of course, the "other side" is then likely to argue the same way. The detection of submarines is necessary only to launch a disarming first strike; to threaten retaliation after a nuclear attack, it is not very effective to be able to destroy submarines that have already launched their missiles. More useful than antisubmarine warfare would be technology on how better to *hide* submarines and make them less vulnerable. This may have to involve a larger number of smaller submarines, each of which should carry fewer warheads than present submarines, so there would be no increase in the total number of nuclear warheads. Such an approach would be the "shallow undersea mobile" (SUM) system proposed by Richard Garwin and Sidney Drell, which would involve a fleet of smaller, more-numerous, quieter, and harder-to-find submarines (quoted by Fallows 1981, pp. 165–66).

A dangerous place to put nuclear missiles is on surface ships.

The Reagan administration has engaged in a program of refurbishing battleships from World War II and equipping them with nuclear missiles. The battleship New Jersey now carries 32 cruise missiles capable of delivering nuclear warheads over a range of 1500 miles (*New York Times*, 29 December 1982). But these easily visible, slow-moving ships, loaded with many nuclear warheads, present a prime target. Instead of giving an opponent the message "You'd better not attack us, otherwise you may face grave consequences," the reverse signal is being sent: "If you destroy our ships in a first strike, you will face a reduced threat. But if you leave them intact, you take grave risks." To send such signals, even if not intended, is imprudent, to say the least.

A totally unnecessary, dangerous development is the reduction of warning time by deploying ballistic missiles closer to their target, on submarines or on land (e.g., in Europe). This has increased the danger of accidental nuclear war by shortening the time in which an opponent can identify a false warning as an error, as discussed in Chapter 1.

A country with no intention of arming for a first strike or to "fight a nuclear war," but whose only aim is to deter a nuclear attack, does not need a large and highly accurate nuclear missile force. A small but survivable arsenal can provide more than adequate deterrence. Solly Zuckerman (1982), the former chief scientific adviser to the British Ministry of Defense, advocates a strategy of "minimum deterrence." He points to the relatively small nuclear forces of Britain and France as demonstrating that even a much smaller force than that of a potential opponent is sufficient to deter a nuclear attack. Of course, the French or British nuclear forces would never be sufficient to initiate a nuclear attack.

Bundy (1982) stresses that "the losses that would be sustained in receiving an attack of 100 megatons far outweigh any 'gains' in delivering ten times as much to an enemy." He advocates a strategy of lesser retaliation against a nuclear attack, to prevent any further escalation and to seek to end a nuclear war as rapidly as possible if it should ever occur. To deter a nuclear attack, a nation need not match the size of a potential opponent's nuclear arsenal. If either side were to limit itself to what is sufficient for deterrence, this could help deescalate the nuclear arms race.

Herbert York, the former director of the Lawrence Livermore Nuclear Weapons Laboratory, saw this very clearly. Questioned in an interview whether the United States had to catch up with the Soviet Union, he replied, "There is parity and, furthermore, there not only is parity, I would go further and say that if the ratio changed by a factor of two either way, there would still be parity" (Scheer 1982, p. 271). George Bush, on the other hand, interviewed during his campaign for the Republican party presidential nomination, took a very different view. He was asked by Scheer: "Don't you reach a point with these strategic weapons where we can wipe each other out so many times and no one wants to use them or be willing to use them, that it really doesn't matter whether you're 10 percent or 2 percent lower or higher?" Bush replied: "Yes, if you believe there is no such thing as a winner in a nuclear exchange, that argument makes a little sense. I don't believe that" (Scheer 1982, p. 261).

The shift that has taken place from a doctrine of nuclear deterrence to a "war-fighting" strategy, with the accompanying "qualitative" arms race to counterforce weapons, is extremely dangerous. Johansen (1982, p. 54) writes, "The MX missile, for example, is designed as an anti-silo weapon. But no one wants to destroy a silo after the missile it houses has left, so the weapon makes most sense for use in a surprise nuclear attack." The same applies to the Soviet SS-18 and SS-19 missiles with their multiple warheads.

Why do we witness all these dangerous and destabilizing developments, which weaken deterrence instead of strengthening it, and thus make a nuclear war more likely? A typical rationale offered is "Of course we would prefer not to have to build all these dangerous weapons systems. But since the other side is building them, we have no choice. We cannot afford to fall behind." This may sound logical and convincing, at first. But on further reflection, this argument is seen to be false. *Even if the other side takes steps that make nuclear war more likely, it does not help one's own side to make nuclear war still more likely.* The proper response is to seek to make nuclear war less likely, and this often requires entirely different measures from what one's opponent does, or what one anticipates he might do. The blind obsession to keep up with, or keep ahead of, the other side is counterproductive in terms of a country's own best security interests.

Richard Pipes (1982, p. 144), a former adviser to the Reagan administration on Soviet and Eastern European Affairs, wrote, "Any evidence that the United States may contemplate switching to a counterforce strategy, such as occasionally crops up, throws Soviet generals into a tizzy of excitement. It clearly frightens them far more than the threat to Soviet cities posed by the countervalue strategic doctrine." Does this mean that a counterforce strategy is a more-effective deterrent because it "frightens" the Soviet leadership more? On the contrary. It could, at some point, frighten them into a preemptive strike. It should be obvious that a counterforce strategy is more frightening to an opponent than a countervalue strategy, because a counterforce strategy makes the outbreak of war more likely. The United States is also more concerned about the prospect that the Soviet Union may acquire a counterforce capability than it is about Soviet retaliatory capacity. It is clear that no sane leader would want to use a retaliatory capability before being attacked, and in this way commit national suicide. This is the reason why a retaliatory countervalue capacity is less frightening than a counterforce capacity. Nevertheless, a countervalue strategy is a far more effective deterrent than the threat of a preemptive counterforce strike. Even if one side should adopt a counterforce strategy, there is no reason for the other side to imitate such a dangerous course, which would undermine its own security.

Some say that sooner or later nuclear war is inevitable. Nuclear war is inevitable only if *both sides* make it inevitable by threatening the other side with a disabling first strike or by failing to maintain an invulnerable deterrent force. As long as at least one side avoids acquiring a first-strike capability and at the same time prevents a first strike by the other side by making its own forces sufficiently invulnerable, nuclear war can be prevented. Here lies some reason for hope.

Even though with nuclear weapons there is no such thing as

"invulnerability without threat," at least there exists the somewhat parallel position of "deterrence without provocation." Unfortunately, the world seems to be moving away from even this faint glimmer of hope.

In spite of the urgent need to avoid unstable deterrence, even "stable" nuclear deterrence is only a temporary bridging measure to gain more time to construct alternative security systems. To ban the danger of nuclear war on a lasting basis, it is necessary to learn to eliminate the causes of war, to move to nonmilitary methods of defense, and to build a global legal framework where disputes can be resolved without recourse to violence.

The policy of nuclear deterrence, which in effect holds innocent civilians as hostages, even in nonbelligerent countries, goes fundamentally against all the values of civilization and must be replaced as soon as possible. Some say this is utopian. But we need to strive for a solution even if it appears difficult, since we do not have many alternatives. As Jonathan Schell (p. 161) has written, "If it is 'utopian' to want to survive, then it must be 'realistic' to be dead."

# 8 Does Balance of Power Promote Security?

A balance of "power" between two opponents is neither necessary nor sufficient for their security. Both sides can be relatively secure with or without a balance of forces, and both sides can be extremely insecure, even with a perfect balance of power. To illustrate this point, several hypothetical calculations involving nuclear forces will follow. (The reader who is not mathematically inclined may wish to skip the calculations, without loss of continuity.) These calculations may seem highly theoretical, devoid of practical experience, and they are. But as Herman Kahn said, "It will do no good to inveigh against theorists; in this field, everyone is a theorist" (quoted in Schell 1982, p. 141).

Some people think that anyone who applies mathematical reasoning to these problems must be out of touch with reality. Obviously, national leaders' decisionmaking is not always cool and rational, and many other factors, including emotions and half-conscious value judgments, influence their behavior as much as or more than rational calculations. Nevertheless, estimates of the risks involved in various courses of action, and of the probabilities of these risks, do have *some* influence over people's behavior. While it would certainly be misleading to suggest that these are the only considerations, it is just as dangerous to ignore them totally.

Suppose, first, that two hostile powers each have 1000 land-based nuclear missiles with a single warhead per missile. Suppose that they have a high target accuracy, so that there is a 90 percent chance that a warhead launched in a surprise attack will destroy its target, an enemy missile in its silo. The probability that two missiles each destroy their own target is somewhat lower. Even if the first missile hits, there is a 10-percent chance that the second missile will miss its target. This reduces the probability of two hits to $.9 \times .9 = 81$ percent. The probability that three missiles will all destroy their targets is $.9 \times .9 \times .9 = 72.9$ percent, etc. The probability that each of the 1000 missiles can destroy its assigned target is $.9^{1000}$ or approximately $10^{-46}$, a virtual impossibility. Neither side could succeed in a disarming first strike and therefore the prospect of retaliation provides a certain stability of deterrence. (This is case 1 in Table 8.1, which gives a summary of this and other calculations.)

This example assumed balanced forces. Even if there is a substantial imbalance, as long as each missile has only one warhead, there is no danger of a successful disarming first strike. Assume, for example, that one side has 2000 missiles, and the other side only 1000 (case 2 in Table 8.1). Clearly, the side with fewer missiles cannot launch a successful first strike; it could not possibly destroy more than half the other side's missiles. But the side with 2000 missiles can now aim two missiles at each enemy silo. If the first one misses, the second still has a chance to destroy its target. The first missile will destroy its target in 90 percent of all cases. In 9 out of 10 of the remaining 10 percent of cases, the second missile will hit the target, even if the first one missed. This increases the probability to 99 percent that one particular enemy missile can be destroyed with two missiles aimed at it. But the probability that *all* 1000 enemy missiles can be destroyed is still extremely low, namely $.99^{1000} = .000043$, or less than one-hundredth of 1 percent. From these calculations, it can be seen that a relative measure of mutual deterrence is possible, with or without a balance of forces.

But with multiple warheads (on MIRVs, multiple independently-targetable reentry vehicles) the situation is totally changed. Suppose that each side again has 1000 warheads, but this time distributed among 100 missiles with 10 warheads each

**Table 8.1 Hypothetical Chances for a Disarming First Strike under Various Assumptions**

| Case Number | Country X | | | | | Country Y | | | | | Stability of deterrence |
|---|---|---|---|---|---|---|---|---|---|---|---|
| | Number of missiles | Number of warheads per missile | Total number of warheads | Probability of destroying a target | Probability of disarming first strike | Number of missiles | Number of warheads per missile | Total number of warheads | Probability of destroying a target | Probability of disarming first strike | |
| 1 | 1000 | 1 | 1000 | .9 | $10^{-46}$ | 1000 | 1 | 1000 | .9 | $10^{-46}$ | stable |
| 2 | 2000 | 1 | 2000 | .9 | .000043 | 1000 | 1 | 1000 | .9 | 0 | stable |
| 3 | 100 | 10 | 1000 | .9 | .999 999 99 | 100 | 10 | 1000 | .9 | .999 999 99 | unstable |
| 4 | 200 | 10 | 2000 | .9 | $1-10^{-18}$ | 100 | 10 | 1000 | .9 | .998 | unstable |
| 5 | 1000 | 1 | 1000 | .9 | $1-10^{-8}$ | 100 | 10 | 1000 | .9 | $10^{-46}$ | unstable |
| 6 | 500 | 1 | 500 | .5 | .04 | 1000 | 1 | 1000 | .5 | .0066 | stable |
| 7 | 1000 | 1 | 1000 | .5 | $10^{-300}$ | 1000 | 1 | 1000 | .5 | $10^{-300}$ | stable |
| 8 | 2000 | 1 | 2000 | .5 | $10^{-125}$ | 100 | 10 | 1000 | .5 | 0 | stable |
| 9 | 1000 | 1 | 1000 | .9 | .9 | 1000 | 1 | 1000 | .9 | .9 | unstable |
| 10 | 100 | 10 | 1000 | .1 | .0015 | 50 | 1 | 50 | .1 | 0 | stable |
| 11 | 1000 | 1 | 1000 | .1 | $10^{-19}$ | 100 | 1 | 100 | .1 | 0 | stable |
| 12 | 1000 | 1 | 1000 | .1 | .9 | 20 | 10 | 200 | .1 | 0 | unstable |

*Note:* If the probability of a successful first strike is low for both sides, deterrence is stable. Otherwise it is unstable.

(case 3 in Table 8.1). Now each side can aim as many as 10 nuclear warheads at each silo on the other side. To guard against the possibility that a missile will fail to fire, the 10 warheads from each missile will be aimed at 10 different targets, so that each enemy silo is targeted by warheads originating from 10 different missiles. As we have just seen, aiming two warheads at one silo increases the probability that it will be destroyed from 90 percent to 99 percent. Aiming three warheads at one silo will increase the probability that it can be destroyed to 99.9 percent, etc. A calculation similar to the earlier ones shows that the probability that all 100 enemy missiles can be destroyed is now $(1 - 10^{-10})^{100}$, approximately 99.999 999 percent, a virtual certainty.

To understand this result intuitively, consider the following analogy. The probability that a warhead will *miss* its target (10%) is less than the probability of getting a 6 in throwing a die (1/6). The probability of missing a target successively 10 times is much lower than the probability of getting 10 sixes in a row when throwing a die 10 times. We all know that this would be an extremely unlikely event. Therefore, it is almost certain that each missile silo would be destroyed, by at least one warhead.

This means that the side which first launches a surprise attack is almost certain to destroy all the opponent's missiles and thus be safe. It could do so even without using all of its own missiles. Whoever hesitates takes the risk of suffering a disarming first strike, with the enormous losses of population that would occur at the same time. It is obvious that such a situation is highly unstable, and both sides are extremely insecure, despite a perfect balance of forces.

We must recall at this point that such considerations apply only if nuclear weapons of relatively "low" yield are used. If the explosions reach hundreds of megatons, even a country that could totally disarm its opponent in a first strike would suffer from the global radioactive fallout and the cooling of the atmosphere (Sagan 1983). Nevertheless, the tendency to build highly accurate "battlefield" nuclear weapons of comparatively small explosive power, which would reduce the effects on the global environment, makes deterrence unstable.

Even the possession of "superior" forces cannot protect a

country in the case of multiple warheads. Consider the hypothetical case where one side has 2000 warheads on 200 missiles with 10 warheads each, and the other side has 1000 warheads on 100 missiles with 10 warheads each (case 4 in Table 8.1). Even the "weaker" side could destroy the more-numerous missiles of the other side in a surprise attack. It could aim 5 warheads at each silo of the opponent. With a 90-percent chance for each warhead to hit the target, the probability of destroying all 200 enemy missiles will then be about 99.8 percent, still close to certainty.

Clearly, if *both* sides were to give up MIRVs in favor of missiles with a single warhead, both sides would be safer. (This point has also been stressed in Lodal 1982). But even one side alone can move independently to restore more-stable mutual deterrence and reduce insecurity for both. If one country alone were to replace its 100 MIRVs by 1000 missiles bearing single warheads, its opponent could no longer launch a successful preemptive first strike (case 5 in Table 8.1). The other side would still be threatened, with 1000 warheads aimed at its 100 missile silos, and would probably want to increase its armaments. But if one side were to replace its 100 MIRVs with, say, 500 missiles bearing single warheads, which also had a lower target accuracy, with a probability of 50 percent that a warhead would destroy its target (case 6 in Table 8.1), then calculations reveal the following: the probability that the country which has 100 MIRVs could destroy all the 500 missiles on the other side is .0066, less than 1 percent. The probability that the country with 500 missiles that are less accurate could destroy the 100 MIRVs of the other side is about 4 percent. Both of these probabilities are now sufficiently low so that neither side is tempted to a first strike, or afraid of one. Therefore, either side alone, or both independently, can take steps to defuse the danger, in their own interest, by moving away from MIRVs toward missiles with a single warhead, and preferably also with lower accuracy. As McGeorge Bundy once pointed out, for military minds who have been trained all their lives to achieve greater accuracy—to "hit the target"—it is, unfortunately, almost impossible to understand that lower target accuracy can provide us with greater security.

The general results described here are not dependent on the particular numbers chosen. With a lower, and perhaps more realistic, target accuracy of 50 percent, we observe the same tendencies. The probability that a disarming first strike could succeed with 1000 missiles on each side is now about $10^{-300}$, a total impossibility (case 7 in Table 8.1). The probability of being able to destroy 1000 missiles of the opponent with 2000 of one's own missiles is about $10^{-125}$ (case 8). But with 100 MIRVs bearing 10 warheads each, the probability of destroying all 100 missiles of the opponent is about 90 percent (case 9). This probability is no longer close to certainty, but is still very high. Given the risks involved in allowing the other side the opportunity to strike first, a decisionmaker might well prefer to accept a 10 percent risk of facing retaliation with one or two missiles.

If the missiles are less vulnerable, then even a much lower number of warheads than the opponent possesses can provide a strong deterrent. Consider, for example, the case where the probability that a missile can be destroyed by a warhead aimed at it is only 10 percent. Suppose one side possesses 1000 nuclear warheads. Whether they are on MIRVs or on missiles with a single warhead does not matter for the following consideration. If the other side has only 50 missiles, 20 warheads can be aimed at each of these missiles. The probability that all 50 missiles can be destroyed in a surprise attack is then .0015, a highly unlikely event (case 10 in Table 8.1). The probability that 100 missiles can all be destroyed is about $10^{-19}$, essentially impossible (case 11). A slightly more involved calculation shows that if there are 200 missiles, the probability that at least 100 among them survive a surprise attack carried out with 1000 warheads is .995, and the probability that at least 90 missiles survive is .99997. Therefore, even a much smaller nuclear force than the opponent possesses can represent a formidable deterrent, if the warheads are dispersed and sufficiently invulnerable. This shows that "minimum deterrence" can be sufficient. But if 200 warheads were to be put on 20 MIRVs, not on 200 separate missiles, then they would be far more vulnerable. The probability that they could all be destroyed in a surprise attack would be about 90 percent (case 12). The resulting situation would be strategically unstable.

It must be stressed again that these are purely hypothetical calculations. At present, no danger of a disarming first strike capability by either the United States or Soviet Union exists, because both sides have not only land-based missiles, but also airborne and submarine-based nuclear arms, which are essentially invulnerable at present. But with efforts in developing antisubmarine warfare, we are moving in this direction.

The preceding calculations have also abstracted from the problem of "fratricide": the probability that a second nuclear warhead can destroy a target may in reality be lower than that for the first warhead to arrive, because the first detonation may damage the second incoming warhead, unless it follows at a proper time interval (SIPRI 1982b, p. 81). But given today's technology, it may not be long before nuclear explosions can be synchronized, if that capability does not exist already. A radio signal, transmitted to all delivered warheads, could bring them to explosion at the same instant, without damaging one another before they explode. Relying on "fratricide" is risky. Furthermore, the probability that a warhead will hit its target can be increased by installing in the reentry vehicle radar devices that can recognize the terrain surrounding the target. Minor course corrections during reentry can then guide a nuclear warhead precisely to its target. Such a system is planned for the Trident II missile (SIPRI 1982b, p. 90). Cruise missiles also possess radar guidance systems and are highly accurate.

Even though the probabilities assumed here represent hypothetical figures, the message is clear. MIRVs are extremely dangerous and destabilizing. It is not necessary to know the actual probabilities of hitting a target, which keep changing, to recognize that it is safer for both sides, in the interest of their own security, not to put many warheads on the same missile. Two nuclear powers who both possess MIRVs can both be extremely insecure, even if they both possess exactly the same number of warheads and missiles with the same capabilities, representing a perfect "balance of power." Similarly, Egypt and Israel in 1967, with vulnerable bomber fleets facing one another, were both very insecure, even if they had had the same number and types of bombers.

To possess a potential for a disarming first strike undermines the stability of deterrence, and thus reduces one's own security as well as that of an opponent. To possess an invulnerable force for retaliation increases the stability of deterrence, and is therefore less dangerous. MIRVs, with their large number of warheads, provide strong capability for attack, but are relatively vulnerable because of the comparatively small number of missiles. For these reasons, MIRVs are destabilizing. Well-dispersed, preferably *mobile* missiles with a single warhead each are less vulnerable and yet do not provide the same capacity for a first strike as MIRVs. They lead to greater stability of deterrence.

The old preoccupation with "balance of power," "parity," "equivalent forces," etc., has become obsolete in the nuclear age. It is far more important to avoid destabilizing first-strike weapons, whether in balanced numbers or not.

The reason why I have given such extensive coverage to a theory of nuclear deterrence is not that I believe that nuclear deterrence can give us security on a lasting basis. Instead, stable peace must be achieved through improvements in relations between states, not through the threat of mutual annihilation. I have intended only to show that certain types of arms buildup that are ostensibly undertaken to strengthen deterrence are actually destabilizing. They *undermine* deterrence and bring war even closer.

## Stability through Strong Defense without Offense

With conventional military forces, we can also observe that a numerical balance is much less important for stability than a predominance of defensive, rather than offensive, capabilities. Behind the concept of "balance of power" lies the fundamental failure to distinguish between offensive and defensive power. It equates "nonaggressiveness" with "vulnerability," and "invulnerability" with "aggressiveness," a confusion that can be very dangerous.

This concept assumes that there is a single variable, "military power," measured by the number of warheads, or missiles, or troops, or by military expenditures, or some aggregate of military forces. Most people believe intuitively that the more "military power" their own side has compared to that of an opponent, the safer they are; that if they have less power, they are in danger; that if both sides have about equal power, both are safe and the situation is stable; but that if one side has superior forces, there is a power imbalance that may lead to war, with the "stronger" side winning. This simplistic concept is illustrated in Figure 8.1, to contrast it with the more-accurate concept to be shown in the next figure. Charts of this type are often found in newspapers to compare the "military forces" of opponents in a war. Yet the notion that one can simply compare numbers is no longer valid (if it ever was). In fact, as we have just seen, both sides can be safe, or both simultaneously totally insecure.

Henry Kissinger said in 1979, "I believe that it is urgently necessary either that the Soviets be deprived of their counterforce capability in strategic forces or that a U.S. counterforce capability in strategic forces be rapidly built" (1982, p. 123). Either of these two measures is intended to restore a "balance of forces," if indeed the Soviet Union currently possesses a counterforce capability. But whereas the first form of balance, with neither side having the ability to destroy the other side's missiles, is relatively secure, the second form of balance, with a mutual first-strike capability, would lead to an even greater danger of war by putting pressure on the Soviet Union to use its missiles or lose them.

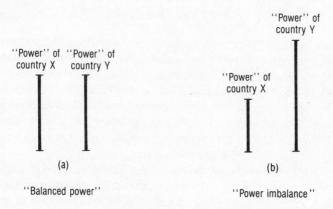

"Balanced power"  "Power imbalance"

**Figure 8.1** The Obsolete Concept of "Balance of Power"

The aggregate concept of "military power" must be divided into two components. In the case of conventional arms, we have *defensive* and *offensive* capabilities, which need not be the same. In the case of nuclear weapons, we must distinguish between offensive *first-strike* weapons and retaliatory (not "defensive") *second-strike* weapons that serve the purpose of deterrence. Again, the two capacities need not go hand in hand, as we have just demonstrated. To speak simply of "military power," without specifying whether offensive or defensive/retaliatory power is meant, creates a dangerous ambiguity. (In the remainder of this chapter, I will be discussing offensive versus defensive conventional arms only, although a similar discussion could be applied to the distinction between first-strike and second-strike nuclear weapons.)

If the defensive capability of either side is greater than (i.e., able to resist) the offensive capability of the other side, then both sides are relatively safe. The situation is stable if both sides must expect to be made worse off by starting a war than by not starting one, because the defensive forces of the other side are sufficient to repel an attack. If either side (or possibly both) has the prospect of winning a war by starting it (because the other side would not be able to defend itself), then the situation is unstable and prone to produce war. The same sort of instability is present even if neither side expects to "gain" anything from war, but if at least one side is afraid of suffering greater losses if attacked first and is therefore tempted to initiate a preemptive strike. Figure 8.2 illustrates this more-accurate picture.

The situation is unstable whenever the offensive capability of one country is greater than the defensive capability of the other, as in (e), (f), and (g). The situation is stable if the defensive capability of either side exceeds the offensive capability of the other, as in (b), (c) and (d). If the offensive capability of neither side exceeds the defensive capability of the other, but is just equal to it, then the situation is neither quite stable nor unstable, and can, perhaps, be called "indifferent," as in (a).

From Figure 8.2 we see that the situation can be clearly imbalanced but stable (d), as long as the defensive capability of each country is greater than the offensive capability of the other.

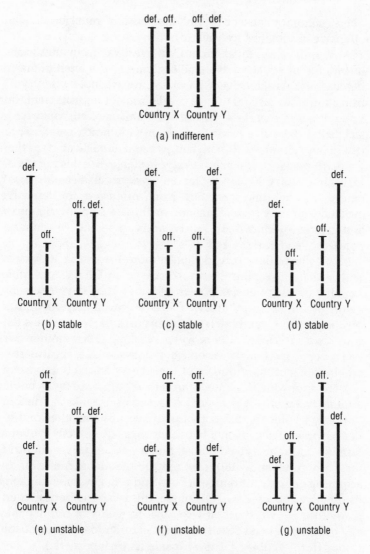

**Figure 8.2** Defensive Capability (def.) and Offensive Capability (off.) of Two Hostile Countries, with Resulting Strategic Stability or Instability

The situation can also be highly unstable and yet balanced (f), if offensive capabilities prevail.

Any country can independently move away from an unstable or indifferent situation to a stable situation, if it strengthens its defense and weakens its offense; see, for example, country X's transition from case (a) to case (b). This is not disarmament, but *transarmament*, a shift away from destabilizing offensive forces to stabilizing defensive forces, which provide much greater security to both countries. If both countries take the same step, then we reach case (c),, which is even more stable. But it is not necessary for country X to wait for any reciprocal measures by Y before it undertakes a shift from offensive to defensive capabilities on its own. Transarmament is a step toward peace and greater international security, and can be undertaken independently and without risk.

As an illustration, consider once more the example of tanks and antitank weapons briefly discussed in Chapter 6. Tanks mainly provide offensive power, although they have also some value for defense. Antitank weapons, at least if they are in fixed positions, serve purely defensive purposes. If two hostile countries have sufficient antitank weapons along their common border to repel any tank invasion, then both are safe, regardless of whether or not the numbers of their tanks and antitank weapons are approximately equal. But if they both have tanks but no antitank weapons, whichever side amasses its tanks at one location may be able to push forward and occupy the other country in a surprise attack, even if both countries have exactly the same number and same type of tanks. Either one of the two countries (or both independently) can reduce the danger of war by acquiring enough antitank weapons and reducing or eliminating its offensive tank forces. (Of course, this is a hypothetical example with only two types of weapons. In reality, a country may still need some tanks for its defense, in order to dislodge hostile troops from occupied territory inside its own borders.)

Situations in which neither side is able to impose its will on the other, even if military capabilities are not balanced, are rather common. For example, Switzerland could never have launched a successful attack against Hitler's Germany. Hitler might have been able to attack Switzerland, but he did not find it in his interest, because the expected losses would have exceeded any possible gain. The Soviet Union, whose military forces are far more powerful than those of the independence fighters in Afghanistan, has so far been unable to break the Afghani resistance, because the Soviet troops are rejected by the local population and are unfamiliar with the local terrain, the language, people's customs, etc. On the other hand, Afghanistan does not have the capability to attack the Soviet Union. Similarly, the United States exhausted itself in Vietnam, yet the Vietnamese could never have attacked the United States' homeland.

"Balanced forces" are not essential for a successful defense of home territory. Agreement on what exactly constitutes "balanced" forces or "parity" is also quite elusive. The negotiations in Vienna between NATO and the Warsaw Pact on mutual balanced force reductions, which have continued without results for a decade, illustrate this fact. Fortunately, it is not necessary for mutual security to maintain a precise numerical balance. It is more important that each side has sufficient, even redundant, defensive capabilities, but not the capacity to launch a successful attack on the other side.

If "balance of power" were a necessary condition for peace, then peace would be impossible. How could there by any pairwise balance of power among 150 countries in the world? "Balance of power" is an ambiguous concept; it is not only useless, but counterproductive, because it diverts attention from the real issues. Much more important is the search for stability through sufficient defensive capabilities, while avoiding to pose any offensive threat.

# 9 Transarmament before Disarmament

In Chapter 3, it was mentioned that some people advocate an arms buildup to achieve security, and others advocate unilateral disarmament to achieve peace. Both base their recommendations on different assumptions. Those who call for more arms ("hawks") believe that they face a threat that is *independent* of their own actions, and that with more arms they can meet that threat. Those who call for unilateral disarmament ("doves") believe that the threat they face emerged as a reaction to their own armament, and will disappear if they disarm. Who is right?

There is a "robust" solution that works regardless of which assumption is correct: *transarmament*, a shift from offensive to purely defensive measures. The notion of *robustness* has been borrowed from engineering: a robust structure does not collapse under stress and is shock resistant. The term has also been used in science. For example, robust statistical procedures give valid results regardless of the underlying probability distributions, which may be unknown. The term is applied here to defense in a precise sense. It denotes an approach to the prevention of war that works regardless of the actual intentions and capabilities of an opponent, whether he has aggressive aims or seeks cooperation, whether he acts independently from what we do or reacts to our policies, whether his offensive and/or defensive capabilities are strong or weak, etc. The search for superiority in offensive capabilities is not a robust defense, for if the opponent reacts to our arms buildup, the consequences make us less secure.

Gray and Payne disregard that point. Calling for a U.S. arms buildup that would guarantee "victory" in a nuclear exchange with the Soviet Union, they write,

> Such a deterrence posture is often criticized as contributing to the arms race and causing strategic instability, because it would stimulate new Soviet deployments. However, during the 1970s the Soviet Union showed that its weapons development and deployment decisions are not dictated by American actions [Gray and Payne 1980, p. 27].

If the Soviet arms buildup were totally independent of what the United States did — which few would argue to be the case — then there might be some logic in trying to "keep ahead" with a rapid U.S. buildup. But in fact the United States has been first to deploy most new nuclear weapons, with the Soviet Union following a few years behind, e.g., the atom bomb, hydrogen bomb, neutron bomb, submarine-based missiles, MIRVs, and cruise missiles. So long as this pattern holds, any U.S. attempt to "keep ahead" is an illusion. Such attempts will be followed by a similar Soviet buildup, bringing greater insecurity to both sides. The effort to "keep ahead" in a race with offensive arms resembles a Sisyphean task: each time an advantage seems to have been attained, it slips away and a new effort is needed to try to achieve it. But it is even worse, because each round is more difficult and more dangerous than the previous one. It is a path toward self-destruction.

On the Soviet side, the same two views may also be present, i.e., that the U.S. arms buildup will proceed regardless of Soviet actions, or that it is motivated by fear of a Soviet threat. Since it is not possible to determine with any certainty which view is more accurate, the best course of action is to seek to maintain an invulnerable deterrent, but one which clearly does not pose a threat of a first strike to the other side, and therefore need not stimulate a further arms buildup.

The worst possible response to an opponent's nuclear first-strike capability is to seek a first-strike capability for oneself. This would make a nuclear holocaust even more likely. A better response is to deny a first-strike potential to the other side by dispersing one's own forces and making them less vulnerable, without acquiring a first-strike capability of one's own.

Unilateral disarmament works if the other side simply reacts, but fails if the other side does pose a real threat. An attempt to "keep ahead" works if the actions of the other side are independent of one's own arms buildup, but fails if the other side makes efforts to keep up. A reduction of one's own threat to the other side but maintenance of a sufficiently invulnerable deterrent, works in either case. In terms of nuclear arms, one type of unilateral shift toward a more-stable deterrence is a move away from multiple warheads to single warheads, as discussed in the previous chapter. In terms of conventional arms, a more-robust defense means transarmament away from offensive to defensive arms.

For disarmament to be effective, it must be mutual. Unilateral disarmament faces three problems: (a) it probably will not be supported by a majority of the people; (b) even if it is accepted, a public backlash may occur if it is not reciprocated, resulting in calls for an even greater arms buildup than before; and (c) it may make war more likely, not less, by making the country defenseless and thus an easy victim of aggression.

Negotiations for mutual disarmament should be pursued with all intensity, but such negotiations are difficult and often disappointing. Einstein compared the disarmament negotiations within the League of Nations before World War II with discussions in a town council which, after a series of fatal stabbings, discusses how long and how sharp should be the knives people ought to be allowed to carry. In this analogy, the town clearly needs a policy force. In the meantime, until agreement is reached to establish one, the best thing individuals can do will be to protect themselves, e.g., by avoiding deserted streets and refraining from threatening others, without waiting for others to do the same.

Similarly, any country can, in its own security interest and without risk, undertake independent initiatives toward transarmament, thereby reducing the threat of war and making a contribution to peace. It is easy to keep peace if others also want peace. But in a militarized world, the safest thing a country can do is to seek good relations with all other countries, while maintaining a sufficient capability for self-defense.

Some argue that it takes two sides to make peace, that no

country can make peace alone without reciprocal steps from the other side. For *active,* mutually beneficial, peaceful relations, this may be true. But it also takes two sides to fight a war. Prevention of war ("negative peace") is less ambitious than achievement of actively good relations ("positive peace"). A war can be prevented even by one side alone, if it maintains a sufficient defense and does not attack the other side.

Before serious disarmament will take place, it is necessary to develop alternative security systems, especially also *nonmilitary* means of defense, which will be discussed in the next chapter. Such measures can be made redundant, for added security. For example, there is no limit to how attractive to a potential opponent we can seek to make peace by offering mutually beneficial forms of cooperation. Taking such measures does not lead to an arms race, because they do not threaten any other country. On the contrary, each country would welcome it if others took similar defense measures, because these measures would increase the security of all. Galtung (1980, p. 214), arguing for a transition to nonmilitary defense, writes "To disarm is to make a society defenseless; to transarm is to change from one type of defense to another." And, "Disarmament does not seem to be the road to peace, but peace may be the road to disarmament" (p. 202).

# *10* Nonmilitary Defense

To dissuade aggression, it is not sufficient to make war disastrous for a potential aggressor; it is equally important *to make peace as attractive to him as possible.* If peace seems to involve unbearable consequences, the incentive not to attack will be weakened, or even reversed.

Aggression can be made less attractive in two ways: by increasing the losses a potential aggressor would suffer if he attacks, and by reducing the gains he may hope to achieve. Similarly, peace can be made more attractive in two ways: by increasing his benefits from maintainance of peaceful relations, and by reducing any losses he may suffer during peacetime.

This gives four different ways in which a would-be aggressor can be dissuaded from his designs: (1) his losses in case of attack may be increased, e.g., through military defense and/or the threat of retaliation; (2) his expected gains from attack may be reduced, e.g., by destroying anything of value before it falls into enemy hands; (3) his losses during peace may be reduced, e.g., by voluntarily changing relations that may be considered unjust by an opponent; and (4) his gains from peaceful relations may be increased, e.g., through trade, provided it is mutually beneficial. These four possibilities, with some examples, are summarized in Table 10.1. To be most effective, defense must not rely on just one of these approaches, but must use *all four* simultaneously. Traditional defense, which has relied almost exclusively on military means, has concentrated on only one of these four—seeking to inflict as heavy losses on an enemy as possible, if he attacks. By comparison, the other three aspects have been neglected. Most countries do employ some of the other approaches, such as maintenance of trade relations with a potential opponent as long as he does not attack. But rarely are these other aspects integrated systematically into an overall defense effort, and they receive much less funding and planning than military preparations.

Galtung (1968, 1980) has called these other efforts *nonmilitary defense.* He points to one grave disadvantage of military defense: that it can instill fear in an opponent, and is therefore likely to lead to an escalating arms race, unless military measures are purely defensive and pose no threat to others. Most arms races in the past have ended in war. In contrast, nonmilitary defense does not create any fear and therefore is not likely to lead to war. If an adversary also shifts to nonmilitary defense, this does not worry us; on the contrary, it is to our mutual benefit. If he seeks to make peace more attractive for us, this does no harm to us.

While deterrence is a policy based on intimidation of an opponent, through the threat of retaliation against his homeland in case of an attack, *dissuasion* is a form of nonthreatening deterrence which, without evoking fear, aims at convincing an opponent that keeping peace is better for him than resorting to war. A variety of such techniques will be described later in this chapter.

**Table 10.1   Four Categories of Methods to Dissuade Aggression**

| If opponent attacks | If opponent does not attack |
|---|---|
| (1) Increase his losses: | (3) Reduce his losses: |
| armed defense and/or retaliation; economic and other sanctions | no exploitation; no humiliation; no threat |
| (2) Reduce his gains: | (4) Increase his gains: |
| nonviolent resistance; industrial sabotage in occupied areas of one's own country; internal unity | scientific, cultural, political & economic cooperation; trade; diplomatic & humanitarian services |

*Do We Face a "Rational" Opponent?*

It may appear that Table 10.1 rests on the assumption of a coolly calculating opponent, who carefully weighs the costs and benefits of various options open to him and then makes a rational choice. But this is not necessarily so. Such an assumption has, rightly, been criticized. For example, Adam Roberts writes,

> Statesmen do not in fact always make careful cost-benefit analyses before deciding on a course of action. They sometimes get obsessed with achieving particular targets and forget altogether about trying to balance books. . . . In some cases where states are concerned as much with *face, reputation* or *high principles* as with their interests by threatening or using force, cost-benefit analysis quickly becomes irrelevant . . . There have been examples of statesmen who up to a certain point have not worried greatly about how many of their own country's soldiers were killed. And in the last resort it is individual statesmen or very small groups, and not whole nations, who make the calculations on which decisions to go to war are based. What is clearly a cost for a nation as a whole may not be regarded equally seriously by its rulers. [Roberts 1976, p. 93, emphasis added].

This observation is very well taken, and perfectly valid, but it does not mean that efforts at dissuasion are to be dismissed as useless. It means, rather, that variables other than simply economic costs and benefits, or even than losses of life, may be more important in seeking to dissuade a potential aggressor. Some countries' governments seem to believe that in any dispute with an adversary, some combination of carrot and stick must exist that will make the opponent accept their proposed solution. If the opponent is offered a sufficient sum of money if he cooperates, and is faced with a sufficiently strong military threat if he refuses to cooperate, he will swing over to their side, they believe. But if the opponent considers the dispute to involve a question of moral or ideological principle from which there can be no departure, then a cost/benefit approach in purely material terms can lead to unhappy misunderstandings. For someone like the Ayatollah Khomeini, for example, who has voluntarily maintained an ascetic life style throughout his life, material incentives may not hold much attraction. What counts in seeking to persuade a decisionmaker is what we can suspect is *important to him or her*, not necessarily what we would consider valuable ourselves. Switzerland's defense doctrine officially recognizes this fact by stating,

> The risks which a potential aggressor must be made to perceive consist in the *loss* of prestige, military forces, war-potential and time, as well as in *running counter* to his ideological, political and economic interests. [General Defense 1973, p. 13; emphasis in original].

It may be difficult to determine exactly what a potential aggressor values most. If we calculate the incentives for dissuasion too sparingly, they may occasionally fail to be effective. A very broad, redundant array of measures, all aimed at making peace more and war less attractive, at maximizing the differential between the two, holds the best promise of preventing aggression.

Ground Zero (1982, p. 173) stresses the weakness of deterrence based on intimidation, since feelings of anger and fear sometimes lead perfectly rational human beings to do irrational things that they later regret. This insight is very important. What it implies is that one should avoid creating fear in an opponent as long as the opponent does not attack, and avoid confrontations that are likely to lead to angry reactions. A firm, steady, reassuring approach provides more security than sudden threats.

The gains and losses mentioned in Table 10.1 are to be interpreted much more broadly than in terms of material values only. They should include prestige or humiliation, and anything else that a decisionmaker may value. The goal of dissuasion is to prove to an opponent that whatever *his* objectives (not ours) may be, he cannot achieve them through aggression. He should be convinced that his true interests, as well as ours, are better served if he keeps peace. This includes showing the value to him of leaving our country free and intact, instead of damaging or destroying it in an attempted conquest.

The following are some examples of nonmilitary defense measures relating to each of the four categories in Table 10.1:

1. Increasing the Losses of an Opponent in Case He Attacks. While this is usually considered a military task, many nonmilitary measures also can have this effect. For example, if a

country hosts international organizations, an attack on that country would also harm international civil servants from many nations, and the aggressor would make enemies throughout the world. This may have been one reason for Austria's efforts to set up a complex of United Nations offices in Vienna.

Kenneth Boulding has made a related proposal, which he calls a system of "guestages," a combination of the words "guests" and "hostages." The United States and the Soviet Union should sponsor exchange visits of young people, including the sons and daughters of the elites, for two-year periods to learn each other's language and study in the other country. This would make more visible the fact that an attack on the other country is automatically an attack on one's own children (which in reality it always is). This should provide a strong motive not to undertake any attack, and would be an even more powerful method of dissuasion than the prospect of harming foreign diplomats. Such an arrangement would be a very useful step to reduce tensions; but one difficulty is that it requires mutual agreement and cannot be undertaken independently by one country alone, unlike other measures described in this chapter.

Other nonmilitary measures to increase an opponent's losses in case he attacks can be economic boycotts, freezing of the opponent's foreign assets, etc. If an opponent commits atrocities, these should be publicized widely, e.g., by inviting foreign journalists to observe and report on the atrocities, thereby undermining the opponent's prestige and eroding his sources of support. For example, in 1979 when Somoza's troops in Nicaragua killed an American journalist in cold blood and this was shown at close range on U.S. television, it weakened the United States' support for Somoza.

2. Reducing the Gains of an Opponent in Case He Attacks. An aggressor seeking to conquer a country will be anxious to seize its factories and infrastructure in the best possible condition. To frustrate such aims, anything of value to an enemy can be destroyed before it can be seized. Bridges, tunnels, and railway lines can be blown up before advancing enemy troops. Stocks of supplies, mines, etc., can be destroyed if they would otherwise fall into enemy hands. During World War II, for example, Sweden threatened, in case of a German invasion, to

blow up the power stations supplying its iron ore mines. This action would have stopped iron ore deliveries to Germany for a prolonged period (Roberts 1976, p. 64). Similarly, "by threatening non-cooperation and a dismantling of railway tracks, Sweden deterred Britain from invading the north en route to Finland in early 1940" (Roberts, p. 119).

Switzerland did not possess any raw materials of significance, but the railway tunnels through the Alps were an important asset. While Switzerland permitted the shipment of nonmilitary goods between Germany and Italy through those tunnels, it made it clear that if attacked, it would blow up those tunnels and make them useless for many years (Schwarz 1980, p. 64ff). This contributed to dissuasion of a German attack. If, instead, the Swiss government had blocked the use of those tunnels to Germany, and if Hitler had believed he could gain access to them through the use of military force, this would have invited an attack.

For such measures to have a dissuading effect upon an aggressor, they must be clearly announced *before* they are taken and must be made credible. A potential aggressor should not be "kept guessing," as certain people propose. To leave one's defensive responses deliberately shrouded in a cloud of uncertainty may deter a risk-averse opponent, but it fails against a risk-taker. A more-robust strategy is to *leave no doubt*.

At a secret meeting in 1943 with the German SS commander Schellenberg, General Guisan, the head of the Swiss army, expressed Switzerland's determination to destroy its Alpine tunnels and fight under all circumstances, if attacked. "Shortly thereafter, the German High Command abandoned its project to attack Switzerland" (Roberts 1976, p. 52). If Switzerland had kept its plans to blow up those tunnels in case of an attack as a "military secret", this would have been a totally useless strategy.

To eliminate any doubt that such sabotage against an enemy would in fact be undertaken, despite the sacrifices required from the invaded country, it may be best to employ certain automatic mechanisms, which would trigger a response, independent of anyone's control, if the agressor should take certain steps (Galtung 1976, p. 398). For example, a trip wire might be set up which would cause a bridge on a frontier to explode automatically if an attempt were made to cross the bridge.

It is not always necessary to destroy something completely to make it useless to an aggressor. For example, it is often possible to make an entire factory useless by removing some small but essential parts from certain machines, parts which it is very difficult, if not practically impossible, to replace. After the invader has been repelled, the factories can easily be restored to working order, by those familiar with the hiding place of the missing parts. It is possible to design industrial plants deliberately in such a way that the removal of a few key items paralyzes them entirely.

To ensure that private entrepreneurs would participate in such sabotage against an occupier and would not, left to fend for themselves, make their own compromises and adjustments with an enemy, Sweden has plans for "war indemnity grants" to reimburse private firms for losses suffered during an occupation (Roberts, p. 121).

A potential aggressor may also attempt to control the population, for example, as manpower for war industries. To frustrate this aim, the population can prepare itself to offer passive, nonviolent resistance. Such techniques have been extensively investigated by Gene Sharp (1973, 1980). Any government, including an occupation force, depends for its functioning on much voluntary cooperation, and may be paralyzed if such cooperation is withheld. It is well known that if employees work strictly "according to the rule book," an organization cannot function. Of course, violent terror can be used to intimidate a population into submission. It takes a great deal of courage to resist an aggressor by refusing to follow orders. But it is not always necessary to refuse orders openly. For example, if an occupation force advertised jobs for certain specialists and simply nobody applied, it would be difficult to identify individuals who failed to respond. It can be made clear to a potential occupier that a constant, large police apparatus would be needed to keep his government functioning, and that such a police force could *not* be recruited from the local population. Clearly, this requires a great deal of internal unity and solidarity among the population.

Proposals for passive resistance have often been criticized with the argument that they fail to prevent aggression and can become effective only *after* aggression has already taken place. Yet the mere *prospect* of having to deal with an ungovernable population can help to dissuade aggression in the first place, by making it clear that the hoped for gains cannot be realized. In this respect, civilian resistance can have a similar effect to military defense along a border.

It is important that people prepare themselves for nonviolent resistance in case of an occupation *before* it takes place, and that they do not rely on improvisation alone (even though skillful improvisation is also important for the success of any type of strategy). Civilian resistance should be practiced regularly, like military defense in maneuvers. Otherwise the population may be at a loss what to do during an emergency, and the credibility and dissuading effect of such resistance is weakened. Such forms of nonviolent resistance, or "civilian-based defense" (Sharp 1980) are essential components of an effective nonmilitary defense strategy.

Strategies of self-sabotage or civilian resistance may seem irrelevant to the security concerns of a country like the United States, which is not worried about occupation, but rather about a nuclear attack. Yet one should keep in mind that a nuclear war could be ignited through the escalation of a local military conflict, perhaps in the Third World, in which both the United States and the Soviet Union became involved. An example is one of Ground Zero's [1982] scenarios of both superpowers seeking to "defend" Iran. If such a war can be averted through a skillful application of nonmilitary defense, without drawing the superpowers into it, this can also improve the security of the superpowers. If Iran can dissuade an attempted occupation of its oil fields by making it clear that it could deny the use of its oil to any aggressor through sabotage, instead of the United States Rapid Deployment Force seeking to "protect" these oil fields, such a strategy can also contribute to greater security for the United States. Threatening the use of nuclear weapons to "guarantee" access to that oil, as the Pentagon had planned during the Carter administration, would risk escalation to a full-scale nuclear holocaust. As Richard Barnet (1981, p. 77) put it, that "would, of course, vaporize the oil along with the civilization that depended on it."

3. Reducing the Losses of an Opponent in Case He Does Not Attack. National leaders go to war not only because of the expectation of some gain, but sometimes because they find a situation intolerable and feel they have nothing to lose. A careful policy of dissuasion should avoid giving any such impression to an opponent.

Former colonies have fought for their independence because they felt their economic relationships with their colonial power were exploitative and unfair. It may be difficult to arrive at a precise definition of what represents exploitation and what does not. But that is not what is essential. What determines people's behavior is whether they *feel* exploited, not whether they "objectively" are. To change a relationship voluntarily that is considered unjust by the other side can help prevent war. Most colonies were, in fact, formally granted political independence without having to wage a war of liberation.

The reduction of economic inequality, both at the domestic and global level, can remove another potential source of conflict. Taylor writes that

> A longer-term threat perceived in Sweden is the growing disparities between the rich industrial world of the North and the poor underdeveloped countries of the South. . . . There is a genuine concern among the more informed Swedish public that international security cannot be attained over the long term while there remain gross inequalities between rich and poor nations (just as the welfare-state psychology suggests that inequalities between rich and poor within states breed conflicts). Sweden manifests its concern for North-South problems by substantial economic development assistance to less developed countries [Taylor 1982, p. 300].

It may have been an unwise policy to impose heavy reparations payments on Germany in the 1919 Versailles peace treaty and to designate Germany as the sole party responsible for World War I. Lord Keynes, still unknown at that time, was a member of the British delegation in Versailles, and in that capacity he warned that such a heavy economic burden would create social unrest. He resigned in protest when his advice was ignored. As it turned out later, he had foreseen correctly. The issue of the war reparations made it relatively easy for Hitler to play on the resulting dissatisfaction among Germans and to campaign on the promise of abrogating the Versailles peace treaty. A more-successful peace policy was pursued by the United States after World War II by granting reconstruction aid to its former enemies, Germany and Japan (as well as to other countries).

If the United States were to plan to wage an "economic and technical war on the Soviet Union . . . as a peace time complement to military strategy" (from "Pentagon Draws Up First Strategy for Fighting a Long Nuclear War", *New York Times*, 30 May 1982), this would reduce the Soviet Union's incentive to keep the peace, instead of promoting it. Sanctions should be reserved for serious violations of agreements and acts of aggression. If sanctions are applied too liberally, they lose their intended effect.

Beside economic reasons, perhaps more serious causes for dissatisfaction are humiliation, fear, and anger. Nor does provocative rhetoric generally further the interests of any country. A Russian proverb says, "Don't tickle a sleeping dog." If the leader of a small nation makes speeches assailing "capitalist imperialism" or "socialist imperialism," this is not prudent, even though he may feel perfectly justified to do so. If a driver approaching an intersection has a green light, but sees a heavy truck passing by without stopping, it is unwise of him to insist on his rights. The expression "defensive driving" is used to denote a careful, farsighted approach, which guarantees that we do not get hurt *even if others make mistakes.* It is the opposite of brinkmanship. Being cautious and not letting others draw us into disaster is not cowardly surrender, it is a strategy that allows us to reach our goals safely. A famous tombstone inscription says, "May he rest in peace. He had the right of way."

In its own interests, a country should avoid humiliating its opponents. Humiliation tends to breed a desire for revenge. During the Cuban missile crisis, the United States refused a Soviet demand that it remove nuclear missiles from Turkey, as part of a formal agreement, in exchange for the Soviet Union's withdrawal of its missiles from Cuba, a gesture that could have helped Khrushchev save face. This was hailed as a great diplomatic victory for the United States at the time. But the humiliation inflicted on the Soviet Union may have induced it to embark on its massive buildup of nuclear missiles. Ground Zero (1982, p. 101) writes, "as Soviet Deputy Foreign Minister Vasily Kuznetzov left one meeting to arrange the departure of the missiles, he remarked to an American negotiator, 'You'll never be able to do this to us again.' " A few months later, the United States removed its aging missiles from Turkey anyway, but ostensibly not as part of any compromise with the Soviet Union. Avoidance of a Soviet humiliation might have better served the long-term interests of United States security.

Initiatives toward compromise by an opponent should not be represented as weakness, otherwise similar initiatives are unlikely to be forthcoming in the future. To encourage desired forms of behavior, such behavior should be acknowledged and rewarded by reciprocity, not portrayed as defeat. For example, an unnamed Eastern European diplomat said in 1946 that a withdrawal of Soviet troops from Austria had to be seen as a voluntary gesture and should not be interpreted as a diplomatic defeat in face of the Anglo-Americans (Rauschensteiner 1979, p. 11).

To enhance its own security, a country should recognize the vital interests of its opponents and allay fears that it poses a threat to those interests. This view is reflected in the following quotation from Ground Zero (1982, p. 193): "Seeing the Soviet Union as a highly security-conscious, almost paranoid nation suggests that as a first step toward reducing the risk of nuclear war we should take pains to persuade the Soviets that we do not pose a threat to their security." (It should be understood that this means no threat to the Soviet Union's security as long as it does not attack the United States or its allies.)

To reduce an opponent's fear as long as he does not attack, governments can initiate a variety of confidence-building measures. Generally, any defense preparation should be carried out more openly and with less secrecy, to show to a potential opponent that it is intended purely for defense and does not pose any threat to her as long as she does not attack (Bay 1981). Military maneuvers can be announced in advance, to allay potential opponents' suspicions that they might be preparations for an attack. A NATO officer once declared, deeply convinced, "You can talk about confidence-building measures only if *both* sides are ready to take them." But while such information should preferably be exchanged on a mutual basis, even if only one side undertakes confidence-building measures, such steps can increase the security of both sides, and are therefore better than none at all. As mentioned earlier, for example, when Switzerland reaffirmed its neutrality at the beginning of World War II, it was in its own interest not to wait for Germany to do the same.

It is clear that not all types of information on defense should be revealed. For example, a country may want to announce that it maintains certain reserves of food and is therefore invulnerable against economic blackmail of that sort. It may want to encourage other countries to do likewise, in the interest of the common security of all countries. But the precise location of these reserves may have to be kept secret, so the supplies cannot be destroyed by an enemy.

One policy that can reduce an opponent's fear of a country as long as he does not attack it is the country's non-alignment. If a country is part of a military treaty with others, an opponent may fear a possible attack from that country during a war, because of its treaty obligations with third parties, and may therefore decide to occupy that country preemptively to eliminate a potential source of danger. If it is clear that a country will fight if and only if it is attacked first, and will not allow its territory to be used by troops from any of the conflicting parties, a potential reason for aggression is removed. Sweden and Switzerland have pursued such a policy, to their advantage, for a long time. (More on this will be said in the next chapter.)

In order not to unnecessarily anger a potential opponent, it is wise to refrain from inflammatory speeches and hostile actions. If another government criticized our leaders, called them "liars and cheats," and portrayed our country as an "evil empire," public opinion would demand a stiffening of our position, resulting in less willingness to seek mutual agreements. Why should we expect other governments to react differently? There may be good reasons to be firm on fundamental principles, but being firm is not the same as being provocative. Provocative words or actions on our part tend to hurt rather than promote our interests and our security.

When the Soviet air defense shot down a Korean civil airliner with 269 people aboard over Soviet waters, allegedly believing it to be a spy plane, this had a chilling effect on the international climate. Instead of seeking to minimize the resulting damage to East-West relations, Soviet commentators further exacerbated those relations by blaming Washington for the incident and comparing the U.S. government to the Nazis, who "forced women and children in front of them" when they made an attack (*International Herald Tribune*, 6 September 1983). Such provocative rhetoric can only damage the Soviet Union's own objective interest in reduced tension with the United States and in mutual arms reductions. In its own interest, the Soviet Union should have offered an apology and a full explanation, should have punished those responsible, and should have voluntarily offered compensation to the victims' families. Instead, they first denied having destroyed a plane, then said it had looked like an American reconnaissance plane, then that it had been no mistake, but the plane had been on a spy mission for the United States. The Soviet response reminds one of the lawyer who had three things to say in defense of his client, who had borrowed a pot and returned it broken: first, that he never borrowed the pot; second, that it was already broken when he borrowed it; and third, that he returned it in perfect condition.

The principle that if we cause anger and frustration, this weakens our security applies on the domestic as well as the international levels. The suppression of ethnic or linguistic groups can create a threat to a country's security, as will be discussed further in Chapter 15. With the approaching possibility of nuclear terrorism, the best (and perhaps only) possible preventive may be to avoid giving anyone the slightest reason for attempting such desperate acts that will threaten the lives of innocent people as well as the lives of the terrorists themselves.

4. Increasing the Gains of an Opponent in Case He Does Not Attack. To increase a potential opponent's stake in maintaining peace, peace can be made even more attractive through scientific and cultural exchanges, and through cooperation in the

fields of medicine, technology, and so on. As gestures of good will, help can be offered after natural disasters, such as earthquakes, floods, or famines. Cooperation can be encouraged on issues of joint concern, such as problems of the global environment or of exhaustible resources.

Students from other countries can be offered fellowships to come and study at one's universities. During such an extended stay, students usually conclude friendships for a lifetime. Such former foreign students may later exercise important functions in their home countries. As businessmen they may choose trade partners and are likely to import products with which they have become familiar. As public servants they may build other forms of international cooperation. It is always useful to have friends abroad.

A country can adhere to norms of international law in its relations with other countries, and renounce the use or threat of force to back its claims vis-à-vis other countries, taking grievances instead before the International Court of Justice. These initiatives may also encourage other nations to do likewise.

### Are Sanctions Effective?

It is valid to ask whether economic incentives or sanctions, praise or condemnation really have the desired effect on other countries' policies. Galtung (1967) has found that external trade sanctions can create an opposite effect from that intended, because they may strengthen the internal unity of a country and foster a feeling of defiance against external pressure. It is clear that if some government, or even a group of governments, set themselves up as self-appointed judges, praising and criticizing the policies of an opponent and rewarding or "punishing" the opponent through the use of economic pressure, the effect may well be opposite of the one intended. Attempts to tell other governments what they ought to do meet with resentment and contempt, particularly when they come from sources that apply a double standard, having previously taken actions similar to those they condemn. This is not what is mean by nonmilitary defense.

Nonmilitary defense means making clear to a potential opponent that one seeks peaceful relations that are also in the opponent's interest, and that, quite naturally, hostile behavior will disturb those relations and be to the opponent's disadvantage. A nation should announce beforehand what responses would be taken against certain threats to its security, and then leave the policy choices to the other side. To have any dissuading value, the possibility of applying sanctions must be apparent in advance. Other nations should not be kept guessing. "Punishments" handed out after the fact, on an ad hoc basis, have no dissuading value.

It is important to grant an opponent a face-saving way out of a corner. Applying pressure and then proclaiming victory if an opponent gives in is certain to induce resistance to such pressure. For example, if the lifting of martial law in a particular country is represented as the result of successful external economic sanctions, this is likely to lead to a prolongation of martial law, because an authoritarian regime will naturally seek to avoid such a humiliating defeat. On the other hand, if a country has a general policy of not entertaining trade relations with *any* country under martial law, and does not single out any particular country as the target, this policy can have the desired effect. It will provide some incentive for all countries to permit civilian governments. An end to martial law in one country will then not be associated with that government's succumbing to direct pressure. (If a government demands an end to martial law in Poland, but not in Chile or the Philippines, this will only be seen as hypocrisy.)

### Is Nonmilitary Defense Sufficient?

In today's militarized world, nonmilitary defense *alone* may not be sufficient to help a country maintain adequate security. But nonmilitary means can certainly *add* to a country's security, without posing any threat to others. Security is strengthened through variety or *redundance* or defensive measures. Those countries that neglect to supplement their military defense with nonmilitary techniques take an unnecessary risk to their security.

A transition to an exclusive reliance on nonmilitary defense, with all countries participating, could be one among several approaches to the elimination of war. Is there any chance that this might ever be feasible?

Karl von Clausewitz, the 19th-century German philosopher of war, did not believe in such a possibility. He wrote that war is to diplomacy what cash is to credit. No matter how rarely actual cash transactions take place, cash must always be ready to back up paper credit, otherwise the credit economy would collapse. Similarly, Clausewitz argued, the power to wage war must always be ready as an ultimate threat, otherwise the whole intricate construct of diplomacy will be "built on sand" and lose its credibility. But this is not necessarily so. The "cash" payment backing up diplomacy can just as well be a sort of real "cash", that is, the delivery or withholding of goods and services, or "positive sanctions" in general. Reliance on war to back up diplomacy has become totally suicidal, and therefore obsolete, in the nuclear age. If one were to apply Clausewitz's argument to the economic realm, one could equally well say, "No matter how rarely the whip is actually used, it will always be needed, as an ultimate threat, otherwise people would stop working." This idea prevailed under the slave system. But that system has long since been abolished in favor of the much less inhumane system of wage labor. The paycheck has replaced the whip as an instrument to induce people to perform various jobs – if they are not motivated to work out of an inner need. Why should nonmilitary means not be able to replace war as an instrument of international relations?

*Some Recent Conflicts*

To conclude this chapter, let us take a brief look at some recent wars and other conflicts to see whether any of the four principles of dissuasion were violated, and whether any of the conflicts might have been prevented.

If it comes to war, usually not just *one* mistake has been made, but a *whole series* of safety barriers have been breached. At each point, if a different decision had been taken, the war might have been prevented. One example is the war between Argentina and Great Britain over the Falkland Islands/Malvinas in spring

1982. Britain might have been better advised in the first place not to conquer a far-away territory that was difficult to defend. Or it could have given the Falklands voluntarily to a Latin American country when most Latin American colonies won independence. Once force had been used by Argentina to seize the islands, however, this was obviously the wrong moment to give away the islands, because that would have encouraged the use of force elsewhere. If Britain were determined to keep the islands, it should have made clearer its willingness to defend them. To protect them with 84 marine soldiers who surrendered without any casualty was not a strong deterrent. Especially since it was known that Argentina laid claim to the islands, a stronger defense posture was indicated, to prevent any temptation to seize the islands by force. For example, preparations could have been made to blow up the air strip and harbor at the first sign of an attempted invasion, and such preparations should have been announced clearly. The fact that Britain's warships took two weeks to arrive left doubt about Britain's determination. While the blame for the invasion lies with Argentina, Britain's position was similar to someone who leaves his bicycle unlocked on the street and is surprised to find that it has been stolen, especially if someone else has been claiming it belonged to him.

The Solidarity union in Poland has been using nonviolent techniques to seek the right to form free labor unions. One problem was that before the institution of martial law, strikes occurred, almost daily, while only a few occurred afterward. For a maximum incentive effect against martial law, the situation should have been reversed: Solidarity should have cooperated with the government, provided it moved toward reforms, granting it sufficient time, but should have made clear its determination to go on a long general strike in case of a military crackdown. Solidarity's leadership did attempt to pursue more or less such a strategy, but many union members seem to have found it emotionally impossible to be more patient.

A successful example of a nonviolent action was the 1942 Norwegian teachers' strike against nazification of the schools. The teachers steadfastly refused to join a compulsory teachers' corporation, even when about a thousand of them were taken to concentration camps and threatened with execution. Quisling, the Norwegian prime minister, realized that if he took stronger action against the teachers, he would further alienate the Norwegian population against his own pro-Nazi regime. The teachers' courage forced him to abandon his plans (Sharp 1973, pp. 88–89).

Israel used some nonmilitary approaches to defense when it returned the Sinai peninsula to Egypt after conclusion of the 1979 peace treaty. But it could have done more: it could have let Egypt derive immediate, clearly visible benefits from the peace treaty. For example, Israel could have shared with Egypt the techniques it had developed for desert agriculture, to help Egypt improve its food situation. This would have cost Israel nothing. Such a move might have strengthened, and possibly helped to power, opposition movements to the governments in other neighboring countries, movements that also wanted to seek peace with Israel. On the other hand, the imposition of embarrassing conditions on Egyptian President Mubarak's planned 1982 visit to Israel was totally unnecessary, and harmed Israel's interests. What other Arab head of state would want to visit Israel, if he could expect to face the same sort of humiliation in the eyes of his own people? The dismissal of elected mayors and shooting of unarmed teenage demonstrators in the West Bank in 1982 undoubtedly won support for those opposed to Israel, and isolated those among the Arab population who might have wanted to cooperate with Israel. Israel's 1982 war against the Palestine Liberation Organization in Lebanon, with its loss of civilian life, has sowed hatred that may erupt again in the future, once the Palestinians gain access to more powerful weapons. There is a pertinent saying, "The only way to get rid of your enemies is to make them your friends." If one does not succeed to turn them into friends, at least one better learn to live with them, for one's own sake. And one should certainly not make *more* enemies.

Before Iraq's 1980 attack on Iran, Iran had violated almost all principles of a prudent dissuasion policy. Iran's regular army had dissolved, making the country appear nearly defenseless. Iran had isolated itself internationally by taking U.S. diplomatic personnel as hostages. No country wanted to provide open support to Iran under those conditions. In addition, the Iranian government had fomented a linguistic dispute in its own country by denying the Arab minority in Khusistan province its request to use Arabic in schools, which led to bloody riots. Again, this added to the appearance of internal division and weakness. Finally, Iranian radio broadcasts called daily on the Iraquis to overthrow their government. (Imagine what would have happened to Switzerland if, at the outset of World War II, it had dissolved its army; detained some foreign diplomats; prohibited the use of the German language with internal riots as a result; and called daily on the German people to overthrow Hitler.) It shoud not be surprising that under these circumstances war appeared more attractive to the Iraqi government than peace. As it turned out, Iraq miscalculated if it expected a quick and decisive victory, and Iran may yet win the war. But if Iran insists on large reparation payments from Iraq, to which it may feel entitled, the seed may be planted for another round of war in the future, just as the Versailles peace treaty's imposition of huge reparation payments on Germany may have been one of the factors leading to World War II.

Does this mean that the victim should be blamed for the aggression it suffered? Certainly not. Clearly, the guilt for the Iraqi attack rests entirely upon the Iraqi government. But in this case the victim might have been able to prevent the aggression by taking a more convincing defense posture—not just militarily, but also diplomatically, politically, and psychologically. Furthermore, the victim, who will suffer, can be expected to have a *greater interest* in preventing aggression than the aggressor, who may expect to benefit from it. While both sides may have some degree of capability to prevent a war, the victim of aggression certainly has a greater willingness to avoid war. For this reason, it may be more promising to investigate what the potential victims of aggression may be able to do to prevent it, instead of making appeals to the perpetrators of aggression, appeals that are likely to fall on deaf ears.

Improved relations with other countries are achieved not by threat of force, but by a search for mutually beneficial undertakings. For example, Japan tried before and during World War II to establish an Asian "coprosperity sphere" with military force, and failed. Since 1945, it has pursued the same goal by relying instead on the attractiveness to other countries of what its economy can offer, and has succeeded.

As another example, the United States in the early 1970s realized it was in its interest to end its hostility toward the Chinese government and its opposition to China's membership in the United Nations. China was interested in purchasing U.S. technology, U.S. companies were interested in doing business with China, and the peoples of both countries were eager to learn more about each other. These factors led to a rapid improvement in mutual relations, with increasing travel and trade.

Let us try to imagine the relations between the two countries today if the United States had sent troops or "special forces" (meaning saboteurs) into China during the Cultural Revolution, to support one faction or another, or the effect if the United States had publicized plans for fighting a nuclear war with China. What would have been the result of an attempt to force the Chinese government to adopt a more market-oriented economic system, through a mixture of threats, criticism, and economic sanctions? It would be naive to believe that this would have had any other effect than the opposite from that intended. Yet some people, who would themselves be the last to submit to such crude pressure, seem to trust in the effectiveness of such methods. Instead, unarmed scientists and artists from both countries opened the way to friendly relations. If the United States had sent troops and B-52 bombers into China and symphony orchestras into Vietnam, its relations with those two countries might have been just the reverse of what they are today: it might have quite friendly relations with Vietnam and rather tense relations with China.

This is a hard lesson to accept for those who instinctively believe that through the use of "hard" force they can achieve anything they want, and that the use of "soft" diplomacy is cumbersome, unreliable and unmanly. But we all need to learn that lesson, for the sake of our survival. Some may suggest that cooperation with a potential opponent is a form of appeasement, which is dangerous, as the experience with the Munich agreement has shown. But cooperation is the exact opposite. *Appeasement means to give in to an opponent when he commits aggres-*

*sion* and thus to encourage more aggression. *Nonmilitary defense,* on the contrary, *means to offer cooperation to an opponent while he keeps peace,* and to make it clear that such cooperation would naturally be lost in case of war. In this way, nonmilitary defense discourages aggression and strengthens peace.

# 11   Entangling Alliances

Military nonalignment was one of the methods listed in the previous chapter to persuade an opponent that he has nothing to fear if he leaves our country in peace. Nonalignment means that we will not attack him during a war, out of treaty obligations with third countries, and will not allow any country to carry out military operations from our territory. We will strongly defend ourselves, but only if we are attacked.

What are some of the reasons in favor or joining a military alliance? Two principle types of reasons have been offered: (a) it is good for the country's security and (b) it is a moral duty. Let us examine the two arguments in turn.

### "Nonaligned Countries Are Weak"

Even among people concerned with preventing war there seems to be some misunderstanding regarding the usefulness of alliances. For example, Bueno de Mesquita (1981, p. 123) has offered a typical statement of the first argument: "Weak nations, through the judicious formation of alliances, may be able to achieve as much security against foreign aggression as some great powers do." In reality, a potential aggressor will weigh the expected *gains* against the expected *losses* in case he attacks. The quoted statement looks at only one factor in a potential aggressor's consideration whether or not to proceed with a foreign military adventure, namely his expected losses. It ignores the other factor—his expected gains, or whether the whole undertaking is worth the risk. If the expected gains are sufficiently small, even a weak deterrent can be sufficient to prevent aggression. (From the discussion in the previous chapter, it should be clear that gains and losses are to be understood in a much broader sense than economic or military values alone.)

To defeat an alliance is usually more difficult than to defeat a nonaligned country. But to win control over an entire group of countries which form an alliance also brings greater gains (in terms of resources, power, pride) than the control of a single small country. To say that whichever objective is easier to obtain will be the preferred one is like saying that since a bicycle is easier to steal than a Rolls Royce, every thief prefers to steal the bicycle. By that logic, Hitler should have attacked Switzerland rather than France, which was allied with Great Britain, since the military forces of the Allies were certainly larger and more powerful than those of a small nonaligned country. On the other hand, he considered France to be of much greater strategic value.

Sweden's official defense doctrine, for example, states, "The defense has to be so strong that the costs to defeat Sweden are out of proportion as compared to the strategic advantages which an aggressor might attain" (quoted in Roberts 1976, p. 92). What counts is the *ratio* between expected losses in case of an attack and the gains to be expected, whether economic, political, ideological, or in terms of prestige, etc. There is no reason why this ratio should be less favorable for a small country than for a large one, or for a group of countries as a whole.

It is clear that sometimes an aggressor may be able to conquer a series of small countries, one by one, if he can concentrate all his offensive power on one at a time. If these weaker countries join forces, they will be better able to resist the aggressor. (This principle, for example, led to the foundation of Switzerland in 1291 as a defense alliance among three localities against expedition forces sent by the German emperor.) Such a defense alliance does not necessarily change the ratio between gains and losses. But it does force an opponent to choose between getting all or nothing, and he may not possess the forces to get all at once, even though he might consider the prize well worth the cost.

Countries which form a defense alliance seek to make the cost of aggression high relative to the *offensive capabilities* of a potential aggressor. Small nonaligned nations seek to make the cost of aggression high relative to the *expected gains* of a potential aggressor. Both approaches can be equally effective in dissuading aggression. The choice faced by a potential aggressor is in a certain sense analogous to the choice faced by a potential buyer. An art collector may not be able to purchase a Rembrandt that is offered for a million dollars, even though she may consider it undervalued. But she may also refuse a painting that sells for one hundred dollars, simply because she does not like it. This analogy again suggests the two approaches to defense mentioned in Chapter 10: (a) make aggression more costly for a potential aggressor and (b) make aggression less rewarding.

A defense alliance can make aggression less likely, because it increases the stakes involved. But if a war occurs nevertheless, the scope of the conflict will automatically widen, because all of a nation's allies will be drawn into it. If a country wants to gain security from joining an alliance, all the other members of the alliance must be equally careful and determined to avoid war. Otherwise the country might be drawn into a war by some other member which is not sufficiently cautious, which takes inadequate preparations for defense and thus attracts aggression, or possibly even takes an aggressive, provocative stance that may lead to war and then involve the entire alliance. A chain usually breaks at the weakest link. Similarly, it will be the most risk-seeking member of an alliance (i.e., the most-vulnerable and/or -aggressive) that may pull the other members into a war.

The problem of choosing allies is analogous to the problem faced by a mountain climber who is considering to go on a joint expedition. If all members of the team are equally skillful and careful, they may be able to save the life of one who slips accidentally, by holding together on a rope. But a single reckless team member who makes an imprudent move or chooses the wrong path may also pull the entire party into an abyss. An experienced mountain climber may be safer alone. Allies must be chosen very carefully. Maybe what is needed on the international scene is an "alliance of non-belligerent countries" (a proposal made by Johan Galtung and Richard Falk).

There may be cases where an alliance has the effect of making any war not only larger but even more likely. This can occur if one of the alliance members feels emboldened by the joint strength of the alliance and embarks on an adventurous foreign policy course that may lead to war. It has been said that the military government of Argentina felt encouraged to attempt a seizure of the Falklands/Malvinas by its perception of having recently gained international support. As it turned out, Argentina did not have as much support as it may have expected, and that war remained limited.

In some circumstances, a military alliance may be compared to a large forest containing no forest-free zones. If a fire starts anywhere, it will spread throughout the entire forest. Nonaligned countries seek to protect themselves against that danger by dissociating themselves from warring parties. They set up a fire break without trees where the fire will exhaust itself and spread no farther. The more such safety barriers, the more localized any fire will remain.

Of course, one must not underestimate the natural impulse to help friends in difficulty, even if they have made mistakes. It is not proposed here to abandon friends when they are in need, but to help them *stay out of war* by making it clear that one's capacity to come to their rescue is not unlimited. We do a service to allies by telling them that if they pursue a policy that leads to war—or invites war—we will not go along with them.

Joining a military alliance can either increase or decrease a country's security, depending on the behavior of the other alliance members. But the arguments in favor of joining an alliance are far less unequivocal than some advocates of military alliances claim. Sweden and Switzerland have avoided defense alliance, as long as other potential members may be less careful in preventing war.

### "Neutrality Is Immoral"

This statement is attributed to John Foster Dulles, Eisenhower's Secretary of State (according to Roberts 1976, p. 79). It expresses the second argument, that it is selfish not to take sides and join other countries in defending themselves, which we will consider now.

It is clear that the European countries are grateful to the United States for helping to free them from Hitler. Some of these countries had neglected to make adequate provisions for self-defense. Yet small neutral countries, if they had joined the war on the side of the Allies, would have suffered from war on their territory, without being able to contribute much to the rescue of others. One may object that if the United States had not fought in Europe, even Sweden and Switzerland would probably have been eventually conquered by Hitler. On the other hand, if all the other European countries had made equally strenuous efforts to resist and dissuade aggression, the war might have been prevented.

Whereas the United States' liberation of Western Europe was clearly welcome, in other cases "outside help" is more questionable. For example, the Soviet Union claims to defend the legitimate government of Afghanistan, at its invitation; similarly, the United States fought long and hard for a South Vietnamese government which did not enjoy universal support in its own country. The danger can arise that two foreign powers support opposing groups in one country, both of which claim to represent the rightful government. To dissuade foreign intervention, the major powers could pursue a policy of "no first intervention," analogous to a policy of no first use of nuclear arms. Johansen (1982, p. 62) writes, "Even without negotiations, one superpower could . . . promise to refrain . . . from sending any of its troops into any nonaligned country, *even if invited*, in return for a promise from the other superpower to show the same self-restraint" (emphasis in the original). He points out that such a policy could have helped to avoid the wars in both Vietnam and Afghanistan. In the long run, on balance, a mutual policy of non-intervention will be in the superpowers' own interest, even though they might believe to be able to gain some short-term advantages from interventions in particular instances.

Advocates of military interventions abroad often explain their position by saying, "We would prefer not to have to intervene in other countries, but the other side continues to intervene, and forces us to keep the line; if we simply sat back, the other side would take over the world." Would that really happen? The superpowers have lost positions of influence by being expelled not by the other superpower, but by the local government or people themselves. For example, the Soviet Union gained a great deal of influence in Egypt after helping to build the Aswan Dam. But Soviet advisers were increasingly resented and were finally expelled in 1972. If the United States had sought to expel them through military pressure on Egypt, they might still be there. Similarly, the American advisers to the Shah of Iran were resented by Islamic fundamentalists as a sort of foreign shadow government. They were expelled in 1979, but not by the Soviet Union. It does not appear true that only military intervention by one superpower can stop the other from dominating a third country.

The Islamic Revolution has had tragic consequences for Iran — but to understand the Iranians' resentment against foreign advisers, we should try to imagine the hypothetical U.S. popular reaction if the Iranian government had helped to overthrow the U.S. government, had installed a fundamentalist Islamic ruler, and had sent Islamic clergymen to advise the U.S. government on how to turn the United States into an Islamic republic. The U.S. participation in overthrowing the Mossadegh government in Iran in 1953 after it nationalized the oil industry may have appeared as a "success" for U.S. global interests — in the short run — but it brought greater problems in the long run. Fortunately, when the Cardenas government in Mexico nationalized the oil industry in 1938, the U.S. government did not intervene; otherwise it might have similar problems with Mexico today.

A more-successful policy than foreign intervention may well be to help the people of other countries to defend themselves against aggression, by providing them with *defensive* (not *offensive*) arms and with information on how they can better protect themselves. Even more important than arms may be for countries to reduce their vulnerability by strengthening internal unity, and by employing a broad-based policy of dissuasion that includes nonmilitary strategies. To enable the people of other countries to defend themselves is a better approach to strengthening peace than for an outside power to take over their defense, sometimes against their wishes.

One of the reasons for the United States' 1983 invasion of Grenada was its fear that the Soviet Union was going to build a military base in the Western hemisphere. But how would the United States have reacted if the Soviet Union had invaded the island of Diego Garcia in the Indian Ocean because the United States was building there a military base in the "Eastern hemisphere"? Another reason for the invasion was the killing of the Grenadian Prime Minister Maurice Bishop and more than 100 civilians. But how would the world have reacted if the Soviet Union had invaded Chile in 1973 after a popularly elected president had been slain in a military coup, together with an estimated 30,000 citizens (even more than in Grenada)? Foreign interventions, even if popular at home, carry the danger that they can escalate into a wider war.

With more than 100 small, independent nations around the world, violent events such as those preceding the U.S. invasion of Grenada are bound to occur from time to time in one place or another. It is in the interest of the superpowers not to allow the whims of a small dictator to draw them into a conflict. If they allow their military policy to be determined by the irresponsible actions of any reckless leader anywhere in the world, the world is not very safe. A policy of intervening in internal conflicts in other countries to restore "socialism" or "democracy" will draw the intervening power unnecessarily into conflicts. If we broke repeatedly into the homes of neighbors to settle family disputes to our own liking, we would get hurt, sooner or later, or at least lose friends.

## A Capsule History of Swiss Neutrality

What led Switzerland to adopt a policy of armed neutrality and non-intervention? It was a peculiar historical experience that brought about the change. For the first two centuries after its founding, Switzerland participated in many wars, partly to repel attempts to subjugate it, partly to conquer other territory. A turning point in attitudes was foreshadowed in 1481 when an emerging internal dispute was settled. The urban member cantons favored the admission of two additional city-states into the confederation, expecting to gain in power. The rural cantons were opposed, afraid they might be drawn into wars in which the cities engaged and would have to supply troops. The conflict threatened to break up the confederation. But at the last moment the two sides agreed to seek mediation from Niklaus von der Flüe, a hermit whose counsel was widely sought and respected. He suggested that the two city-states be admitted and be entitled to receive assistance in their defense if they were attacked from outside, but not if they became involved in war because they intervened abroad. That Solomonic judgment was acceptable to all sides.

What triggered a lasting shift in foreign policy was a strange historical coincidence. In 1515, two Swiss armies, one fighting on the side of the French king and the other on the side of an Italian duke, found each other situated on opposing sides of a battle at Marignano in northern Italy, and almost completely annihilated each other. When the few wounded survivors brought news of this event back to Switzerland, there was deep horror and indignation and a realization of the futility of war. The killing of "enemies" had not had the same psychological impact. This was not even a civil war, where people wanted to fight each other; it was just a senseless, unintended, mutual massacre. The conviction gradually emerged that the best way to keep out of war was not to become entangled in disputes between other nations; that it was preferable to seek to solve any problems with other nations through peaceful negotiations or, if negotiations failed, through binding legal arbitration. Attacks from abroad were to be discouraged through the defense readiness of a strong militia army that would fight only inside its own territory.

As time passed, positive experience has further strengthened the Swiss people's conviction that these policies represent a successful approach to avoiding war, that it is best not to interfere in disputes among other nations and to solve domestic problems internally. The abhorrence against foreign interference is very deep. During a brief civil war between Catholics and Protestants in November 1847, some Jesuits called on the Austrian emperor to intervene. The conflict was settled before any intervention took place, but the popular anger against this appeal to a foreign power to meddle in an internal dispute caused the Jesuit order to be banned in Switzerland for more than a century. Proposals to lift the ban were repeatedly turned down in popular referenda, until the Jesuits were finally readmitted in 1973.

Switzerland's policy of armed neutrality has served it well. With the exception of a temporary occupation by Napoleon's armies from 1798–1815 and the 1847 civil war, it has enjoyed almost five centuries of peace since the battle at Marignano, while many wars raged in Europe.

Switzerland learned to adopt a peace policy the hard way, through its own early mistakes. Is it possible to learn from the experience of other nations, or must all nations first repeat similar mistakes themselves? It may well be that after a nuclear world war, with the slaughter of hundreds of millions, the world will come to realize the futility of war in general. But that may be too late.

# 12 Forms of Power and Resistance: Military, Economic, and Psychological

In earlier chapters we have considered almost exclusively how a country can dissuade military aggression, or protect itself if dissuasion fails. But countries which seek to exercise power over other countries employ not only military force, but also a whole range of other means. Among them may be economic pressure, bribery, false propaganda and rumors, etc. A variety of approaches can be used to resist these various forms of power. This chapter will first offer a classification of these various forms of power and resistance, and then mention some examples of defense against economic and psychological pressures.

Galtung (1980, pp. 58–63) distinguishes between power-over-oneself and power-over-others. Following the classical distinction, he divides power-over-others into power through rewards (the "carrot") and power through punishment (the "stick"). Both rewards and punishment can be in the form of material or nonmaterial means. If nonmaterial rewards (e.g., praise) and punishment (e.g., criticism) are combined into a single form of "persuasive" power, one obtains a three-fold classification of power-over-others: (a) normative power, based on persuasion; (b) remunerative power, based on bargaining; and (c) punitive power, based on force. Galtung mentions that immunity against these three forms of power can take the form of self-respect, self-sufficiency, and fearlessness, respectively (the opposites of submissiveness, dependency, and fear).

Military threats are a particular form of punitive power-over-others, and we have examined various ways to resist them. But a country that wants to preserve its independence must also be able to defend itself against economic pressures (a form of remunerative power) and against psychological or ideological influence (a form of normative power).

For someone to exert power-over-others, he or she must have both the subjective desire and the objective capability to exert power. In Table 12.1, a distinction is made between the subjective and objective components of each of these three forms of power-over-others, extending Galtung's classification. Resistance to each of these three forms of power also requires both the subjective will to resist and the objective ability, as shown in the Table. I will briefly discuss each of the components and offer a few examples.

1. Military power. Some countries, even though they possess powerful offensive arsenals and armies, have not used these forces to invade other countries. Other countries, under an aggressive leadership, have attempted invasions but did not possess the objective means or the strategic skill to carry them out successfully. The greatest danger stems from countries with great offensive power whose leaders have the urge to use it.

2. Economic power. Greed is a desire to take away from others, offering them nothing in return, in a parasitic relationship. Greed differs from enterpreneurship, which involves a sense for discovering mutually beneficial opportunities that others may have overlooked, and through this perceptive skill and initiative provides benefits for others as well as for the entrepreneur.

The harm done by *monopoly power* to those dependent on it has been extensively analyzed. Galtung (1980, p. 170) cites Andrei Sakharov as having stated that he "agrees about the dangers of monopolistic capitalism, particularly when there is one monopoly for the whole field of production: the state."

3. Psychological power. Arrogance is the idea that one knows what is good for others, without taking their opinions into account. The opposite is empathy, a sincere desire to under-

**Table 12.1   Forms of Power and of Resistance to Power**

| | Power-over-others | Resistance |
|---|---|---|
| **Military (punitive)** | | |
| Subjective component | Aggressivity | Will to defend; fearlessness |
| Objective component | Offensive arms, skills in offensive strategy | Defensive arms and skills |
| Combination | Military threat | Indomitability |
| **Economic (remunerative)** | | |
| Subjective component | Greed | Modesty of wants; self-restraint |
| Objective component | Monopoly power, manipulative skill | Resourcefulness, Ingenuity |
| Combination | Exploitation, economic blackmail | Self-reliance |
| **Psychological (normative)** | | |
| Subjective component | Arrogance | Self-respect, self-conviction |
| Objective component | Control over media, propo-gandistic skill | Knowledge, access to media |
| Combination | Mind control, demagogy | Autonomy |

stand others, to listen to their concerns, and to help them if help is welcome. There is a difference between preaching to others, and sharing knowledge and insights with those who wish to listen.

The objective capability of exerting psychological power over others requires skillful propaganda, and is enhanced through control over the mass media.

The objective capability of exerting power of any type thus has two components, the material means (control over media, financial wealth, offensive arms) and the necessary skill to use these means (skills in propaganda, in bargaining and in offensive strategy). Possession of any of these components of power is likely to enhance other components. For example, wealth permits the acquisition of more arms; and arms can be used to strengthen an exploitative relationship that brings in more wealth. Money can buy control over the media, and this control can be used for further enrichment. Also, one of the first positions seized in a military coup is usually the national radio and television station. Aggressivity, greed, and arrogance tend to go together and mutually reinforce one another.

The combination of all these six components is "power-over-others." The proper response to such power is not to exert power in reverse (to "dominate so as not to be dominated"), but to make oneself invulnerable by using all six parallel components of resistance against power. Let us briefly review each of these.

1. Resistance against military power. Fearlessness, to be justified, must be backed up by the capability to defend and protect oneself.

2. Resistance against economic power. The objective component of self-reliance (see, for example, Galtung, O'Brien, and Preiswerk 1980) may be called "resourcefulness," the ability to provide for oneself if necessary, without exploiting others or depending on the good will of others. It is strengthened by access to the necessary physical resources, technical knowledge, skill, ingenuity, etc. Self-reliance, or *potential* self-sufficiency, is different from autarky (i.e., permanent self-sufficiency) in that self-reliance does not mean to cut off mutually beneficial economic relationships. Rather, it means to be prepared and able to

sever an economic relationship if it is inequitable. The subjective aspect of self-reliance is modesty, voluntary simplicity, so as not to be attracted by unnecessary material rewards offered. Self-reliant in terms of food is someone who can either produce much, or survive on little, or preferably both.

3. Resistance against psychological power. In order not to be influenced by others' value judgments, a good portion of self-respect is helpful. But it is also useful to have more experience and objective knowledge than someone who attempts to assert his influence. An illustration is the fact that advertisements for baby milk powder easily influenced mothers with little education in the Third World, who were misguided to substitute it for much-healthier mother's milk. The use of this powdered milk under Third World conditions (with contaminated water and excessive dilution by the uninformed mothers) has caused the death of many infants. Had these mothers been better informed about the health hazards involved, they could have formed their own independent judgment and would not have naively accepted the advertisements' claims that artificial milk made babies strong and healthy. In a similar way, well-informed people are not easy victims of any propaganda. The ability to resist hostile propaganda is further enhanced by decentralized access to the media, in the form of call-in radio braodcasts, a diverse press, people-to-people communication via telephone, etc. This is the opposite of centralized control over the media.

The six components of resistance against power also mutually reinforce one another. Economic self-reliance in sectors that are vital for survival and for a prolonged defense effort strengthen military defense capability, and vice versa. Self-respect strengthens a population's will to defend itself and reduces vulnerability to economic incentives, and so on.

A complete system of pure defense should seek to strengthen all six components of resistance against foreign powers, but should seek none of the six components of power over others, to prevent any widening of a conflict. Such a system may be characterized, in brief, as *invulnerability without threat*. We will now discuss briefly how countries can reduce their vulnerability to hostile economic and psychological pressures without exerting similar or other pressures on other countries.

*Reducing Economic Vulnerability*

To reduce its vulnerability to embargoes of vital commodities, a country should avoid depending on the use of military force to restore the flow of these commodities. Such a response would escalate the conflict and draw the country into an open war. In its own interest, the country should instead make itself invulnerable against such pressures without posing any threat to other countries. Some methods to achieve invulnerability against a potential cutoff of imports are (a) the stockpiling of reserves of vital commodities, (b) the development of stand-by domestic production capacity, (c) the exploration of possible substitutes, and (d) plans to reduce nonessential consumption of these commodities, should it become necessary.

Switzerland has such a plan for food, and resorted to the plan during part of World War II. Food is perhaps the most vital of all commodities. During peacetime, Switzerland imports nearly 50 percent of its food consumption. In case of a cutoff of imports, food would be immediately rationed, requiring about a one-third reduction in daily caloric intake. Meat consumption would be drastically reduced to arrive at a more-efficient calorie conversion factor through a more-vegetarian diet. (To produce one calorie of beef requires seven to eight calories of grain.) Grassland would be converted gradually, in three yearly phases, into cropland. In the meantime, the food deficit would be bridged with reserves of nonperishable food, which are constantly being renewed in peacetime. Similar programs exist for fuel, certain minerals, and other vital commodities.

A buildup of food reserves is not directed "against" any other country. Any potential adversary is most welcome to use a similar defense program. This does not pose a potential threat, as would a buildup of offensive arms. Switzerland has not created these plans because of any special virtue. In its case, such emergency plans are simply a necessity, because it would never have the military capability nor the desire to invade its neighbors to get the food supplies it might need in a crisis.

Up to now, the great powers have not been forced to adopt similar policies. They have found it more convenient to depend on certain supplies from abroad, and to point to their military might as a deterrent against any attempt to strangle their economies by withholding vital imports. But military force cannot accomplish everything. For example, it is impossible to patrol an oil pipeline that is hundreds of miles long, day and night, to prevent its destruction. A few determined saboteurs could easily blow it up, and could do so repeatedly. To *guarantee* oil imports by military means is very difficult, if not impossible; it is much easier to keep oil flowing with economic incentives. More than that, in an age where any local war carries with it the danger that it might escalate into a confrontation between the superpowers, the risks of such a policy may have become too great. A genuine strengthening of a country's national security is much better achieved if the nation makes itself less vulnerable to economic pressures, through plans for potential self-sufficiency in case of emergency. Plans to go to war to secure imports are a dubious contribution to a country's real security.

One argument says it is too expensive to stockpile essential commodities against a trade embargo. Indeed, it may well be unnecessarily expensive to continue with the normal standard of living under those circumstances. But to make preparations to survive, even if at a more-frugal level, should not be overly expensive. Furthermore, such expenses should be considered part of the defense budget; viewed from that perspective, these expenses are not high at all. For example, Sweden's "economic defense" expenditures for the stockpiling of food, various strategic materials, fuel, and heating oil comprise no more than 2 to 3 percent of its total defense budget (Roberts 1976, p. 103). If such expenditures can help prevent war, especially in our nuclear age, they are modest.

To make one's transportation system less-vulnerable against aerial bombings, it is useful to have a dense transportation network, so that if any branch is destroyed, numerous alternative paths will lead to a given destination. The Ho Chi Minh trail, for example, operated on this principle, and it proved to be practically impossible to interdict the flow of supplies to South Vietnam, despite heavy American bombing. Similarly, industries are less vulnerable if they are geographically dispersed, not concentrated in a few metropolitan areas. Of course, it is not suggested here to close down existing industries and move them elsewhere. What is proposed is a policy that favors the construction of industries in a less-vulnerable pattern as new plants are added.

It is also useful to have an industrial structure that is rich in alternatives for any source of supply. Any particular industry should have several plants, preferably located in different parts of the country. If there is only a single source of supply, its loss can paralyze a whole chain of industries. For example, if there is only one coal mine, and its output is interrupted, as a result of war, natural disaster, or merely a domestic labor dispute, this can also paralyze the steel and chemical industries and a long series of subsequent industries that depend on intermediate inputs from those branches for their production. Alternative sources of supplies, or plans for the use of substitutes (which may be more expensive, but better than nothing) can, through redundance, make the economy more robust and resilient and therefore less vulnerable.

An example of an extreme case of vulnerability was Chile's dependence on spare parts for its fleet of trucks. The country is long and thin, stretched between the ocean and the Andes, and its entire economy is critically dependent on transportation, mainly provided by trucks. Chile had no capacity to produce spare parts for these trucks, and almost no reserves. It depended on imports essentially from one country, the United States. Difficulties in obtaining spare parts, which the truck owners attributed to the policies of the Allende government (and an ill-conceived plan to nationalize the trucking industry) led to a truckers' strike, which received financial support from the CIA. This strike paralyzed almost the entire Chilean economy and contributed to Allende's overthrow by the military in 1973. Foreign trade can be helpful, and generally increases people's welfare. But *dependence* on imports, particularly from a single source, or on exports to a single buyer, is not advisable.

A policy of greater self-reliance is not to be confused with a policy of economic autarky. Someone is self-reliant who keeps candles in case the electricity is interrupted. Autarky would be practiced by someone who refused to use electricity out of fear that it might be cut off—and possibly even made his own candles.

Self-reliance is perfectly compatible with a large volume of foreign trade, for mutual benefit, which can be a factor strengthening peace. But a country should not make itself totally dependent on trade for vital goods. There is no need to produce goods constantly at home, as long as they can be imported more cheaply. But it is useful to have a stand-by capability to produce those goods oneself, or to use substitutes, or to do without them entirely. It will be in a country's interest to have *potential* self-sufficiency in such vital areas as food, energy, medical supplies, essential transportation and communication, and defense.

The legitimate question can be raised whether it does not better serve the interests of peace to create a more *interdependent* world. Greater integration in the economic as well as in other spheres generates joint interests and better mutual understanding. Those countries that maintain substantial trade relations are generally on better terms with one another than those which isolate themselves economically from each other. Dependence on trade may even be used as a method of nonmilitary defense, as was Sweden's threat to destroy its iron ore mines in case of a German invasion, and can thus help prevent war.

On the other hand, wars have sometimes been fought over foreign raw material supplies. For example, if the United States feels vitally dependent on oil from the Persian Gulf region and believes it must intervene there with a rapid deployment force if the flow of oil is ever interrupted, this might lead to a war, possibly involving the Soviet Union as well. If the United States could become self-reliant in energy, for example by saving some of its Alaskan oil for an emergency, this could strengthen peace.

Which of the two arguments is right? Does trade promote peace or war? It depends on whether the economic relationship is helped or hurt by war. If economic exchange can take place in peace but would suffer in case of war, then economic interdependence strengthens peace. This is the case for the bulk of mutually beneficial trade. But if a flow of goods may be interrupted during peacetime and one of the parties is so dependent on those goods that it is prepared to go to war in an attempt to restore that flow, then dependence on trade can be a cause of war.

The recommendation, then, is to strengthen mutually beneficial relations in trade and many other areas, but not to make oneself or others so vitally dependent on those relations that they would risk war to restore or preserve them. It should be made very obvious that war would *hurt* those relations, and not improve them. If interdependence is constructed in that way, it will indeed strengthen peace.

## Reducing Psychological Vulnerability

The people of a country may lose their independence, even if no military or economic pressure is applied against them, through psychological or ideological subversion or "superversion" (from above). Subversion means that the less-privileged members of society are instigated to rise up against the ruling elite. Superversion could be called the opposite: an elite being led to represent the interests of a foreign power, instead of the interests of the country's own population.

The best defense against such dangers is a country's internal unity. Clearly, to be effective, such unity must be voluntary. It cannot be enforced by one group over another, otherwise the "unity" is only superficial and will dissolve at the first opportunity. Dictatorial regimes sometimes seek to justify their suppression of human rights with the excuse "We must be united in face of our enemies." But what is required for true security is not the false "unity" of a police state, but close bonds of true sympathy and solidarity throughout the society. Such unity is strengthened through social justice. Even a poor country which cannot offer its people much in terms of social services can distribute more fairly whatever it has. Also, people are happier if they have at least some voice in helping to decide the policies that shape their own lives. Giving them such a voice is not expensive.

If a country is internally divided, the people's will to defend their government is seriously weakened. Unless people have something to defend that they value dearly, they will not want to resist. For example, under Batista's dictatorship in Cuba, there were enormous differences between rich and poor, and the country was torn by dissension. Batista is said even to have failed to pay his soldiers regularly, a highly imprudent move on his part. When Castro secretly landed with a small band of guerillas, he gradually gained more supporters and was able to topple Batista's government, because the army dissolved almost without a fight. A reverse example is offered by Austria after World War II. Since it was apparent that there was no substantial pro-Soviet faction in the Austrian population that could form a Soviet client regime, the Soviet Union agreed to withdraw its troops in 1955 and let Austria become an independent, neutral country. On the other hand, in Afghanistan a pro-Soviet government seized power, and internal power struggles occurred before the Soviet intervention in 1979.

It is much more difficult to carry out a *coup d'état* in a country with a decentralized, federal structure, and with many partially overlapping organizations than it is in a country with a highly centralized, hierarchical form of government. A federal structure has not only vertical channels of communication, but also many horizontal ones. With such a form of government, it will not be possible to control the country by replacing a few people in key positions. Change can come about only gradually, since the approval of all the various groups involved is needed. A federal structure is also much less vulnerable to a possible paralysis of the goverment through the elimination of a small group or even of a single leader. If the leadership of one area is lost, only a relatively small part of the whole is leaderless, and other, still-functioning parts of the system can step into the breach. For this reason, a federal structure of government is less vulnerable to a strategy of "decapitation" aimed at its leadership.

People are less susceptible to hostile propaganda if they are well informed. Accurate and comprehensive news sources are important. Manipulated information that tries to hide setbacks and negative developments loses credibility and may, after a while, have the opposite effect from that intended. An uncensored and diversified press can uncover cases of corruption or abuse of power, and in this way may help prevent the growth and spread of such decay. In this sense, it can perform a function analogous to that of white blood cells in the human body, which attack disease germs before they can multiply and spread through the body, and in this way keep the body healthy and resistant.

The best defense against outside attempts to win power over a population through psychological or ideological means is to develop a high degree of internal social justice. This, again, threatens no other country. If a potential opponent improves his security by developing greater internal justice, we have reason to be not frightened, but relieved. A country with less internal tension also tends to be less aggressive toward the outside.

# *13* General Defense

"General" defense means the combination of all legitimate means, military as well as nonmilitary, against all possible forms of external threat, whether these threats be military, economic, political, or psychological in nature.

The countries whose defense policies come closest to this concept are Sweden (whose defense doctrine is called "total defense"), Switzerland (with its "general defense"), and Yugoslavia (with its "general people's defense"). Sweden and Switzerland were among the few countries in Europe able to keep out of World War II, and Yugoslavia was able to avoid a Soviet intervention, despite its political break with Moscow.

The defense concept to be outlined next is particularly well suited for small countries with no ambition to "project power" around the world. It will hold no attraction for the United States or the Soviet Union, as long as they see themselves in a global role as protectors of a large "sphere of influence." But the superpowers would certainly be involved in fewer wars if small countries were to become more self-reliant in their own defense and did not rely on a superpower for their "protection." Assuming responsibility for the defense of many small countries can draw the superpowers into war, possibly even into a direct confrontation.

As mentioned earlier, defense has the dual task of dissuading aggression and protecting what it intends to save. These two tasks are closely related, because if dissuasion is effective, protection will be maintained; and if a country is less vulnerable, this will also help it resist submission and serve to dissuade an attacker in the first place.

Four possible approaches to defense, listed in the order of decreasing levels of violence, are

1. retaliation against the civilian population of the aggressor by means of mass destruction, possibly including nuclear, biological, or chemical weapons;
2. frontal defense from the border inwards, using regular armed forces;
3. guerilla attacks against foreign occupation forces inside the country's own territory; and
4. nonviolent civilian resistance and other means of nonmilitary defense.

General defense is a combination of the second, third, and fourth of these levels. It excludes warfare against the civilian population of an aggressor, on the grounds that this would violate the international law of war. For example, Switzerland's defense doctrine states that it "takes all its general defense measures *in accordance* with the provisions of the law of war and international law. This entails the prohibition of any recourse to indiscriminate conduct of war against the population of the opponent" (General Defense 1973, p. 23). That provision will be observed even if the aggressor breaks it. Moreover, holding innocent civilians as hostages is more fitting for terrorists, not something that most people would embrace wholeheartedly in good conscience. Roger Fisher (1982, p. 234) of the Harvard Negotiation Project has made that point vividly. He proposed that the secret code needed to launch nuclear missiles, which is carried in an attaché case by a Secret Service agent near the U.S. president at all times, be implanted in a capsule near a volunteer's heart, and the volunteer would carry a butcher knife instead of the code in his attaché case. If the president decided that he had to launch those missiles, which could kill tens of millions of human beings, he would first have to kill one human being with his own hands. When Fisher explained his idea to military planners, they replied that this was terrible—it could distort the president's judgment and he might never push the button.

General defense consists only of defensive measures to improve a country's own security without posing a threat to a potential opponent's homeland. Let us examine each of the three components of general defense somewhat more closely, starting with category (2).

*Militia Army*

A type of army that is most suitable for defense inside a country's own borders is not a standing professional army, but a militia of militarily trained citizens who perform their regular civilian jobs during peacetime but can be mobilized if the country is in imminent danger of attack. This system makes possible a very large army if the need should arise, at comparatively modest cost. Roberts writes that "the current official figure for the total mobilizable strength of the Swedish armed forces is 750,000 or just over 9 percent of the total population. But in normal times only about 13 percent of this force is actually under arms" (1976, p. 96). Sweden's mobilization can be completed within 72 hours (p. 98). The figures for Switzerland are similar. About 80 percent of all men between age 20 and 50, all those who are not physically or mentally impaired, are members of the militia, representing about 10 percent of the total population. They keep their uniforms, personal weapons, and ammunition at home. In an emergency, the entire militia can be mobilized within 48 hours. In Yugoslavia, many women are also required to serve in territorial defense, and most adults between 16 and 60 (55 for women) that are not assigned to the armed forces are obliged to serve in civil defense capacities, such as in the provision of shelters, medical care, etc. According to a Yugoslav statement, as much as 70 to 80 percent of the population would be engaged in various forms of resistance in case of an attempted invasion (Roberts, p. 182). As a further expression of Yugoslavia's determination to defend itself to the last, its constitution states that "No one has the right to recognize or sign the capitulation of the country or the capitulation of the armed forces" (Roberts, p. 187).

These militia armies are trained to fight *only inside their own territory*, where they enjoy the support of the local population, have shorter supply lines, are intimately familiar with the terrain, and so have many advantages over an invader. (If all countries were to adhere to this simple condition, war would be eliminated.)

Officers are chosen from the ranks, which reduces the cleavage between higher and lower ranks. It also makes a military coup almost unthinkable, because if the leadership of the army is representative of the entire population, it is hard to see "against whom" the army could stage a revolt. The Greek army, whose colonels staged a coup in 1967, also had a high proportion of conscripts, but its officers consisted of a full-time professional corps. In this respect the Greek army differed from a citizen army in which most officers also pursue a civilian career, like the ordinary soldiers (Roberts, pp. 36, 243).

A citizen army in itself provides no guarantee that it will perform only defensive functions, unless it is "coupled with a clear political will to avoid offensive military operations" (Roberts, p. 228). That a citizen army does not automatically refrain from crossing its borders can be seen from the conduct of the Israeli army. Although it was officially modeled after the Swiss army, it invaded portions of Egypt, Jordan, and Syria in 1967, and Lebanon in 1982.

### Guerilla Forces

These form the next category of "general defense" and are small, highly autonomous units that could harass an occupation force if the regular army should be defeated or forced to retreat. They would force a potential occupation army to keep constantly in a state of alert, and impede its movements through acts of sabotage. Guerillas would prevent an invading army from enjoying its victory, and prepare the way for eventual liberation of the territory.

The same criticism of civilian resistance has been leveled against guerilla warfare—that it offers no protection against an initial invasion, in contrast to frontal military defense along a borderline. Guerilla warfare is said to "accept invasion" and to become effective only after a country is already occupied. But again, if a potential aggressor knew that, even though he might encounter little difficulty in invading the country initially, he would nevertheless face constant problems in trying to hold the occupied territory, this might be one of the factors dissuading him from attempting an invasion in the first place.

If an invader has overwhelming force and is very brutal, it may be necessary to abandon violent resistance temporarily and give top priority to saving people's lives. Violence is the one level of conflict on which the opponent will have greater expertise. For example, when two Czechs in 1942 threw a bomb that killed the German chief of the Security Service branch of the SS, the Germans, in retaliation, killed some 3000 people, including the entire male population of the village of Lidice (Roberts, p. 232).

## Nonmilitary Defense

This final category is often hardly recognized as a method of defense. For example, the fact that Switzerland was able to keep out of World War II is usually attributed not to its "defense effort" (meaning military defense) but more to lucky circumstances. Even Hitler found it useful to have a place where banking transactions, which were still needed during the war, could take place, and a neutral location where representatives from the Allies and the Axis powers could meet to sense each other's positions and exchange information. But if one studies official Swiss documents on defense policy, it becomes clear that this is not merely "luck" but a deliberate aspect of a comprehensive defense strategy. The aim was to prove to all sides that invading Switzerland would hurt their interests as well, not only the interests of Switzerland.

Another typical example of an effective nonmilitary approach to defense is provided by Hong Kong, which is extremely vulnerable and militarily weak. China has maintained a long-standing claim over Hong Kong, ever since it was taken away from China by the British in 1841. But Hong Kong's special role as a banking and foreign trade center for China has made it advantageous for the Chinese government to leave Hong Kong untouched. Even if sovereignty over Hong Kong should formally return to China in 1997, it will be in China's objective interest not to disturb the economic system of Hong Kong. Many other small countries would similarly do more for their security if, instead of spending large sums for modern weapons, they were to carve out for themselves a useful function they could perform for their neighbors, a function that their neighbors would not like to see disappear.

One should strive to make peace more attractive *with all available means*, even excessively. If the other side does the same to us, we are not afraid of that, but welcome it. Yet we need not wait for the other side to do so first, or even to do so at the same time.

## Strength through Redundancy

*All* purely defensive efforts should be undertaken, even efforts that are insufficient in themselves. In combination with other efforts, they may just be able to tip the balance against aggression. Every effort, however small, is worthwhile; even if such efforts cannot guarantee the prevention of war in themselves they will *reduce* the risk of war and *add* to security.

The reason for combining several different approaches to defense, instead of choosing only "the" most effective one, is that diversity and duplication are general methods for reducing vulnerability. If one method fails to work, others may be able to take over as a back-up. Redundance increases resilience.

Another reason for combining military and nonmilitary forms of defense is to preserve a democratic social structure, which allows for a maximum amount of personal freedom and choice in which no group imposes its will on any other group. For this reason, conscientious objectors who condemn violent forms of defense should be permitted to contribute to their country's security through nonviolent methods, if that is what they believe in. For the same reason, adherents of nonviolence should not impose their views on the rest of society and should accept "conscientious objectors against nonmilitary defense," who believe that only force can effectively deter aggression. The two forms of defense should be closely coordinated and support each other, not work against each other.

General defense means to seek friendly relations with every other country, but to be prepared to defend oneself if necessary, without threatening other countries. The goal of smaller, nonaligned countries is not to be able to match the military forces of a potential aggressor, but by a policy of dissuasion to show that even though it might be possible to defeat their armed forces, the cost of doing so would far exceed any potential benefits. Sweden's official defense doctrine, which was quoted in Chapter 11 and which is similar to the policy of other small neutral countries, says that the costs to defeat Sweden must be out of proportion as compared to the advantages an aggressor might attain.

The expression "out of proportion" indicates a pessimistic, cautious approach, which seeks to take no chances. The costs of aggression should not just barely equal or slightly exceed the expected gains, but should exceed them by a wide margin. This is to prevent wars by miscalculation. If the two opponents in a war were able to calculate their gains and losses precisely, and if they acted rationally, there would never be any actual fighting. Both sides would know in advance who was going to win (if there were any winner at all), and the losing side would give in, sparing both sides the loss of life and physical destruction. War is always a "negative-sum game", because whatever one side may gain is less than what the other side loses. (On the other hand, peaceful cooperation is a "positive-sum game", since both sides will gain.)

If a war erupts, it is always due to some misperception, at least by one side, possibly by both. This does not mean that it is always irrational to fight and lose; without resistance one might have been forced into even greater concessions. But misperception by at least one side is involved in any war, since there always exists some compromise that would have left both sides better off than if they actually went to war. To prove this assertion, it is sufficient to give one example, like in a mathematical existence theorem: if the two conflicting parties, without actually fighting a war, were to adopt the peace treaty that finally emerges, *both* would suffer less. At least one side must have overestimated its offensive or defensive capabilities, or underestimated the offensive or defensive capabilities of the other side. To prevent a potential aggressor from miscalculating that he could defeat us, it is better to have a defensive capability that is substantially greater than the minimum needed for dissuasion.

### "Worst-Case" and "Best-Case" Analyses

The following quotation appears to state the same principle in a different context:

Military planners tend to err on the side of caution, to assume the worst, to prepare for anything. This is referred to as worst-case analysis, and it seems to be the working rule of thumb on both sides. Since you can't *know* what the other side will have in its arsenal ten years down the road, better play it safe, figure what the other guy *could* do and plan to be ready for that . . . In trying to estimate Russian military capabilities, the Pentagon has a special category for the worst case called the greater-than-expected threat, or GTET . . . If the U.S. best estimate is that the Soviet Union will have seven thousand ICBM warheads by 1987, the Pentagon will try to plan U.S. force levels sufficient to meet a somewhat greater number, say eight thousand to ten thousand warheads—just in case . . . This systematic overcompensation [is] called alarmist by some, prudent by others [Ground Zero 1982, pp. 64–65; emphasis in original].

Does not the same principle underlie the concept of general defense—to *err on the safe side*? There is one fundamental difference. General defense seeks to err on the safe side by employing purely defensive measures, which pose no threat to anyone. To overcompensate with *offensive* arms is not to err on the safe side. If both sides adopt that practice, it inevitably leads to an arms race, which may spell doom for both sides.

The recommendation to overcompensate by building up offensive arms is based on the assumption that the other side is engaging in a preplanned arms buildup, which is independent of what our side does; that they are proceeding at the maximum feasible rate permitted by their economy and their technological innovations. An alternative and even more-dubious presupposition that may underlie the tendency to overcompensate with offensive arms is that the other side can be convinced that it is losing the arms race and will therefore give it up, realizing its futility. If either of those assumptions hold, the recommendation to overcompensate for the other side's buildup may yield what is sought, a margin of superiority. Yet if the other side should react to our side's arms buildup, then a further buildup is the worst recommendation, leading to greater insecurity for both sides. It cannot be determined with certainty which assumption actually holds.

Some suggest that military planners should also perform

"best-case analyses," and not always assume the worst. But that may also be risky and underestimate a real danger. Some people with good intentions advocate "taking a risk for peace." But to strengthen peace is to *reduce the risk* we face, not to increase it. There is nothing risky in taking purely defensive measures without threatening others, and in strengthening mutual interest in peace. What is risky is to threaten or even to attack others. Hitler took grave risks. There is no risk in peace. The risk is in war.

## A Robust Analysis

Instead of a best-case or a worst-cast analysis, I would propose a *robust* analysis, to explore what measures can truly provide security regardless of unverifiable assumptions. A robust, truly risk-averse approach is to overcompensate with *defensive* measures, but to avoid posing a threat to the other side. This type of approach does not fuel an arms race, nor does it attract aggression through defenselessness. It can provide security, regardless of which assumption about the other side's behavior is true.

To seek security through a "balance of power" is not a robust approach. It fails if one's "power" is inferior, and also fails if it is excessive, because it generates fear and leads to an escalation of the arms race. One has to balance on a knife's edge so to speak. Let us recall the earler analogy of a robust engineering approach. An engineer will make an elevator cable thicker than is absolutely necessary to guarantee that the elevator will not fall. But seeking security through a balance of power is like trying to design the right cable for an elevator knowing the cable might break either because it was too thin (too weak) *or* because it was too thick (too stiff). This would be a very risky elevator to ride on indeed. Seeking security by maintaining "parity" with an opponent is a delicate balancing act. It is not like stepping away from the edge of a cliff back onto firm ground. It is rather comparable to an attempt to cross an abyss on a tight rope, stumbling neither to the left *nor* to the right—on a rope that in addition may break at any moment. What kind of "security" is that?

A robust, safe approach to national security is to take a broad, redundant array of defensive measures that pose no threat to other countries, and to avoid generating fear among potential opponents by reassuring them—through deeds, not merely words—that their security is not threatened as long as they don't attack us. Such measures can be compared to regaining firm ground, far from the abyss of nuclear war.

# *14* The Costs of Defense

It has been argued that a defense not based on the threat of retaliation, but on purely defensive measures, is possible but extremely expensive. Even if a purely defensive military posture were more expensive than an offensive posture or reliance on deterrence through threats, it might still be well worth adopting. An advantage of such a policy is that it does not provide any reason for an arms race, and therefore does not buy short-term security at the expense of greater insecurity in the longer run. If a defensive posture is more likely to preserve peace, it is worth greater expenditures: when survival is at stake, cost considerations become secondary. But in actuality, a purely defensive military posture is less expensive, not more expensive, than an offensive posture.

Table 14.1 contains a comparison of the defense expenditures of selected countries. This table shows, for example, that Switzerland's military expenditures are less than half the world average, measured as a fraction of its gross national product. Even though some expenditures (e.g., a portion of people's time served in the army, which is partly compensated for by their employers) are not covered by the military budget, the cost of defense is still not high. Sweden's and Yugoslavia's defense budgets are somewhat higher, but are still in line with the world average.

Countries that have recently fought wars on foreign soil, on the other hand, can be observed to have higher military expenditures than the world average. This refutes the contention that a defensive posture is too expensive.

It is not necessary for a country to be rich to adopt a purely defensive military posture. When Switzerland changed to a posture of armed neutrality in the 16th century, it was very poor.

Another argument favoring the construction of offensive arms instead of a more-defensive posture is the reverse, namely that military expenditures are good for the economy and prevent unemployment. (This line of reasoning has also been used to criticize disarmament proposals.) Underlying that argument is a misunderstanding of Keynesian economics. Keynes argued that when the economy stagnates and has unused production capacity (as during the Great Depression of the 1930s), the government can revive it by placing orders for goods and services to supplement insufficient private demand, and by financing those orders through deficit spending. The income to firms and individuals so generated will then be used by them for additional purchases, yielding a multiplier effect. This will help the economy to extricate itself from stagnation, and the higher tax revenue generated by an economy working near full capacity can be used to pay back the government's deficits. This device of deficit spending was meant to be used only intermittently, however, to pull the economy out of recessions or depressions, not on a permanent basis. Furthermore, there is no reason that the government's orders for goods and services should be for anything useless. Typical expenditures would be for roads, schools, hospitals, and other infrastructure projects, in fact, any public goods and services that tend to be neglected by the private sector of the economy because they are privately unprofitable even though society needs them.

De Grasse (1983) has found that spending for defense not only produces nothing that consumers can buy, but is also a very poor way of creating jobs. He estimated that in the United States $1 billion spent by the Pentagon creates 28,000 jobs. The same expenditure would create 32,000 jobs if spent on public transportation, 57,000 jobs if used for personal consumption, and 71,000 jobs if spent on education. Thus, a shift of $1 billion from education to military purposes causes a net loss of 43,000 jobs. (In quoting these figures I do not imply that a reduction of military spending would *automatically* lead to a corresponding increase in government spending for social purposes. To do so requires a clear political will and plan for action.)

**Table 14.1   An International Comparison of Defense Expenditures**

| | Military Expenditures in US $ million[a] | Latest year available | Military Expenditures as fraction of GDP in percent[b] | Latest year available | rank | Population in mid-1980 in millions[c] | Approximate per capita military expenditures in US $[d] | rank |
|---|---|---|---|---|---|---|---|---|
| Oman | 1,444 | | 22.3 | 1980 | 1 | 0.9[e] | 1,650 | 2 |
| Saudi Arabia | 22,458 | | 16.5 | 1979 | 3 | 9.0 | 2,495 | 1 |
| China | (37,200) | | 14.8f | 1980 | 6 | 976.7 | 38.1 | 64 |
| N. Korea | 3,424 | 1980 | 14.1 | 1976 | 7 | 18.3 | 187.1 | 26 |
| Israel | (2,462) | | 14.0 | 1980 | 8 | 3.9 | 631.3 | 6 |
| Iran | (4,040) | 1980 | 10.9 | 1977 | 12 | 38.3 | 104.1 | 41 |
| Iraq | (2,675) | 1979 | 10.4 | 1977 | 13 | 13.1 | 204.2 | 24 |
| Egypt | (1,539) | 1980 | (9.6) | 1979 | 14 | 39.8 | 38.7 | 62 |
| USSR | (118,800) | | (9.1) | 1979 | 15 | 265.5 | 447.5 | 9 |
| S. Korea | 3,519 | | 6.0 | 1980 | 24 | 38.2 | 92.1 | 44 |
| USA | 134,794 | | 5.8 | | 27 | 227.7 | 590.2 | 7 |
| Pakistan | 1,307 | | 5.2 | 1980 | 29 | 82.2 | 15.9 | 79 |
| Britain | 19,901 | | 5.0 | | 32 | 55.9 | 356.0 | 15 |
| Yugoslavia | 2,936 | | (4.6) | 1979 | 36 | 22.3 | 131.7 | 32 |
| France | 23,633 | | 4.2 | | 40 | 53.5 | 441.7 | 10 |
| Nigeria | 1,869 | 1980 | 4.0 | 1980 | 42 | 84.7 | 22.1 | 73 |
| W. Germany | 25,509 | | 3.4 | | 46 | 60.9 | 418.9 | 11 |
| Sweden | 3,157 | | 3.1 | 1980 | 53 | 8.3 | 380.4 | 12 |

| | | | | | | | |
|---|---|---|---|---|---|---|---|
| India | 3,991 | 2.8 | 1979 | 57 | 673.2 | 5.9 | 106 |
| Italy | 8,184 | 2.5 | | 64 | 56.9 | 143.8 | 29 |
| Indonesia | 1,426 | 2.3 | 1980 | 67 | 146.6 | 9.7 | 95 |
| Philippines | 688 | 2.1 | 1980 | 73 | 49.0 | 14.0 | 84 |
| Switzerland | 2,000 | 2.1 | | 73 | 6.5 | 307.7 | 17 |
| Canada | 4,227 | 1.8 | | 80 | 23.9 | 176.9 | 27 |
| Bangladesh | 140 | 1.3 | 1979 | 97 | 88.5 | 1.6 | 119 |
| Austria | 847 | 1.2 | 1980 | 101 | 7.5 | 112.9 | 38 |
| Japan | 9,461 | 1.0 | 1979 | 106 | 116.8 | 81.0 | 46 |
| Hong Kong | 196 | .6 | 1980 | 113 | 5.1 | 38.4 | 63 |
| Mexico | 782 | .5 | 1980 | 114 | 69.8 | 11.2 | 89 |
| Brazil | 1,234 | .5 | 1980 | 114 | 118.7 | 10.4 | 92 |
| Costa Rica | 19 | .5 | 1980 | 114 | 2.2 | 8.6 | 99 |
| Mauritius | 1.9 | .2 | 1978 | 1978 | 118 | 0.9g | 2.0 | 117 |
| World totals | 518,000 | 5.1 | | | 4,181 | 124.0 | |

aFigures from the 1982 *SIPRI Yearbook*, pp. 140–45. If no other year is indicated, figures are for 1981. Figures in parentheses are estimates.

bFigures from the 1982 *SIPRI Yearbook*, pp. 150–53. If not otherwise indicated, figures are for 1981.

cExcept where indicated, figures from World Bank, *World Development Report*, 1982.

dFigures derived from division of column one by column six.

eFigure not listed by World Bank. Information from Bureau of the Census, *Statistical Abstract of the United States*, 102nd ed. (Washington, D.C., U.S. Dept. of Commerce, 1981), p. 868.

fFigure not listed by SIPRI. Figure derived from division of column one by the GDP figure. GDP information taken from World Bank, *World Development Report*, 1982.

gFigure not listed by World Bank. Information from *Statistical Abstract of the United States*, 1981, p. 868.

If defense expenditures could be reduced because of an improvement in the international situation, this would not lead to a permanently higher level of unemployment. Other government expenditures for public projects could absorb the jobs no longer needed for military requirements. For example, the production of transportation equipment, of medical instruments, or the exploration of space could make use of skills similar to those needed to produce weapons.

Even if the government would not increase its spending in other areas to compensate for a reduction of military spending, the loss of jobs would be only temporary. Private demand for goods and services tends to adjust gradually to available production capacity. For example, since the early 19th century, the per capita production capacity of the U.S. economy has increased about 20 times, yet—as William Baumol once put it—this has by no means led to a 95 percent unemployment rate. Demand has slowly adjusted to the newly feasible supply, and leisure time has increased. There is no sign that people's demand for consumption goods is approaching any absolute limit.

A *sudden* reduction of total demand, or a shift in demand from one type of product to another, can bring some temporary unemployment, unless it is accompanied by plans for the conversion of industries to meet existing demand in other areas, or newly created demand. To make plans for shifting to a more defensive military force structure or for mutual disarmament politically feasible, attention must be given to the problem of economic conversion (Melman 1983). The least amount of retraining is needed for unskilled and semiskilled workers, who can be reassigned to almost any new type of work. The most relearning has to be done by managers and engineers, who must adjust to the harsher environment of a competitive civilian market. (It has been said, ruefully, that engineers who have been working for defense contractors can think in only three dimensions: meters, kilograms and seconds—but not in dollars.)

Not only the workers and managers of the arms industry must be given other forms of employment but, in particular, the military establishment. From this point of view, a proposal for general and complete disarmament made by Khrushchev— "sending all the generals into retirement"–could be disastrous. As Johan Galtung pointed out, these generals might find a way to make themselves needed again–e.g., by instigating a war. If disarmament is to be carried out successfully, new roles for the members of the military-industrial complexes must be found, for example in peace-keeping or in economic conversion, not only to provide them with a source of income, but also, and perhaps more important, as a source of social esteem. Otherwise disarmament would face their formidable opposition.

Defense expenditures are far from being a boon to the economy as a whole. They instead represent a burden to it, because military hardware cannot be consumed or used for the production of other goods. Defense expenditures must be financed either through taxes (causing a reduction in average living standards through lower disposable incomes), or through deficit spending (causing inflation), or both. This burden is certainly worthwhile if it can guarantee our security and survival. Yet some arms buildups have reduced, rather than increased, our security. Whatever portion of the public budget is deemed necessary for defense should be spent carefully, in such a way that it truly helps to increase national security, not to create a risk for security.

World military expenditures in 1981 exceeded US$ 500 billion (SIPRI 1982a; see Table 14.1). Wassily Leontief and Faye Duchin (1983, p. 66) have concluded that

> Virtually all economies are able to increase total output and per capita consumption as they progressively reduce their military spending. . . . If moreover the rich regions transfer part of the resulting "savings" to the poorest of the less developed regions in the form of developmental assistance, this transfer of income would result in increased worldwide levels of production, trade and consumption. [But they also warn that] only if the transfers of resources just described are accompanied by changes in the *structures* of the poor economies might the economic prospects for the future of the poor less-developed regions appear less gloomy [emphasis in original].

More is required than a transfer of money alone.

Defense expenditures are justified if they can help preserve a country's independence and save the lives of its people. But seen from this angle, they must be put into some perspective. Other expenditures, for example for public health, can also help save lives and sometimes more effectively. I would like to give only one striking example. In 1981, an estimated 17 million children under the age of five died worldwide from preventable diseases and from malnutrition and its consequences (Grant 1982, p. 9). This silent death toll, which is seldom mentioned in the news media, is the estimated equivalent of more than 200 Hiroshima bombs being dropped every year (Zimmerman and Leitenberg 1979). UNICEF has estimated that less than $100 per child could have bought improved diets, basic health care, and safer sanitation and would have saved most of these children's lives. That amounts to $1.7 billion worldwide. A single nuclear-powered aircraft carrier, which is of dubious value for true defense, costs $3.5 billion (U.S. Department of Defense 1982, p. N-15). These figures speak for themselves.

# 15 Conflict Resolution

Independent measures, which have been mainly discussed up to here, can accomplish a great deal more for the prevention of war than is generally assumed. Still, there are limits to such measures. Certain things can be achieved only through mutual cooperation.

In this chapter, some methods of conflict resolution will be briefly explored: some ways of negotiating successfully without giving in; the role of transnational institutions; how to overcome domestic conflicts that may invite foreign intervention; some principles of fair sharing; and the role of peace research.

*Successful Negotiations*

The key to success in negotiations with an opponent is to come up with imaginative proposals that hold something attractive *for both sides*; for if the opponent would lose something by accepting a proposed solution, we can hardly expect him or her to agree to it.

Negotiating tactics can be divided into four basic approaches, shown in Table 15.1, depending on whether a negotiator seeks to satisfy the interests of both sides (position 1), of only his or her own side, (position 2), of only the other side (position 3), or of neither side (position 4). (It may be interesting to note the structural analogy among Tables 15.1 and 3.2, and Figure 5.2.) Many believe that to "win" in negotiations one has to be "tough" (i.e., take a "hawkish" stand); that if one is too "soft" ("dovish"), one will lose. But that simple idea looks at the wrong dimension. The most-succesful approach is that of a "peacemaker." The most-irrational position is that of the "warmonger." Yet we are far too familiar with that last form of behavior.

**Table 15.1   Four Negotiating Tactics**

|  | Ignore own interests | Promote own interests |
|---|---|---|
| Promote negotiating partner's interests | (3) "Dove":<br><br>try to reach agreement at any price by giving in prematurely and sacrifice your own interests | (1) "Peacemaker":<br><br>seek imaginative solutions that can satisfy your own needs as well as those of the other side, and reach agreement without giving in |
| Ignore negotiating partner's interests | (4) "Warmonger":<br><br>try to deny the interests of the other side at any price, even if this means that you have to sacrifice your own interests | (2) "Hawk":<br><br>promote only your own interests and fail to reach agreement because you have nothing attractive to offer to the other side |

Some may doubt whether it is possible to meet simultaneously the interests of both sides in negotiations. But, in fact, opportunities for mutual gains are abundant. In discussing possibilities for mutually beneficial cooperation between the United States and the Soviet Union, Deutsch cricitizes

> an underlying view which hampers the attempt to strengthen cooperative bonds: *the view that anything which helps them hurts us.* Clearly, it helps them if their control over their nuclear missiles is such as to prevent accidental firings. But does this harm us? Clearly, it helps them if their children have available the Sabin polio vaccine. But does this harm us? [Deutsch 1983, p. 28; emphasis added].

Schell (1982, p. 288) writes "for both superpowers—and, indeed, for all other powers—avoiding extinction is a common interest than which none can be greater." This common goal ought to provide a solid basis for negotiations aimed at preventing a nuclear war.

If negotiations are to be successful, they must offer each side some gain, *in each side's own view*. For this reason, for example, a disarmament proposal that requires the Soviet Union to shift its main missile force from land-based to submarine-based systems is unlikely to be negotiated successfully. It may well be that such a shift would objectively increase the security of the Soviet Union. But that is not what counts. Unless the Soviet leaders believe such a shift to be in their interest, they will not agree to it. So far, there is no indication that the Soviets have been convinced that it would be better *for them* to place less reliance on land-based missiles. A more-likely path to agreement on nuclear arms reductions may be to propose an equal, mutual ceiling on the number of warheads, and to leave it to each side to decide how it will base them—whether on land, submarines, or bombers, or on what combination of them—to make its own system least vulnerable, *in each side's own perception*. Under such a proposal, each side would likely begin to dismantle its most-vulnerable and least-reliable weapons, which would have the advantage of reducing strategic instability.

To achieve success in negotiations, it is helpful to be explicit about one's interests, but to remain flexible about the concrete solutions by which those interests are to be met. Fisher and Ury (1981) give the following example from daily life: suppose a husband and wife want to build a house together. If an architect asks each of them separately to draw his or her preferred floor plan, it will be almost impossible to reconcile the two different plans. But if he asks each to specify the number and purpose of rooms he or she needs, the architect may be able to come up with a design that meets the interests of both.

Fisher and Ury offer an application of this principle to the solution of an international conflict and show how an innovative approach may meet the interests of both parties in negotiations. During the 1978 Camp David peace negotiations, an impasse appeared to have been reached.

> Israel insisted on keeping some of the Sinai. Egypt, on the other hand, insisted that every inch of the Sinai be returned to Egyptian sovereignty. . . . Looking to their interests instead of their positions made it possible to develop a solution. Israel's interest lay in security; they did not want Egyptian tanks . . . on their

borders . . . Egypt's interest lay in sovereignty; . . . after centuries of [foreign] domination, Egypt was not about to cede territory to another foreign conqueror. . . . Egypt and . . . Israel agreed to a plan that would return the Sinai to complete Egyptian sovereignty and, by demilitarizing large areas, would still assure Israeli security [Fisher and Ury 1981, pp. 42–43].

Fisher and Ury's example illustrates once more that if one wants the other side to agree to a proposed solution, it is in one's own interest to have something attractive for the other side in the proposal; otherwise, the other side is not likely to accept it. For this reason, if we are interested in reaching an agreement, it is to our own advantage to try to explore and understand as fully as possible the interests of the other side, as the other side really perceives them. The real interests of our opponents need not be identical with their declared positions, but it may also be quite different from how *we* would perceive their interests if we were in their position. It will not help us to approach the other side with an attitude of "We know what is good for you." While it is helpful for mutual understanding to try to place oneself in the other's situation, for example by playing reversed roles, it is still necessary to carry out a *dialog* to explore how the other side really sees its interests.

To understand the interests of the other side does not mean that we give something away. On the contrary, it helps us to achieve what we want by simultaneously meeting the interests of the other side. This is particularly important in the field of security. Countries which have long avoided war have taken great care not to be seen as a threat by others as long as they leave them in peace. If we want to be secure, we must think of a way in which others can also feel secure, otherwise we will not remain secure for long. I once tried to discuss the problem of stable vs. unstable deterrence with a professor who teaches nuclear strategy at a U.S. military academy. He broke off the discussion by saying, "*Our* task is to defend ourselves. How the Russians are going to defend themselves is *their* problem; we cannot figure it out for them." This short-sighted attitude, which is likely to be found on the Soviet side as well, is partly responsible for the precarious situation into which we have maneuvered ourselves. The race between the superpowers to keep ahead in nuclear weaponry, without giving much thought to how the other side is going to assure its perceived security in any other way than by building up a huge nuclear arsenal, has brought us to our present predicament. To regain real national security, the superpowers will have to think of measures that improve the security of both sides at the same time.

If we want to reach a lasting agreement, it is in our own interest to leave the other side a face-saving way out of any impasse that may develop during negotiations, and not to seek to humiliate it. For example, as was discussed in Chapter 10, it might have been better for the United States to permit Krushchev a face-saving withdrawal of Soviet missiles from Cuba, by agreeing formally to some reciprocal step, than to force him to back off—a humilating response that may have contributed to the subsequent intensification of Soviet military expansion.

For an agreement to be stable, it should be firmly anchored in each side's self-interest. Each side must be convinced that if it were to break the agreement, it would *itself* lose something, not only the other side. A signature on a document does not necessarily make an agreement "binding." For many, the loss of honor or good conscience that would be associated with breaking an agreement may be sufficient to keep them from breaking it, but not necessarily for all. *It is not wise to rely on a nation to keep agreements that go against her interests.* It is not even enough that each side would lose if it broke the agreement; each side must also clearly *perceive* it that way. For example, as the course of history showed, it was objectively not in Hitler's interest to break the non-aggression treaty with the Soviet Union in 1941. But blinded by his early victories, Hitler did not see it that way. For the Soviet Union's non-aggression treaty with Germany to be effective, it ought to have been backed up by a stronger and more clearly visible defense capability. "Trust" alone is not a good basis for a lasting agreement; it is important to take precautions not to be cheated. But this does not in any way imply that one should seek to cheat or threaten the other side. According to Deutsch (1983, p. 30), his research suggests that the approach most likely to elicit cooperative behavior, and which also appears to be most effective in reforming aggressive criminals, is a firm and self-confident, but calm and nonbelligerent, attitude.

Being cautious is not to be confused with being hostile, or with presuming the worst intentions on the part of those with whom we deal. We can very well seek friendly relations with them. But it would be unfair even to our best friends if we were to put them deliberately into a situation where they are tempted to cheat.

An agreement based on blind trust is probably worse than no agreement at all, because it may penalize those who keep it and reward those who break it. For example, when the U.S. government called for voluntary restraint in wage and price increases to fight inflation, John Kenneth Galbraith mocked that he hoped the next step would be voluntary taxes—he would be the first not to pay them. For the same reason, it is important that arms control agreements include adequate provisions for verification of compliance. This does not mean that it is necessary that verification be 100 percent reliable; it is sufficient if there is a reasonable risk that violations might be detected. For example, the detection of tax evasion is far from perfectly reliable, but cheaters are discovered and punished occasionally, and this is sufficient to induce most people to pay their taxes. Even though that system is not ideal, it is preferable to no tax system at all. Similarly, with arms control agreements, it is desirable to seek constant improvements in verification procedures, but even if verification is not yet perfect, this is no reason not to keep and seek to expand existing agreements. The situation would be much worse in the absence of any agreements whatsoever. For this reason it would be useful, for example, to resume negotiations aimed at a comprehensive nuclear test ban treaty.

If two countries are engaged in a series of negotiations, it is counterproductive to begin with the most-difficult and -controversial issues. Success is far more likely if those issues are addressed first where there is the strongest common interest, and where agreement is relatively easy to achieve. As Churchill once put it, it should be possible to settle something before settling everything.

Some people think that areas of agreement are less important and no precious time should be wasted on them, that all effort should be concentrated on dealing with the crucial points of disagreement. But such a negotiating strategy is likely to fail. Unless areas of common interest are also stressed, it will be much more difficult to find solutions in those areas where interests are opposed. On the other hand, if some agreements in relatively noncontroversial areas have already been reached, a favorable climate will have been created for negotiations on more-difficult issues.

For example, in arms control and disarmament negotiations between the United States and the Soviet Union, it is best to start with topics where there is a very strong and easily visible joint interest. One such area is the prevention of the spread of nuclear arms to more and more countries, and particularly into the hands of terrorists — a field where unilateral measures cannot achieve much. If even one country makes technology and raw materials for the manufacture of nuclear bombs available to others, nuclear bombs can spread. To prevent this, *all* potential leaks must be blocked. The common interest of both superpowers, and of most other countries, has made conclusion of the nonproliferation treaty of 1968 possible. A further strenghtening of the inspection mechanism of the International Atomic Energy Commission, to prevent the dissemination of weapons-grade uranium and plutonium, particularly to terrorist groups, is an area where there seems to be little reason for disagreement between the superpowers and where an early treaty might be reached.

Another area of strong joint interest is the prevention of nuclear war by accident. Many steps in that direction can, of course, be taken independently by each side, in its own interest. But certain measures require mutual cooperation. For example, the 1963 establishment of a direct communication link between the White House and the Kremlin (the "hot line") could not have been implemented by one side alone. Agreements on similar issues, such as regular high-level or even summit meetings, could be mutually beneficial. Also, the exchange of information on how to effectively prevent technical malfunctions that could lead to false attack warnings or accidental missile firings should be noncontroversial.

A further area where negotiations could be fruitful would be the joint exploration by both the United States and the Soviet Union of measures to make their nuclear forces less vulnerable to a surprise attack.

On the other hand, the effort to achieve balanced force levels through negotiations over how many weapons of one type are equivalent to how many different weapons of the other side are almost designed to fail. Each side will claim that the weapons of the other side are more dangerous, so that the other side will have to make deeper cuts. As Johan Galtung said, there is only one way to find out with certainty how different weapons compare—by trying them out in a war. Past disarmament negotiations have not only failed easily but may even have been counterproductive by searching for a precise "balance." Each side prefers to add to its arsenal in areas where the other side has more, instead of destroying weapons of which the other side has less. Disarmament negotiations reveal where these gaps are, and may thus lead to more armament (Galtung 1984). As was shown in Chapter 8, numerical parity in weapons is neither sufficient nor necessary for security. It is far more important to avoid destabilizing weapons systems that may precipitate a war. Negotiations with the aim of establishing a perfect "balance" may divert precious energy and time from other, more-important and more-promising areas.

Since national security is an extremely sensitive area, burdened with emotions, it may be useful to spend some effort as well on other areas where mutually beneficial cooperation between the superpowers is possible. Examples are the exchange of scientific information, or direct cooperation in such areas as the peaceful exploration of space, medical research, pollution-free manufacturing techniques, and the development of new energy sources. Some joint work is going on in all of these areas, but such forms of cooperation could be greatly expanded for mutual benefit.

## The Role of Global Organizations

To solve global problems that no single country can tackle alone, global organizations must take over. Some global problems entail potential dangers to human survival that are not related to military technology: an accumulation of carbon dioxide in the atmosphere caused by excessive burning of fossil fuels worldwide could lead to a greenhouse effect, warming up the earth and melting the polar ice caps. Coastal areas would be flooded, and the earth's climate and food production patterns could change in unpredictable ways. Another danger is that certain industrial pollutants could deplete the ozone layer that protects life on earth from excessive ultraviolet radiation. The result would be not only an increase in skin cancer, but also a higher rate of possibly lethal mutations, in humans as well as in animals and plants. No country can prevent such potential catastrophes alone. As long as one major industrial power continues to accumulate carbon dioxide or to deplete the ozone layer, all nations will be affected.

About six thousand years ago, one of the first advanced civilizations emerged in Egypt. A possible reason was that the irregular flooding of the Nile valley was a problem that no single farmer could attack alone. Cooperation on a very large scale was necessary to build a dam to store the water and release it in a controlled way. Similarly, the need has now arisen for the emergence of some form of global organization to deal effectively with the global problems facing all of humankind.

To deal with problems that no country can solve by itself will require the establishment of more global institutions. The first such global organization, which has operated successfully for more than a century, is the World Postal Federation, which was founded in 1875. Since then, a great variety of international organizations have developed, both at the governmental and nongovernmental levels, most notably the League of Nations and the United Nations; but a number of others are still needed. One issue that can be dealt with successfully only at the global level is disarmament. Galtung (1984) has proposed a U.N. agency that would not only work toward the elimination of offensive arms, but also help member countries to defend themselves without becoming a threat to other countries. Maybe such an agency could be more successful than the disarmament agencies have been so far, because member countries would perceive it to be in their obvious interest to cooperate with such an agency.

Many global institutions still wait to be created. But at the same time as the need for them has increased, it has also become much easier to communicate at a global level. It is hard to imagine that when the United States was founded two centuries ago, the fastest method for a message from New York to reach Washington was via horseback and took ten days. A message to England took three months by sailboat. Today, any point on earth can be reached in seconds by telephone, and personal contacts among people from different parts of the world have increased enormously. While technology has created many global problems, it has also provided better means to solve them.

One difficulty that hampers negotiations at the global level is that the negotiators themselves do not always suffer directly from a lack of agreement, and therefore tend to prolong the negotiations. For example, at a U.N. conference negotiating a new wheat agreement, including provisions for food aid to regions in conditions of famine, the delegates failed to reach agreement but were apparently very well fed. The Catholic church has developed an efficient mechanism to achieve rapid agreement on the selection of a pope—perhaps after centures of trial and error. The cardinals are simply locked up until they announce their joint decision. (Maybe we should lock up the disarmament negotiators in Geneva until they have reached agreement.)

## Solving Internal Conflicts

While certain issues can be dealt with effectively only at the global level, because they affect all countries, many other problems can be solved just as well at a regional or local level. It is best to leave decisions to the *lowest* level that includes all those affected by the decision, because those who benefit or suffer from the outcome have the greatest incentive to choose wisely. Also, if they make a wrong choice, they have no one but themselves to blame. This reduces a potential source of conflict.

Methods to resolve conflicts peacefully, through negotiations, are needed at the domestic level as well as at the international. International wars often grow out of unresolved domestic conflicts. Foreign powers which support one or the other of the parties to the conflict may then become involved. Roberts (1976, p. 67) writes, "Acute internal divisions, whether political or ethnic, often provide a cause or an excuse for wars and crises. This was true in Czechoslovakia in 1938, in Poland in 1939, and in South

Vietnam in the 1960s." One might also add to this list the internal power struggle in Afghanistan in 1979 that offered the Soviet Union an excuse for intervention, the suppression of the Arabic minority in Iran in 1980 that may have contributed to Iraq's decision to attempt an invasion, the violent coups in the Dominican Republic in 1965 and in Grenada in 1983 that led to U.S. intervention, and many other examples.

The peaceful resolution of internal conflicts is an important precondition for the prevention of international wars. The several schools of thought on how this is best to be done correspond roughly to the four basic approaches to negotiations listed in Table 15.1. A "hawkish" position holds that a firm, unyielding attitude by the government against any form of opposition is the best guarantee for stability; severe punishment of anyone who tries to upset the status quo will prevent things from getting out of hand; and any compromise would only encourage increased demands. A "dovish" position holds that the best response is to give in to all the demands of the opposition, to avoid any dispute. Such a position may encourage excessive demands by a minority, at the expense of the majority. The worst position, that of the warmonger, in effect declares a war on the opposition, with all the resulting suffering this brings to both sides. The most-promising position is the first, yielding to legitimate demands that are supported by a majority, while resisting unpopular demands that a minority may seek to impose by violent means. Let us compare this last approach with one that could be described as "hardline" or "hawkish."

An internal conflict developed in the Jura region of Switzerland in the 1950s and '60s. A Catholic, French-speaking minority in the northern part of the canton of Berne felt dominated by the Protestant, German-speaking majority in the rest of the canton. A separatist movement gained in strength. The people were warned by the government in Berne that they would suffer economically if they separated. But the best judges of what is in their true interest are the local people themselves. Some politically motivated cases of arson began to appear. If no solution to this problem had been worked out, there is little doubt that eventually it might have led to a civil-war-like situation, as it exists in Northern Ireland today. But after long talks and delays, the government of Berne finally agreed to hold a referendum in the contested region. Of the six districts, the three northernmost voted to form their own independent canton. The three southern districts had majorities in favor of remaining within the canton of Berne. After that vote, each community along the new borderline could choose whether it wanted to remain in the district in which it found itself, or switch over to the other side. Several communities changed to one side or the other. In 1978, the new canton Jura was founded and welcomed into the Swiss Confederation. Since that time, the conflict has subsided.

A similar problem, although at a more-advanced stage, exists in Northern Ireland with the strife between Catholics and Protestants. The Catholic minority feels dominated by the Protestant majority and favors joining the Catholic Irish Republic. The Protestant majority understandably is opposed to such a step, fearing its fate as a minority in Ireland. This conflict has intensified over many years and finally led to street fighting and political assassinations. It might be worth trying the solution that worked in the Jura: allow each community to decide its own future, and help those who are caught on the wrong side to migrate if they wish. Instead, attempts have been made to suppress the violence with armed force, and the killing continues. When some Catholic prisoners went on a hunger strike to back up their demand to be treated as political prisoners, British Prime Minister Margaret Thatcher took an unyielding position and allowed them to die, creating martyrs. Their memory will further intensify the bitter feelings of the Catholics. The present approach of the British government does not seem to lead to an end of the conflict.

Permitting change is not the same as succumbing to violence. On the contrary, it means to provide an opportunity for peaceful change and for reason to prevail, and in this way removes the root causes that breed violence. Gene Sharp (1973, p. 10) writes, "Relying on destructive violence to control political power is . . . just as irrational as attempting to use a lid to control steam from a caldron, while allowing the fire under it to blaze uncontrolled."

An important condition for the preservation of internal peace is a fair treatment of minorities. Linguistic minorities, for instance, should be permitted to use and teach their own language and practice their cultural traditions. If they are prevented from doing so, frustration is built up and creates a source of conflict. Fatal riots broke out in the Khusistan province of Iran when the use of Arabic in schools was prohibited. A similar problem exists in the Basque region of Spain, where the imposition of the Spanish language has contributed to the emergence of a separatist movement and acts of terrorism. Switzerland has made a conscious decision to permit minorities to use their own language. The smallest language group, speaking Romansch, comprises only 1 percent of the population, about 50,000 people, who are scattered in various mountain valleys. Elementary school textbooks are printed in five different dialects of Romansch, and children are taught in their own dialect during the first three school years. From a purely economic viewpoint, this makes no sense; but from a political viewpoint, it may well be the right thing to do.

An institution that can help keep domestic peace is the office of an ombudsman. He must be an impartial, incorruptible, and respected personality who will give serious consideration to people's claims if they have a grievance against some government agency, and must have the legal power to redress any wrongdoing. The Scandinavian countries have had a good experience with this institution. On the other hand, if there is a sluggish bureaucracy that is unresponsive to justified complaints, terrorist groups may emerge. If all roads to peaceful change are blocked, the use of violence may appear as an attractive alternative. Mechanisms for peaceful change serve the function of a safety valve that allows pressure to escape, before it can reach excessive levels that may lead to an explosion.

Treating the opposition with respect, even if one does not agree with all of their proposals, can help reduce tension. When President Mubarak took office in Egypt, he released a group of opposition writers and intellectuals from detention, met with them, listened to their complaints, and promised to do his best to work toward solutions to the country's problems. This gesture helped defuse a tense situation. On the other hand, when a group of Indian peasants entered the Spanish embassy in Guatemala to call world attention to their plight of losing their land, the government did not attempt to hold a dialog with them; they were burnt alive. Such acts of repression will certainly fuel other peasants' desire to seek change through armed force.

The forces that seek an improvement in the situation of the underprivileged can either be channeled into constructive directions and absorbed into the government, or be suppressed with violence. Suppressing them may appear as the simpler and quicker solution, but that approach only tends to postpone the problem. Unless the injustices are removed that lead people to risk their lives in order to change their society, dissatisfaction will grow and make the problem worse in the long run. The following analogy may illustrate this point. If a mountain torrent causes destruction, its power can be channeled into productive uses for irrigation and power generation, or an impenetrable dam can be built to block its flow. As the water level rises behind the dam, the dam must be built higher. But ultimately the pressure of the water will build up to such a level that it will break through any wall and cause much greater destruction than would have occurred in the absence of an attempt to block it. Similarly, if an attempt is made to block inevitable social change by force, the violence and destruction will ultimately assume much larger proportions than if the needed reforms had been undertaken in time.

If a "friendly" government in another country has lost popular support, another nation can either try to prolong its life by economic and military aid, even intervening in its support, until the inevitable bitter end occurs, at great human cost; or it can seek to build good relations with a newly emerging, more-popular government. The same two types of approaches have also been tried in the economic field, and this may give a clue as to which approach works better. European countries and the United States have tended to extend the life of obsolete industries through subsidies until they finally collapse, causing even greater economic disruption. Japan does the opposite. When an industry is no longer competitive and is in difficulty, the government helps the affected companies to move into *new*, more future-oriented industries. It might be worth trying the method Japan has used so successfully in its economic policy in the field of foreign policy as well, in choosing with which groups to build good relations. One difficulty is, of course, that there is more emotional attachment to a certain political party that may have lost its popularity than to a certain branch of industry that may have lost its competitiveness.

*Fair Sharing*

Some standard mechanisms exist by which disputes can be arbitrated in a fair way. A traditional method is "cut and choose." If one cuts a cake into two pieces and the other is free to choose one, neither side has any grounds for complaint. That method can be generalized to more than two participants (see, for example, Baumol 1981). Such methods would be useful, for example, in settling disputes over inheritances. Quarrels often arise among heirs over certain sentimental values, for example, who can keep the parents' house, and who receives only money as compensation. If there are two heirs, one could divide the inheritance into two portions he considers of truly equal value to him. The other heir could then choose which option she prefers. There would be no cause for argument or regret, and the income of inheritance lawyers would diminish.

The same method could be used to solve certain international disputes. Two countries may want to build a joint steel plant, to take advantage of scale economies. But each would prefer to have the plant on its own territory, to create jobs and to give greater assurance of future supply. Potentially beneficial forms of economic cooperation often break down over such disputes. A simple solution would be the following: one country estimates how much it would be worth to it to have the plant on its own soil, and how much compensation it would be willing to pay to the other country for letting it have the joint plant. It can choose the level of compensation in such a way that it is *indifferent* to either having the plant and paying the compensation, or receiving the same amount of compensation from the other country and not having the plant. Then it can let the other country choose. In this way, the dispute could be settled in a fair, amicable way, with no later regrets.

Sometimes the market can be an effective tool for conflict resolution. People need not agree with each other on the values of various goods. If people place *different* values on different goods, they can both benefit from an exchange. They would be ill-advised to try to convince the other side that their own relative evaluation is correct. For example, when the U.S. government bought Alaska in 1867 from Russia for $7,200,000 it would not have cared to argue with the czar that Alask was really worth a great deal more.

## On the Role of Peace Research

Innovative ideas and proposals for preventing or solving conflicts peacefully are much needed. Deterrence or defense, even nonmilitary defense, is only a last resort to seek to prevent a war when a conflict has already reached an acute stage. To use an analogy, to prevent a child from being a delinquent, we rely primarily on education. Detainment in a "correctional facility" is only a last resort, if education has failed. Similarly, prevention of war through deterrence or dissuasion should be only a last resort, if it has not been possible to resolve a conflict in other ways. Much more work needs to be done on the prevention of serious conflicts at a very early stage, when it is generally easiest to do something about them. An important role in this endeavor needs to be played by conflict and peace research.

At the United Nations Second Session on Disarmament in 1978, then Secretary General Waldheim appealed to all nations to make available 0.1 percent of their military expenditures for disarmament research and education. Even that relatively modest amount is not devoted to peace research in most countries. Yet research and education for the prevention of war could probably contribute a great deal more to countries' security than could marginal additions to their military hardware. The prevention of a nuclear holocaust is certainly worth a greater effort.

Peace research now depends mainly on individual efforts and voluntary contributions. Let us try to imagine the state of military defense if it depended on individual actions and voluntary donations. Still, this is no reason for despair. In the last century, the slave traders and slave owners prospered materially, while the people who freed slaves and worked for the abolition of slavery did so out of commitment to a social vision, voluntarily. In spite of their apparent disadvantage, they were successful in the end.

# 16   What We Can Do

It has been said that theory without action is lame. Conversely, action without theory is blind. Another saying states that "Nothing concentrates the mind like the prospect of imminent disaster." The growing awareness of the danger of a nuclear holocaust must give rise to informed actions to avert it before it is too late.

## Motivation and Capability

Before any change can take place, it is necessary for people to become conscious of the need for change and to be motivated to do something. Without the traumatic experience of the fratricidal battle at Marignano, Switzerland might never have extricated itself from the war system. Deutsch (1983, p. 24) writes, "It is difficult to induce a therapeutic change in a pathological social or psychological process until the pathology is recognized as such and seen to be unacceptably harmful." Schell (1982, p. 148 and 150) quotes Pascal's observation that "It is easier to endure death without thinking about it than to endure the thought of death without dying" and says that this observation perfectly describes our response so far to the peril of extinction. He points out that "If one nuclear bomb had gone off each year in one of the world's cities, we can well imagine that public attitudes toward the nuclear peril would now be quite different."

The first step is thus to increase people's awareness that there is a problem. Many physicians have joined efforts to make the public aware of the medical consequences of nuclear war, and of the fact that the only meaningful medical response is its prevention. Other professions also contribute to raising the public consciousness. Since the thought of nuclear war is unpleasant, most people have tried to push it out of their minds. But being conscious of the danger can lead to the motivation to do something about it. It can generate an interest in a shift toward safer foreign and defense policies, which reduce the likelihood of nuclear war.

To be successful, any strategy for change must be supported by a coalition of forces that is both interested in carrying out that change and, at the same time, capable of implementing it. Any proposal that ignores this, no matter how well intended, is utopian and mere wishful thinking. By saying that someone must be *interested* in change in order to be willing to work toward it, I do not imply that this motivation must be based on "self-interest." Altruistic motives also exist. Many people have dedicated themselves to a cause out of concern for others, or to defend principles in which they believe. Even so, it is naive to expect people to make an effort for something in which they are not interested.

The groups who have the power to bring about war or peace are, typically, a country's foreign policy and defense establishments. But they may have little interest in a change of course, because present policies have brought them to their positions of power and privilege. Other groups may be strongly motivated to seek a better approach to the prevention of war, but may lack the power to implement it. Typically, these are citizens' groups who want to prevent a nuclear holocaust, and who don't want to kill, or dominate, anyone else. The two groups, those who are able to implement change and those who are in favor of it, do not always overlap. How can they be brought together? Generally, the solution is to make the powerful more motivated, and the motivated more powerful.

The range of potential actors may be classified into governmental groups (local and national governments and intergovernmental organizations such as the United Nations), and into nongovernmental groups (individual citizens and private associations, such as professional societies, business firms, labor unions, religious groups, etc., at the local, national, and international levels). In the following, I will discuss some possible strategies toward the prevention of war that can be pursued (a) by individuals, (b) by nongovernmental associations of various sizes, (c) by national governments, and (d) by intergovernmental organizations.

The most powerful among these four groups are national governments. Changes at that level would have the most far-reaching effect. But such change may also be the most difficult to accomplish. A more-successful strategy may be to bring about change by working through private groups, and through local governments and international organizations. From such a broad basis, it may ultimately be possible to bring about a change in national governments' approach to the prevention of war.

### Individual Actions

As individuals, we can better inform ourselves about the consequences of war, and about various approaches to its prevention. We should seek information from a great variety of sources, and not rely on any single source. The probability that several *independent* sources will provide the same false information is much lower than the possibility that a single source could be wrong. If we have the opportunity to travel abroad, we can seek first-hand information by talking with people and finding out how others see a problem. We should keep an open mind, and try to learn from the experience and insight of others. (This book, as stated in the introduction, is intended as a contribution to such an open discussion.)

We can organize informal discussion groups among our friends and co-workers. If we have some information that others are lacking, we can share it with them, if they care to listen. But if we try to impose our own views on others, we will only antagonize them. We should be eager not only to talk, but also to *listen*. To be effective, we must try to understand the views of others, rather than prematurely attributing evil motives to those who disagree with us. Unless we are prepared to listen to others and take their concerns seriously, they will not listen to us either.

Roger Fisher stated that

> We in the peace movement do not always practice what we preach. I am always ready to tell friends at the Pentagon that it does no good to call Soviet officials idiots, but am likely to add,

"Don't you see that, you idiot?" We who are concerned with reducing the risks of war often think that our job is to "win" the war against hawks . . . . But our task is not . . . seeking to win a war, but to gain a peace [Fisher 1981, p. 227].

To advance peace, we must help others to solve their legitimate problems at the same time, or else we will not succeed.

The attitude of many people, that problems of national security are so complex that they are best left to the experts in the government, is dangerous. The larger the number of independent people who concern themselves with a problem, the more likely is it that all aspects will be taken into account and the truth finally emerge from an open discussion. A good example of this is the discussion about the fallout from atmospheric nuclear tests in the late 1950s and early 1960s (Commoner 1963). At first, the U.S. government kept test results classified and made them accessible only to a small group of government scientists. The public's concern over possible radiation hazards was brushed aside with the contention that radiation from fallout was far below the natural level of radioactivity in the environment. When the secrecy was partially lifted in 1954, a much larger group of independent scientists could begin to study the problem. They found that direct radiation from fallout was indeed negligible, but that the radioactive isotope strontium-90, which has a similar chemical structure to calcium, found its way from low-level deposits on grassland through cow milk in higher concentrations into the bones and teeth of infants, where it represented a substantial health hazard. A report of the Atomic Energy Commission in 1957 concluded that "Fallout from tests completed to that date would probably result in 2,500 to 13,000 cases of serious genetic defects per year throughout the world population" (quoted in Commoner 1963, pp. 17–18). The widespread public protest over these radioactive baby teeth contributed to the conclusion of the 1963 atmospheric test ban treaty.

It is true that the partial test ban treaty did not slow down the arms race significantly. Underground nuclear tests, which are still permitted under the 1963 treaty, have continued since then at a higher annual rate than earlier atmospheric tests. The treaty must be seen as an anti-pollution measure rather than an arms control measure. Nevertheless, it shows that a public debate can force governments to take corrective measures. Let us hope that the growing debate about the effects of nuclear war, which are incomparably more serious than the effects of nuclear testing, will lead to measures to its prevention.

Science advances through a constant process of independent verification or correction. If errors are kept secret, they cannot be discovered. In a similar way, the more people take an independent look at a problem and do not blindly trust in authorities, the more likely it is that viable ideas for possible solutions will be generated and ultimately prevail.

We can talk about our ideas to the people we meet in our daily lives; we can write letters to local newspapers. With some preparation, we can give talks at schools or various clubs. We may sometimes be hesitant because we do not have enough expertise. But others, not necessarily more qualified, are always less scrupulous and make their views known loudly. If we keep silent, we allow them to gain control. We can vote for representatives who are concerned with peace, and even campaign for them. We can write letters to government officials. In suggesting this, I have no illusion that one pleading or angry letter will change the mind of a politician. But many officials are basically sympathetic to the cause of peace. Giving them support in their effort will strengthen their position. Political leaders are under constant pressure to give attention to many competing issues. Unless it is made clear to them that the prevention of war is of great concern to their voters, they may instead give priority to daily short-term problems and to issues pressed by special interest groups. We may also express our appreciation to elected officials if they have taken a step in the right direction. A letter of support may often be more effective than a letter of protest, and will encourage them to go further.

### Strategies for Peace Organizations

To become stronger and more effective, we can associate ourselves with *groups* of likeminded people. There are two opposite approaches to the formation of a coalition. Either we can seek to form a group all of whose members are in strong agreement on almost every issue. Such a group will be able to agree on a comprehensive plan of action but will necessarily remain small, because few people agree with each other on everything. Another approach is to concentrate on a single issue and to seek an alliance even with people with whom we disagree on other issues. Such a coalition will be able to agree only on a limited plan of action, but it will be very broad-based and powerful. Neither of these two extremes is the most desirable. An all-inclusive coalition may not be able to agree on anything of importance, and a highly sectarian group will totally lack the power to implement any of its proposals. The ideal is a coalition that is sufficiently small so that it can agree on some important issues, but is still large enough so that it has the strength to implement them.

If the precise borderline between success and failure is unclear, it is preferable to be on the safe side. We will want to make sure that the public is on our side and supports our proposals, even if these proposals may not go as far as we would ideally wish. It is better to be successful on the issues that are absolutely essential for survival, than to be overambitious and to fail completely. This situation can be compared to the choice of how much to load on a boat. The more we load on it, up to a certain point, the more we can carry to the other shore. But if we overload the boat just a little, it will sink and everything is lost. In assessing the potential success of a policy proposal, it is difficult to know precisely where that breaking point is located. Therefore, it is preferable to ensure that one can win the support of a sufficiently strong majority, and not to be too exclusive. To use another analogy, the harder one spans a bow, the farther one can shoot an arrow. But if one spans the bow a little too hard, it breaks.

To ensure success of a movement, the best method is to build a very broad, strong coalition and to aim at the most important issue on which there is broad agreement. Highly controversial issues are better avoided, for they can easily split a coalition and lead to failure. The stronger a coalition and the more modest its objective, the more likely is success. The weaker the coalition and the more ambitious its goals, the more likely is failure. A weak coalition and a modest goal, or a strong coaliation and an ambitious goal, are apt to produce an uncertain outcome.

A Chinese diplomat, when asked by a Western colleague why the Chinese were so successful, is said to have replied: "You try to catch ten flies with one finger and don't catch any. We use all ten fingers to catch one fly, and catch it." Sometimes the best is the enemy of the good. Striving for perfection can result in missing opportunities for improvements that would have been feasible.

In choosing our goals, we must not only consider what would be desirable, but also what is feasible under given circumstances. Wishing alone does not help. Paul Warnke, the chief U.S. negotiator for the SALT II treaty, when criticized for not having sought greater concessions from the Soviet Union, replied that he certainly wished that he could have extracted greater concessions from the Soviet negotiators, but that one had to be realistic about what one could expect from the other side. He said he also *wished* he could fly – this would save him many plane tickets.

In calling for the formulation of modest goals, I do not mean goals that are irrelevant to the achievement of our fundamental objective, the prevention of war. Modest goals are not palliatives that detract from the principal goal. "Modest" means to concentrate on what is absolutely essential, and to omit for the time being other proposals we may consider as desirable, but for which the majority of the public is not yet ready.

Consider the following example. Almost everyone, with the exception of a few perverted minds, wishes to prevent nuclear war. But far fewer people would agree on the desirability of a world government. If we call for the formation of a world government to prevent nuclear war, this is an overambitious goal that is likely to fail to win sufficient support. But if we show that the threat to initiate nuclear war makes a preemptive nuclear attack on one's own country more likely, there is a greater chance that enough support can be built to desist from such a suicidal policy.

Similarly, a call for complete unilateral disarmament makes the task of militarists too easy. It will not be hard for them to convince the public that the peace movement lives in an illusionary world, out of touch with reality, and that only military strength can guarantee their country's security. It is important for the peace movement to stress that it is equally or even more concerned about national security than the militarists, but that only peace, not war, can give security.

The peace movement should certainly not oppose all forms of defense. This would isolate it from the general public, which has a legitimate fear of aggression. Rather, it should emphasize that there are better forms of defense than the acquisition of offensive capabilities. It must be emphasized that certain measures taken in the name of defense actually reduce a country's security. The acquisition of nuclear missiles with a first-strike capability, even if they are not intended for that use, makes a nuclear war more likely and thus reduces everyone's security.

Some people argue that one should demand more than one actually expects to achieve in order to achieve at least something. The image in their minds is a labor union bargaining for a new wage contract. The union may ask for a substantial wage increase as a starting position, so that after some compromise the increase will still be acceptable. But this comparison leaves out the role of the general public. If there are two contending proposals, the public will lend its support to the proposal that appears more reasonable, rather than mediate toward some middle ground. If the peace movement makes unrealistic demands, it will isolate itself from the public and may drive it to support a bellicose government. In the same way, if a splinter group makes unrealistic demands in the name of the peace movement, such as a call for complete unilateral disarmament, it will not only isolate itself, but may well discredit the rest of the peace movement at the same time, and thus do a disservice to peace.

Many members of the peace movement have denied the existence of any serious threat of foreign aggression, in order to counterbalance the exaggerated claims of danger from the military establishment. But in belittling the existence of a potential danger, they have isolated themselves from people who are worried about possible aggression. Even those who do not themselves believe there is a serious threat will be more effective in achieving their goal of preventing war if they address people's fears, admit the possibility of a danger, and offer plausible ways to meet it. The way to meet a possible threat is through the ability to resist such a threat, without becoming a threat to others in the process. Sweden and Switzerland were able to avoid involvement in World War II not by denying the existence of a German threat, but by preparing against it, while taking care not to be seen as a threat themselves.

To build a broad coalition for a new approach to the prevention of war, the issue must be made relevant to people's primary concerns. Research among middle-class high school students in the United States (Philomena Fischer, 1984) has shown that their main concerns relate to their future careers, their economic situations, and their family lives. Providing them with information about the arms race did not make them more peace-oriented, but rather more hawkish. The number of those who accepted war as being sometimes necessary increased significantly after they saw a slide show about the dangers of the nuclear arms race. Unless individuals understand that if there is a nuclear war there will be neither career for them nor family life, the issue of nuclear war may always seem remote. It is necessary to make the problem of war and peace relevant to people's main concerns. If we want to change people's attitudes, we must start from where *they* are, not where we are. Many political movements seem to overlook this fact and consequently lose touch with people.

There may seem to be some contradiction between seeking to relate the issue of war and peace to people's other concerns and, on the other hand, to limiting oneself to the key issue, the prevention of a nuclear holocaust. The solution to this apparent contradiction is to build an *inclusive*, not an exclusive, alliance. Clearly, there are many important issues to be addressed, such as human rights violations, poverty, unemployment, discrimination against women or minorities, etc. All these issues are to a greater or lesser extent connected with each other, and with the problem of building peace. But if all these issues are addressed at the same time, it may then become difficult to reach agreement on what should be done concerning each one of these issues, and disputes over secondary problems may internally weaken a coalition. One should certainly connect the problem of war and peace with these other issues, but not make it a condition for joining that everyone agree with each proposal made. If one tells people "you are part of our movement only if you agree with this *and* that *and* that proposal," the movement becomes very weak and splintered. But if anyone is welcome to join who is committed to work for peace, *or* for solidarity with the Third World, *or* for women's rights, *or* for more jobs, etc., *or* in favor of all these, then one can build a very broad-based and strong movement.

Many members of the peace movement talk only to themselves; others try to convert the most-bellicose members of society to their own cause. Neither of these audiences is the most fruitful to address. While it is easy to agree with other members of the peace movement, this does not add new strength. It is very difficult, if not impossible, to persuade a convinced militarist that there also exist nonmilitary approaches to national security. Attempts at discussion with a closed mind bring no result, exhaust our energy, and are discouraging. The most-important group of people to address have not yet made up their minds and are just beginning to concern themselves with the danger of war. They have mental flexibility, and may realize that a rapidly accelerating arms race and threatening speeches are not the best approaches to the prevention of war.

Organizations that can reach many people, and which in most countries enjoy a certain independence from the government, are schools, churches, unions, and the news media. Because of their great influence, they have a particular responsibility to educate people about the problems of war and peace, and to contribute to the prevention of war. An example of such an effort is the 1983 pastoral letter on war, armaments and peace by the U.S. National Conference of Catholic Bishops Ad Hoc Committee on War and Peace.

To sustain a movement, it is important that there be some early, even if modest, successes. If the first goal is too difficult to achieve and takes too long, some people will become discouraged and drop out, but a small initial success will encourage people to increase their efforts. An example of a small but feasible step toward the prevention of nuclear war is a policy of no first use of nuclear weapons. Another small but important step is a mutual verifiable freeze on nuclear weapons. To aim immediately at a more-ambitious goal, such as complete mutual nuclear disarmament, could weaken the peace movement, because it is unlikely to be realized soon. Of course, small steps must be planned as part of a comprehensive, long-term strategy. One must not relax efforts after the first insignificant success, but keep working toward larger goals. The partial test ban treaty of 1963 had the unfortunate result of leading to the dissolution of the strong antinuclear movement that had developed in the early 1960s, even though that treaty had little effect on the nuclear arms race.

As was mentioned earlier, the profit motive is one factor behind the arms race. But it would be totally false to conclude that all large corporations benefit from the arms race and support it. A call for the dismantling of all transnational corporations, as some have made, is counterproductive. These corporations are unlikely to disappear. A group that indiscriminately opposes all transnational corporations creates a formidable opponent to itself. It will exhaust its resources long before these corporations exhaust theirs. A more-successful strategy is to make a distinction between those corporations who profit from war and those who are interested in preventing war, because their businesses would suffer in case of a war. The corporations who would suffer from war are a far greater majority. Seeking their support for measures to prevent war can add strength to that cause. And as was mentioned earlier, business corporations can also strengthen peace by engaging in trade between countries with tense relations, for example in East-West trade. The peace movement should seek to isolate the corporations that profit from war, and not isolate itself. It should unite itself and split the opposition, not split itself and unite the opposition.

In addition to the profit motive of arms manufacturers, another factor behind the arms race is the constant flow of new inventions by scientists and engineers working in weapons development laboratories. One approach to halt the arms race is to try to interrupt that flow of destructive innovations. Scientists who work on such new weapons can be isolated and criticized by the scientific community. This approach should certainly be pursued with all vigor. But to be entirely successful, such a movement would have to be able to prevent *all* scientists from working on the development of new weapons. Anything that requires cooperation from every single member of a group is difficult to achieve. It is much easier to succeed with something when the support of even a few individuals can make a difference. An example is the invention of cheap and effective conventional defensive arms. Such an invention would not require the cooperation of the entire scientific community. A small group, even a determined individual scientist, may succeed in this.

To stress this point, consider the following analogy. To achieve absolute silence in a concert hall, each one of the several thousand people in the room must desist from coughing or moving. But to fill the room with beautiful music, a small orchestra, or even one soloist, is sufficient.

Inventions for peace can take many forms, not just the development of purely defensive arms. Ideas for conflict resolution, for just settlements of disputes, for the creation of international law that is acceptable to all sides, etc., can be generated by individuals or small groups. To create inventions for peace is easier, for the reason explained, than to prevent all inventions for war. To generate good ideas is easier than to suppress bad ideas.

Sometimes, a small, dedicated group can achieve far-reaching success. When the West German government announced it would build a nuclear fuel reprocessing plant near Gorsleben, a group of activists camped on the planned construction site in an attempt to block construction. One day they were forcefully removed by the police. The members of the group thought their effort had been futile. But a month later, the interior minister canceled the project "because of popular resistance."

Many criticize the peace movement in the West by pointing out that no comparable popular movement is tolerated in the Soviet block. This is unfortunately true. It would be much better if there were strong independent peace movements in both East and West. But suppression of such movements in the East is no reason to suppress them also in the West. The members of the peace movement do not aim to weaken their own side and to make their own country defenseless, but to achieve security for everyone through a stable peace. A strong, independent peace movement can make sure that governments do not embark on a dangerous course leading to war. The United States was better off for having extricated itself from the Vietnam War, partly because of the strong domestic antiwar movement. Similarly, the Soviet Union could be much better off if a domestic antiwar movement could convince the government to withdraw its troops from Afghanistan. Having an independent peace movement that can help to correct erroneous policies should be seen as a strength of a free society, not a weakness. *Avoiding war does not harm us, but help us.*

To be effective, a peace movement cannot afford to limit itself to a critique of current foreign and military policies. It must offer feasible *alternatives.* It is usually much easier to criticize than to devise a better solution, but criticism alone does not show a way out of the present danger. Most people agree that nuclear weapons are undesirable. But without a credible alternative approach to defense, they will not be prepared to reduce their reliance on nuclear arms. One small step toward the possible implementation of alternative security policies is the formation of *alternative security commissions,* groups of specialists and people with political experience or plain common sense, who can combine their insights and work out concrete proposals on building a safer world.

Rather than calling for unilateral disarmament, which makes a country defenseless and can therefore increase the danger of war, it is more realistic to call for *transarmament,* i.e., a shift to a nonthreatening form of defense, which offers greater security than a threatening military posture.

We should also develop visions of a better alternative future. Motivation for the prevention of war should be based not only on the fear of war, but also on the desire for a better world. The question of setting goals must involve everyone. We must overcome the false idea that there is one single ideal form of society that is the best for everyone, for all times. (Galtung [1984] has noted that this false idea, which is rooted in occidental religions, seems to be shared by both the left and the right of the political spectrum.)

Generally, a strategy for change is more successful if it seeks to work with those who are dissatisfied with the present situation, not with those who benefit from it. As Robert Johansen put it, it would have been unrealistic to expect plantation owners to take the lead in the movement to abolish slavery. To avoid military involvement abroad, it may be fruitless to argue with weapons manufacturers who profit from the supply of arms. It will be more effective to work with people who don't want their sons or husbands to die for a questionable cause. People who enjoy privileges will rarely be persuaded by moral arguments to give them up voluntarily. But they will change when they realize that change is inevitable.

I have concentrated on examining what the victims of war can do to prevent it, and have devoted little space to criticizing those who are responsible for war, because those who are motivated to prevent war are more likely to act against it than those who justify war. It is always easy to blame others, but determining who is responsible for a problem usually does not show the way to a solution. More important than to argue who is at fault is to figure out what *we* can do to prevent war, regardless of whether we are guilty or not.

*Peace Strategies for National Governments*

After these general observations about the type of initiatives that nongovernmental groups can undertake, let us summarize what a national government can do to prevent war. Basically, it can protect its country's national security without reducing the real or perceived security of other nations.

Measures for the prevention of war can be divided into mutually negotiated steps and independent steps. Any government will do well to participate constructively in mutual negotiations for disarmament and for the strengthening of international law with other governments. But at the same time it should take independent measures that are feasible without risking its own security. Measures that do not depend on an agreement with other governments can be taken more quickly and easily.

Any change that can be undertaken by individual decisionmakers, one at a time, occurs more easily than a change that depends on the simultaneous action of many decisionmakers. This is also true within countries. For example, production technologies, which can be changed by individual firms, one at a time, have been developing continuously and rapidly. But changes in a country's social and legal order, which depend on the simultaneous consent of many different forces in a society, occur only rarely, in big shifts at a time. This is why changes in the social and legal organization of production lag behind changes in the technology of production, and sometimes have a tendency to adjust in sudden bursts, rather than smoothly. For example, the abolition of slavery in the United States occurred only after the transition from a plantation economy to an industrial economy requiring factory workers had already advanced significantly. The abolition of slavery did not precede the growing demand for wage labor. A similar phenomenon can be observed at the international level. Different nations' defense policies and military preparations change constantly, in a gradual fashion. But changes in the international legal order, such as the creation of the United Nations, occur only after long intervals, in a one-time major shift, because they require the simultaneous agreement of many independent governments. The creation of a new world order that is less prone to war is highly desirable, but will be more difficult to achieve than gradual shifts in individual countries' defense postures and foreign policies.

If governments were to wait for the moment when all countries simultaneously gave up the use of violence, they might have to wait for a long time. The world might not survive til that moment. To blame others for a lack of progress and to wait for them to take the first step seldom bring results. Any government interested in avoiding war can take steps in that direction, without waiting for others, by giving up the use or threatened use of violence in its relations with other countries, while at the same time not permitting other nations to use violence against itself.

Table 16.1 gives a brief overview over some of the measures that individual nations can undertake, which have been discussed in earlier chapters. Some of these measures are listed separately for the superpowers and for other nations, because they play very different roles in the world today. Of course, to be of greater use, these general measures would have to be adapted to the specific conditions of each country; but as basic

**Table 16.1    A Summary of Proposed Measures for the Prevention of War
That Can Be Taken Independently by Nation-States**

| For the superpowers | For other countries |
| --- | --- |
| Abolish first-strike nuclear weapons (e.g., MIRVs) while maintaining a survivable nuclear deterrent until mutual nuclear disarmament can be achieved. Withdraw "battle-field" nuclear weapons, which would lower the nuclear threshold. | To avoid becoming a target in a nuclear war, do not permit the super-powers to station any first-strike nuclear weapons on your territory. |

*Transarm:* shift from offensive to defensive conventional arms (e.g., anti-tank and antiaircraft weapons) that can help prevent aggression without being useful in carrying out aggression.

| | |
| --- | --- |
| Help allies to become more Self-reliant in their defense; Guard against being drawn into a war by a belligerent small nation, whether it is an ally or an adversary. | Keep out of conflicts between other nations. Strengthen pure self-defense. Prepare for self-sabotage and guerilla warfare in case of occupation. Avoid being a pawn in the global struggle for "spheres of influence." |
| Seek to build good relations with *popular* governments, not with "friendly" dictators. | Strengthen internal unity by resolving domestic conflicts peacefully, striving for economic justice, and granting rights to minorities. |

Reduce your vulnerability: increase economic security by maintaining stockpiles of vital imports and developing alternative sources of supply. Plan to use substitutes and rationing schemes in case of an emergency instead of relying on military interventions to secure foreign supplies.

Make yourself useful — even indispensable — to other nations if you are left in peace, through mutually beneficial trade, scientific cooperation, cultural exchange, assistance in case of natural disasters, etc.

Approach negotiations in an imaginative way to obtain agreement by having something attractive to offer to *both sides.*

Avoid waiting until conflicts reach an acute, violent stage, but seek to anticipate potential problems and solve them early, using legal means and fair arbitration whenever possible.

principles, they should be applicable in a wide range of circumstances.

Obviously, these measures will not all be taken at once. They may require a long, gradual process. But any move in these directions, along any or all of these dimensions, adds to security.

There are two aspects to a defense that does not threaten other nations. One aspect is the choice of armaments, the other the choice of military doctrines and foreign policies.

A country can reduce the danger of war, without increasing the risk to its own security, by strengthening its defensive capability while deliberately avoiding the acquisition of any offensive potential. While offensive arms, such as aircraft carriers, can be used to attack remote territory, they are of limited value for territorial defense. Such weapons, which are likely to provoke retaliatory measures from opponents who feel threatened by them, do not add to a country's security. They do add to a country's ability to dominate others and to play the role of a self-appointed world police force. But fighting wars abroad on behalf of other governments is very different from helping other countries defend *themselves*, by providing them with purely defensive arms.

Those countries that now rely on nuclear deterrence are not likely to undertake unilateral nuclear disarmament. While making every effort to seek verifiable mutual disarmament, these countries can still take, in the meantime, certain independent steps to reduce the danger of nuclear war and to improve everyone's security, including their own. It is in the strong interest of any such country to make it absolutely clear that its nuclear weapons are not usable to carry out a preemptive first strike, but serve exclusively the purpose of deterring the use of nuclear weapons by other nations. For this reason, it is essential that these nuclear arms be made as invulnerable as possible, so there can be no pressure to use them or lose them. Greater target accuracy is not only unnecessary, but in fact counterproductive to a country's own security. It will instill fear of a preemptive attack in an opponent and may therefore induce him, during a grave crisis, to launch a preemptive attack first, out of fear of suffering even greater losses by waiting to be attacked. What causes this fear in an opponent is a mere first-strike *capability* on our part. We need not actually intend or announce that we would strike first. An opponent's behavior is determined by his *perceptions,* regardless of whether they are justified.

If a retaliatory nuclear force is sufficiently invulnerable, and if that invulnerability is made known to a potential aggressor, there is no need to match the number or size of the opponent's nuclear weapons. What counts is not how much a country can destroy, but whether it will be able to retain a credible deterrent even after suffering a potential surprise attack. To avoid an escalating nuclear arms race, one can achieve that purpose even with a substantially smaller nuclear force than that of a potential opponent. There is no need for overkill capacity. As Churchill once put it, it does not matter how many times the rubble bounces; once is too many.

In terms of military doctrine and foreign policy, the principle must be *never to be the first to resort to arms,* and never to be the first to escalate to the use of nuclear arms. Confidence-building measures to reassure potential opponents that they have nothing to fear from us as long as they do not attack us, improve our own security, even if we take the measures independently, without waiting for agreement on reciprocity. To dissuade aggression, a country should also seek to make peaceful cooperation as attractive as possible to a potential opponent.

A combination of a strong but nonthreatening and nonprovocative defense with efforts to seek mutually beneficial relations is a truly robust approach to defense, which works regardless of whether the leaders of other nations are motivated by aggressive intensions, fear of aggression, or by a desire to cooperate.

No political leader is likely to pursue deliberately a policy with the aim of waging nuclear war. It is too obvious that this would be suicidal. The greater danger stems from the possibility that governments pursue a path that will ultimately lead to war. After a certain point of no return has been reached, there may be no other exit from such a path. To avoid sliding onto such a dangerous collision course at a very early stage is the main task of a responsible government.

*International Organizations*

To conclude this chapter, let us briefly examine what various international organizations and the global community as a whole can do to prevent war.

A key point in order to make international negotiations successful is to concentrate on areas where mutual gains for all participants can be achieved. Highly divisive issues, where one side's gains are by necessity another side's losses, are best left off the agenda, or at least put aside until a better negotiating climate has been created through successes in other areas. It may often be the best approach to agree to disagree on a certain issue, rather than constantly to reiterate well-known and irreconcilable positions.

Prime examples of a divisive issue are incompatible claims over territory or mineral rights. One side's gain of territory is by necessity another side's loss. To focus negotiations exclusively on a territorial dispute is likely to lead to a failure. A better approach is to precede such negotiations by an exploration of areas where the countries can mutually benefit, such as mutually beneficial trade, the sharing of technological knowhow, or the joint exploration of natural resources. Once a solid basis for joint interests has been established, the countries may be able to settle a territorial dispute peacefully, because they are aware that they would lose the benefits from mutual cooperation if they failed to agree.

A legal order governing the use of global commons, such as the ocean and seabed resources, is in the joint interest of all countries. As the U.S. National Conference of Catholic Bishops (1983) pointed out in its pastoral letter, "If future planning about conservation of and access to resources, like that involved in the Law of the Sea, is relegated to a pure struggle of power, we will simply guarantee conflict in the future."

The strongest common interest of all nations lies in the prevention of nuclear war, including the possible outbreak of nuclear war caused by some accident. Negotiations in this field should be given much greater attention. The focus should not be on a comparison of different weapons systems, where the interests of the two superpowers are naturally opposed to each other, with each side claiming that the other side's weapons are more threatening. Rather, the emphasis should be placed on measures that simultaneously make both sides more secure, such as preventing accidental missile launchings or seeking to keep nuclear arms out of the hands of terrorists.

Other areas of common global interest lie in the prevention of natural catastrophes, such as a greenhouse effect from the excessive burning of fossil fuels, in protecting the ozone layer from industrial pollutants, in finding solutions to the food and energy shortage, and so on. The emphasis in international cooperation should be on common threats and common opportunities, not on divisive issues.

One inexhaustible resource that permits mutual gains, and which has not yet been adequately exploited, is useful information; for example, in the fields of agriculture, medicine, peaceful industrial technology, etc. Unlike physical resources, which must be taken away from one party to be given to another, information, once it has been created, can be duplicated without limit at virtually no additional cost. Knowledge about more-efficient production processes can be made available to any number of countries, without having to be taken away from anyone. A better use of this rich resource could help improve people's living conditions everywhere considerably.

A particular example of a beneficial exchange of information is in making defense measures more transparent, which reduces mistrust. There is no reason to keep the *existence* of defensive preparations secret. On the contrary, they are better made known, to dissuade aggression. Some secrecy about detailed plans may still have to be maintained if the knowledge of these defense plans would make it easier to counteract them.

All countries can benefit from greater exchange of knowledge and of views. Restrictions to the flow of information across borders, or to international travel, should be reduced. But this does not mean that borders, or areas of legal competence, should be less-clearly defined. Ambiguity creates misunderstandings that may cause conflicts.

Another measure at the international level from which countries can derive mutual benefits is the creation of effective international law. Care must be taken that such law is not directed against one group or another, but is just and in everyone's interest. Galtung (1980, p. 396) writes, "as far as humanly possible, peace proposals should be directed against the peacelessness of social structures, not against fellow human beings."

In many areas, it has long been recognized that adhering to rules or accepting the decision of a neutral arbitrator benefits everyone. For example, as Howard Kurtz, who promoted the idea of a U.N. observation satellite, once pointed out, if two passenger planes are potentially on a collision course, they follow the directions of an air traffic controller who guides them to safety, even if the controller has no enforcing power. No pilot in his right mind would signal to another pilot, via radio, "Watch out, our plane is bigger," even if their respective countries were bitter enemies. Similarly, national leaders may sooner or later come to recognize that their country's security is better served if they accept the decisions of a neutral arbitrating body, than if they pursue a collision course that may end in mutual destruction.

The international community should take a more-active role in eliminating potential sources of conflict at an early stage. It is necessary to develop mechanisms for the peaceful resolution of conflicts before they have reached an acute stage. The United Nations should not limit itself to firefighting operations after a catastrophe has already occurred. It is equally important to develop "fireproof" structures. This does not mean that firefighting ought to be neglected, but we can and must go beyond it.

# Conclusions

The main theme of this book has been to show that to be secure, it is necessary to find a way that enables others to be secure at the same time. For as long as other countries feel threatened by us, they will seek to eliminate that threat.

A widely held belief maintains that to be secure, a country should take a threatening posture vis-à-vis potential adversaries; that the less secure an opponent is, the more secure we are. But if our country is perceived by others to be a threat to their security, to such an extent that they wish we would disappear from the face of the earth, and if they have the means to make us disappear, we are not very secure. To be truly secure, we must make peaceful relations so attractive that others would be disappointed if we did disappear.

Should we abstain from threatening other countries out of altruism? There is no need for altruism. It is in our *own* best self-interest not to represent a threat to others. Some people argue that self-interest is not a solid foundation for stable peace, and that instead the observance of moral principles is needed. It is clear that the prevention of war is a profoundly moral issue. What I have stressed here is that it is *also* a matter of self-interest, because moral arguments are often dismissed as being utopian. There is no contradiction between morality and self-interest. Self-interest is not to be confused with "selfishness." Whereas *selfishness* implies that someone seeks advantages *at the expense of others*, true self-interest has no such connotation. The prevention of war is not only in our own interest, but also in the interest of others.

The greatest weight is carried not *only* by a practical or *only* by a moral argument, but by a combination of the two, both pointing in the same direction. Such a combination of reasons brought about the end of slavery in the United States: a moral outrage over the inhuman conditions under which slaves were held, and a need for free wage labor in growing industries. Moral considerations coincided with the self-interest of the elites. In the same way, a combination of reasons against war — the moral consideration of not wanting to destroy life on earth, and the self-interest of wanting to survive — may help bring about an end to war as a political institution.

Some argue that since war has been with us with only a few brief interruptions throughout recorded history, it must somehow be rooted in human nature. They conclude that there will be wars as long as human civilization exists. But using the same logic, it might have appeared in earlier periods that slavery, cannibalism, and human sacrifice were institutions that corresponded to human nature and were here to stay. The argument that it is impossible to abolish war is equally fallacious.

I have sought to show that the prevention of war is by no means an impossible goal. While it takes two sides for active peaceful cooperation, it also takes two sides to fight a war. One side alone can prevent war if it maintains an adequate, but nonprovocative defense. No country needs to wait for others to take the first step toward peace. A whole range of measures exists to reduce the danger of war that any country can take independently, without having to wait for others. Such measures do not reduce its security; on the contrary, they improve the security of everyone.

The question naturally arises why such measures have not been implemented more widely long ago. The problem is not so much that people in power are genuinely concerned with preserving peace but don't know how to do it. Usually they know very well how more-peaceful and -democratic societies could be constructed, but they are not primarily interested in peace. They are more concerned with consolidating their own power. To develop concrete strategies and feasible plans for action to cope with this problem is a task that yet needs to be done.

To preserve peace and common security, it is necessary to make it clear that aggression cannot succeed. But it is equally important to make it credible that we do not pose any threat to others as long as they leave us in peace. To threaten others, or even to allow them wrongly to believe they are threatened, can be suicidal in the nuclear age. The old idea that in order to protect its own security a country must threaten the security of other nations has become obsolete, if it was ever valid at all. In the nuclear age, we are either all secure, or no one is.

Oskar Morgenstern, the cofounder of game theory with John von Neumann, disappointed about the slow acceptance of their new ideas, once observed sadly: "Obsolete ideas do not die out in people's mind; they disappear only when the people holding those ideas die out." But with the dangerous idea that threatening others brings us security, we may not have time to wait for that moment. Unless we can overcome that false idea soon, we may all die out.

# Appendix: Some Simple Models of Arms Races

In Chapter 6 on the dynamics of arms races, it was argued that offensive arms contribute more to an arms race than do defensive arms. To support that argument, a few simple models of an externally stimulated arms race between two countries are presented here.

Three different types of assumptions are made: (a) both countries are motivated only by their concern for national security; (b) the two countries are motivated by the desire to conquer each other, through superior offensive power; and (c) one of the two countries seeks conquest, while the other merely seeks to defend itself. For each of these three types of assumptions, a continuous and a discrete model are discussed. In the continuous model, countries have a whole range of options open to them, spending an arbitrary portion of their production for arms. In the discrete model, they have only two choices, either to arm or to disarm. A mathematical treatment of the continuous models is given in Fischer (1981).

As is customary in models, it is necessary to simplify drastically from reality to be able to draw any conclusions. We assume here that the world consists of only two countries of equal size, and that their economies consist of only two sectors, a military and a civilian sector. The military sector uses goods from the civilian sector as inputs. The civilian sector is self-sustaining, using inputs from itself, but it cannot use any outputs from the military sector for production, since military goods can neither be consumed nor are they productive capital goods. The smaller the fraction of the given output from the civilian sector that is used for military purposes, the faster the economy can grow, because more will be available for investment in the civilian sector and for consumption.

The military sector produces weapons, which have a dual effect. They increase the security of the country producing them, and reduce the security of the other country. If the weapons are predominantly offensive, they reduce the other country's security by more than they add to a country's own security. If they are predominantly defensive, they add more to a country's own security than they reduce the other country's security.

In the first model we assume that each country is concerned only with maintaining its own security. Each country faces a dilemma. The less it spends for military purposes the less secure it will be, but the faster its economy can grow (which is seen here as a desirable goal, ignoring possible problems of pollution, stress, etc.—another model abstraction). The more it spends for military purposes the more secure it feels, but the slower the growth of its economy. If it spends too high a proportion of its total output for military purposes, the civilian economy will be weakened so much that it cannot any longer sustain the military sector and will undermine its security in the future. In this dilemma, it is assumed that each country will seek to keep some balance between security and prosperity.

Let us call the two countries X and Y. Assume X spends a certain amount to build arms, which are offensive and reduce Y's security by twice as much as they increase the security of X. If Y builds the same type of arms in response, it will want to build twice the quantity of arms X built, to restore its security to the original level. This is represented in Figure A.1.

Consider the following example. Suppose it takes two tanks, on average, to intercept one attacking tank. (A military rule of thumb says that an aggressor needs a superior force to overwhelm a defender. But the attacker can choose the point of attack and concentrate all his forces there, while the defender must protect the entire border, and may therefore need more tanks.) If X builds 100 tanks, Y will want to build 200 tanks to restore its security to the original level. But now X's security is threatened by Y's offensive arms. To compensate X will need to build four times the original amount of arms, further threatening Y's security, and so on. The result is a spiraling arms race. However, this process cannot go on unchecked. Ultimately, the burden on the civilian economy will become so heavy that a country will be forced to keep a ceiling on military expenditures to prevent ruining its civilian economy. The result of these pressures is Y's optimal schedule of military expenditures in response to X's expenditures, shown in Figure A.2.

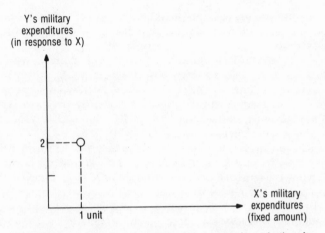

**Figure A.1**   Arms expenditures in Response to Opponent's production of a Given Amount of Offensive Arms

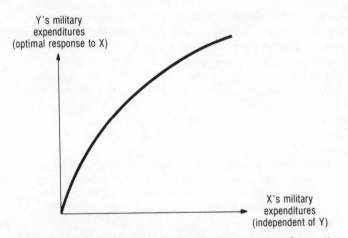

**Figure A.2**   Optimal Schedule of Arms Expenditures in Response to Opponent's Production of a Variable Amount of Offensive Arms

With the use of purely or mainly *defensive* arms, on the other hand, the situation is quite different. The acquisition of defensive arms by country X may slightly reduce the security of country Y. But Y can restore its level of security by acquiring a *smaller* quantity of defensive arms than X. While these arms may pose some additional threat to X, X can restore its security by an even smaller quantity of additional arms, etc. Soon this process will come to a halt. For example, if X seeks to protect itself by stationing a chain of fixed antitank guns along its borders, country Y need do nothing in response, as long as it does not plan to invade X. Neither does Y need any tanks nor antitank weapons, because X's purely defensive arms pose no threat to Y. In the real world there is often a tendency to respond to a new defensive weapon on the other side by constructing a more-powerful offensive weapons system to counteract its effect (Galtung 1980, p. 190). But such a response is necessary only for offensive purposes.

If X had produced defensive arms that reduce Y's security by half as much as they increase X's own security, and Y had responded with the same type of defensive arms, then Y would need to build only half as many arms as X to restore its security. This is shown in Figure A.3.

By the symmetry we have assumed, X's optimal response to Y's arms expenditures is exactly the same, in mirror image, as Y's optimal response to X's arms expenditures. These optimal responses, for various degrees of offensive or defensive arms, are shown once more in Figure A.4.

The only point where the mutual arms expenditures are in balance is where the two curves shown in Figures A.4(a) and (b) intersect. This is where X's original arms expenditures are identical with what it would

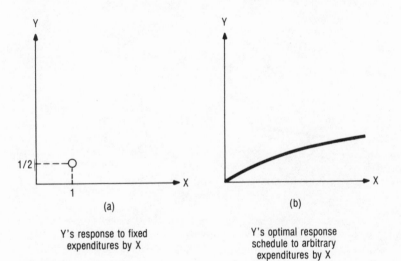

| (a) | (b) |
| --- | --- |
| Y's response to fixed expenditures by X | Y's optimal response schedule to arbitrary expenditures by X |

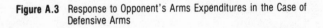

**Figure A.3** Response to Opponent's Arms Expenditures in the Case of Defensive Arms

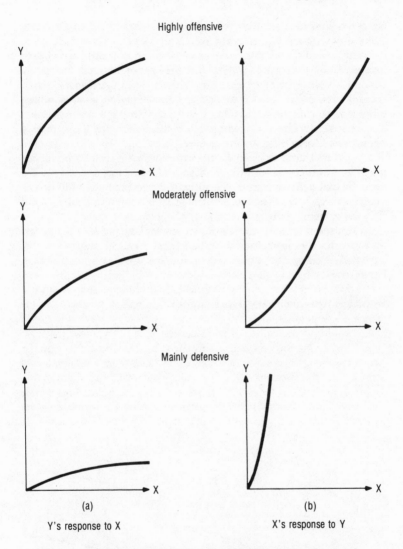

**Figure A.4** Optimal Responses to Arms Expenditures for Various Degrees of Offensive and Defensive Arms

want to spend in response to Y's expenditures that X provoked. These balance points are shown in Figure A.5.

These equilibrium points will soon be reached from any arbitrary starting point. Suppose X starts with arms expenditures less than the amount A shown in Figure A.5(a). Then Y will spend more than X spends in response. This again causes X to increase its level of military spending, and so on, until both X and Y spend the amount A. Similarly, if X starts out with an amount of military spending larger than A, then Y will spend less than X does in response, and X will now find that it can afford to invest more of its output in the civilian sector of the economy, and so on, until both X and Y spend the amount A. The result is that if X and Y both use sufficiently defensive arms to protect their security, there is no arms race at all, indicated by the intersection at point zero in Figure A.5(c).

The question naturally arises, how defensive is "sufficiently" defensive? In the simple models described here, a precise answer can be given. As long as the acquisition of arms reduces the security of the other country by an equal or lesser amount than it increases the country's own security, the arms are sufficiently defensive. This would correspond to "intermediate" types of arms in Figure 5.1, which are not very defensive at all.

One could, in principle, define a "degree of defensiveness" for every type of arms, as the amount of security the arms add to the country acquiring them, divided by the sum of the increase in a country's own security and the decrease in the opponent's security. From Figure 5.1, it is apparent that this index is 0 for purely offensive arms, 1 for purely defensive arms, and 0.5 for intermediate arms. It is negative for superoffensive arms and greater than 1 for superdefensive arms. In

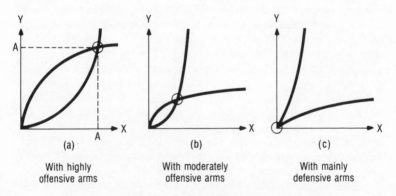

| (a) | (b) | (c) |
| --- | --- | --- |
| With highly offensive arms | With moderately offensive arms | With mainly defensive arms |

**Figure A.5** Equilibrium Points of Mutual Arms Expenditures

reality, it may be difficult to assign a precise "degree of defensiveness" to any particular weapons system. But, fortunately, this is not necessary. To be safe it is preferable not just to seek the minimum degree of defensiveness necessary.

As can be seen from Figures A.5(a) and (b), the more offensive the arms used are, the higher is the mutual level of arms expenditures and the less secure both countries are, because their military spending cannot keep up with the level that would be needed to restore their security. (But trying to keep up with that level would only make things worse, because it would lead to further arms expenditures by the other side, and even greater insecurity.)

It will be observed that there is a second equilibrium point in Figures A.5(a) and (b), at zero arms expenditures. This is indeed a solution far preferable to the other equilibrium points indicated. Both countries could spend nothing for arms, enjoy maximum feasible economic growth, and be perfectly secure. Unfortunately, in the absence of any agreement, that equilibrium is not stable. If one side deviates ever so slightly from zero arms expenditures, the other side will find it in its interest to spend some more, and so on, up to a level where the requirements of the civilian economy put enough downward pressure on mutual arms spending.

The interesting result is that if the arms used are sufficiently defensive, there is no need to wait for the result of lengthy negotiations. Each country will begin to disarm out of self-interest.

As was briefly mentioned in Chapter 6, and is argued at greater length in Fischer (1981), if the two countries seek to conquer each other instead of merely seeking to maintain their own security, then they prefer offensive arms that can be used to attack their opponent. In that case, the mere *availability* of cheap and effective defensive arms will not necessarily bring an end of the arms race. But it is sufficient that *one* of the two countries is interested only in its own defense. If that country can render the offensive arms of its opponent useless, while not posing a threat to the other side, it can force an end to the arms race.

The types of mutual reaction curves of arms expenditures shown in Figures A.2 to A.5 have been discussed extensively in Lewis F. Richardson's (1960) classicial analysis of arms races. One difference is that Richardson considered linear response functions, represented by straight lines, and did not take explicitly into account the ultimate limits imposed by economic capacity. He added all arms expenditures of any type, making no distinction between defensive and offensive arms. Also, he began his analysis by assuming various reaction functions and then deriving their implications for an arms race. In this model, these reaction functions are derived from a country's economic structure, from available weapons technologies (defensive or offensive), and from a country's strategic objectives (conquest or defense).

One interesting result from Richardson's analysis might be called the "law of escalation." According to this principle, overreaction leads to unlimited escalation. To state the result more precisely, assume that country X responds to a given amount of arms expenditures by country Y by spending p times as much as country Y, and Y responds to arms expenditures of X by spending q times as much as X. If the product, p.q, is greater than or equal to 1, the arms race will have no finite limit. Richardson concluded that in this case it must either lead to war, or end with the economic ruin of one or both countries. If p.q is less than 1, then the arms expenditures of both countries will reach a finite ceiling, and the arms race will not go out of control.

It is not necessary that *both* sides do not overreact. If one side is sufficiently restrained, it can compensate for a moderate overreaction by the other side. For example, if X spends 50 percent more than Y as a reaction (p = 1.5) and Y spends only half as much as X in reaction (q = 0.5), we obtain p.q = (0.5)(1.5) = 0.75, less than 1, and the mutual arms expenditures will gradually slow down. But if both sides overreact, even only slightly, escalation is inevitable. For example, if both X and Y spend 10 percent more than their opponent as a reaction (i.e., p = q = 1.10), we find p.q = 1.21, greater than 1, and the arms expenditures will keep growing from period to period, without limit.

This law can be applied to many more situations than arms races. We know, for example, that an uncontrolled chain reaction in a nuclear bomb occurs if each atom emits, on the average, more neutrons than it absorbs or that are lost to the outside, resulting in a reaction factor of more than 1. If there is enough absorbing material in between (with a reaction factor of less than 1), the chain reaction can be held under control.

Not only arms expenditures, but hostile acts in general offer a good application of the law of escalation. The Old Testament proposes the rule "an eye for an eye and a tooth for a tooth" (a reaction factor of 1). This is more bellicose than the counsel of the New Testament to practice patience and restraint. But it must be seen as progress over what was once the going practice—two eyes for an eye, etc. The important moral message is "no more than an eye for an eye."

Hitler threatened that he would avenge every British bomb dropped on Germany a hundred-fold. With a reaction factor of 100, it is difficult to prevent escalation. By contrast, the Swiss defense doctrine (General Defense 1973) emphasizes the importance of preventing automatic escalation through appropriate, *not excessive*, but sufficient reactions, if peace is to be kept in the nuclear age. The Yugoslav news agency, commentating on the Israeli air raids on Lebanon in response to the 1972 Munich Olympic killings, stated, "Increased counterterrorism does not eradicate terrorism, but justifies and stirs it up" (Roberts 1976, p. 212). This is not an arbitrary value judgment, but a simple mathematical law. The essence of defense vs. deterrence can be compared to protecting one's eyes in order to keep them, instead of destroying someone else's eyes in retaliation.

To my knowledge, no formal analysis of the arms race has so far made a distinction between offensive and defensive arms. The unit of account has either been military expenditures, or missiles, or numbers of warheads, etc. But to find a way out of the false dilemma between "too much" or "too little" military spending, I consider the distinction between defensive and offensive arms to be crucial. The solution is more defense and less offense, to achieve security without an escalating arms race.

## The Arms Race as a Prisoner's Dilemma

The arms race has often been compared with a "prisoner's dilemma game." A good description of that dilemma, which reflects the essence of many situations in the real world, can be found in Morton Davis (1970, pp. 93ff). Briefly, this dilemma can be illustrated by the following story, from which it got its name. Two prisoners are accused of a bank robbery. If they cooperate and both deny their involvement, they will each be convicted of the minor charge of the illegal possession of arms, which carries a one-year prison sentence. If they both confess to their crime, each is sentenced to five years in prison. But if one confesses and the other denies it, the one who confesses is immediately released because of his assistance in convicting the other. The other is sentenced to ten years in prison, for lying in addition to his crime. Some reflection shows that each of the two prisoners will be tempted to confess, not knowing what the other will do, and will spend five years in prison, even though both would be better off if they denied the charge and were released after one year.

This story is not the most-fortunate illustration of this type of dilemma, because in the optimal solution, the two prisoners would lie and thus violate society's moral code. This may give the wrong connotation that there is something immoral about cooperation or "collusion." Normally, the cooperative solution that yields the better outcome for both parties is in no way detrimental to the rest of society, but is preferable for everyone.

It will be shown here that an arms race with offensive arms does indeed correspond to a prisoner's dilemma, but if cheap and effective defensive arms are available, the dilemma resolves itself.

We simplify in the following by considering only two choices open to each country, either to arm or to disarm. These two choices for each country give rise to four possibilities, listed in Table A.1, for the case of offensive arms.

In the absence of any mutual agreement, X does not know whether Y will arm or disarm. If Y arms, the two options open to X are (1), if it arms, or (3), if it disarms. Since X does not want Y to be able to force it into concessions (outcome 3), it will reluctantly prefer outcome (1) in Table A.1 as the lesser of two evils, even though that means heavy arms expenditures, without any perfect guarantee of security. Thus, in this case, X will arm. If Y disarms, the two options available to X are (2) or (4). X is likely to prefer to be able to force Y into concessions and will not mind the (in this case modest) arms expenditures required. Therefore, regardless of what Y does, X always prefers to arm. By the perfect symmetry of the situation, Y will apply the same considerations and also prefer to arm. The result is outcome (1) in Table A.1, where both countries feel insecure and are burdened with arms spending. But it is clear that instead of (1) both would prefer outcome (4), where both countries are secure without arms spending.

It has sometimes been said that if we could only understand the causes of the arms race, we would be able to solve the problem. But as the above discussion shows, we may perfectly understand the problem and yet be unable to reach the preferred solution.

If the two countries could reach an agreement to disarm, both would be better off. This is the purpose of disarmament negotiations. But with mutual distrust and in the absence of reliable verification, it is difficult to reach agreement. Brams, Davis, and Straffin (1979) have shown that improved technologies for the verification of arms control agreements make such agreements more attractive and are in the interest of both sides.

Charles Osgood (1962) proposes an alternative strategy to help move the world from position (1) to position (4) in Table A.1, in case negotiations are stalemated. He calls it graduated and reciprocated initiatives in tension-reduction (GRIT). Either side would begin with a small step of arms reductions, which do not undermine its security, and wait to see whether the other side responds. Once the step has been reciprocated, a further reduction in tensions could be tried, and so on, to turn the arms race into a "peace race." Such initiatives are certainly welcome and can be attempted without much risk. But the discussion of Table A.1 shows why it may be difficult to succeed along such a path.

**Table A.1   Four Possible Outcomes with Offensive Arms**

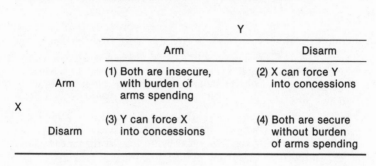

|   |   | Y | |
|---|---|---|---|
|   |   | Arm | Disarm |
| X | Arm | (1) Both are insecure, with burden of arms spending | (2) X can force Y into concessions |
|   | Disarm | (3) Y can force X into concessions | (4) Both are secure without burden of arms spending |

The discussion so far has assumed that the leaders of the two countries X and Y make their choices (to arm or disarm) under the assumption that the other side will not react to what they do. Their decisions are based on a rather short-sighted, or "myopic" way of thinking. Brams and Wittman (1981) have investigated the consequences of a "nonmyopic" analysis that takes into consideration what the next countermove of the opponent might be. In that case, the preferred solution (4) in Table A.1, where both sides disarm, can be a stable equilibrium. Starting in position (4), X might at first prefer to arm and move to position (2) where it can dominate Y. But that is Y's least-preferred position, and Y would then certainly also arm to move to position (1), which is worse for both than (4). Looking ahead at the expected reactions to X's move, X will prefer to remain at the original position (4), where both disarm. So will Y, by symmetry. It appears that this evolution in political thinking still lies ahead of us—if we do not abort evolution before reaching that stage.

An easier path to disarmament is transarmament, a shift from offensive to more defensive arms. Transarmament can be implemented by either side independently, without any reduction of its security. Rather, it will improve a country's own security as well as that of its opponent. The possible outcomes if both countries defend themselves only with defensive arms are shown in Table A.2.

If Y arms itself with purely defensive arms, there is no real or perceived threat to X, and no need for X to respond. X will prefer outcome (3) (disarm) over outcome (1) (arm), to save itself the unnecessary arms expenditures. Similarly, if Y disarms, X cannot gain any advantage over Y by having defensive arms; X cannot force Y into any concessions, and will again choose to disarm, preferring outcome (4) to outcome (2). Regardless of what Y does, X now prefers to disarm. The same consid-

**Table A.2    Four Possible Outcomes with Defensive Arms**

|  |  | Y | |
|---|---|---|---|
|  |  | Arm | Disarm |
| X | Arm | (1) Both are secure, with burden of arms spending | (2) Both are secure; X spends for arms, Y does not |
|  | Disarm | (3) Both are secure; Y spends for arms, X does not | (4) Both are secure without burden of arms spending |

erations apply to Y. Therefore, there is no dilemma here. What each side does, based on its own narrow and short-sighted interest, is also in the best interest of the other.

Let us next consider the mixed case where one side uses offensive, and the other defensive, arms. If country X uses defensive arms, while Y uses offensive arms, the four possible outcomes are shown in Table A.3. In this case, X would prefer to arm if Y does (so that X can defend itself), and to disarm if Y also disarms (because now X has no need to defend itself). Y would prefer to arm if X disarms (Y can dominate X) and to disarm if X arms (Y cannot dominate X). What should they do? What strategic planners typically do in such situations is to perform a conservative "worst-case analysis" (corresponding to what is called a "minimax strategy" in the mathematical theory of games).

If X disarms, the worst that could happen from X's viewpoint is that Y arms and could force X into concessions [outcome (3) in Table A.3]. If X arms, assuming that it has effective defense to protect itself against any potential aggression from Y, X will be secure but burdened with arms spending [outcome (2) in Table A.3]. This is the lesser evil, compared to being threatened by Y. Therefore, X will choose to arm itself defensively.

If Y arms, the best that could happen is that it could force X into concessions, if X disarms [outcome (3) in Table A.3]. But the worst is that Y will be burdened with useless military expenditures, if X arms [outcome (1)]. If Y disarms, it will be secure and not burdened with military expenditures, regardless of what X does. Therefore, Y will prefer to disarm, considering the worst-possible outcome for each of its choices.

The result of this combination of X's and Y's choices will be outcome (2) in Table A.3, where X arms and Y disarms. One may object that if Y disarms, there is no need for X to keep up its defense expenditures, and

**Table A.3    Four Possible Outcomes with Defensive Arms on One Side and Offensive Arms on the Other**

|  |  | Y (offensive arms) | |
|  |  | Arm | Disarm |
| --- | --- | --- | --- |
| X (de-fensive arms) | Arm | (1) Both are secure, but with burden of arms spending | (2) Both are secure, X spends for arms, Y does not |
|  | Disarm | (3) Y can force X into concessions | (4) Both are secure, without burden of arms spending |

X would be better off to disarm also. But the likely consequence would be that then Y would arm itself offensively, and be able to force X into concessions. To guard against that possibility, being averse to risk, X is better off to maintain its defense, unless Y also considers to use only defensive arms.

We can conclude from this that while mutual agreement is sufficient to end the arms race, agreement may not be necessary. If an effective defensive technology can be found, it may bring an end to the arms race, even in the absence of any mutual agreement.

*A Computer Tournament*

Even as long as there is a true prisoner's dilemma situation (such as an arms race with offensive arms), it is possible to elicit cooperation from the other side, if one uses a skillful strategy that rewards cooperation and discourages noncooperation.

Robert Axelrod (1984) has conducted an interesting study, in which he asked game theorists around the world to submit a computer code describing how they would play a sequence of repeated prisoner's dilemma games against a hypothetical opponent. A preview of some of the results has been given by Douglas R. Hofstadter (1983). The programs describe how they would cooperate or defect, depending on the other player's past moves. Table A.4 shows the "payoff matrix." The assigned goal was to score as high an average payoff as possible over the tournament against all other entries.

If the other player has chosen all her moves in advance, or plays randomly (e.g., by flipping a coin to decide her next move), the best one can do is to defect constantly. But if the other player responds to our

**Table A.4    Payoff Matrix for a Prisoner's Dilemma Game**

|  |  | Player B | |
| --- | --- | --- | --- |
|  |  | Cooperates | Defects |
| Player A | Cooperates | (3,3) | (0,5) |
|  | Defects | (5,0) | (1,1) |

Note: The first figure in each cell indicates the payoff to A, the second figure the payoff to B.

moves, we may be able to induce cooperation by the way we react to the other player's past behavior. This would increase the average score of both players.

Axelrod received 62 entries, and had them play against (or "with") each other several thousand rounds of the game on a computer. The winning entry was the simplest of all, a program called "TIT FOR TAT," submitted by Anatol Rapoport. It starts out by cooperating, and then simply repeats what the other player did on the previous move. If he cooperated, he is rewarded with cooperation. If he defected, he is punished with a one-time defection on our part.

Axelrod discovered that the programs that did well all had the following four characteristics in common

1. they never initiated noncooperation;
2. they did not passively accept noncooperation, but retaliated immediately;
3. they did not retaliate excessively and escalate a conflict, but immediately sought renewed cooperation after retaliating once; and
4. they were simple and transparent, so that their strategy was easily recognizable by other players.

TIT FOR TAT has all these four properties. Concerning the last property, Axelrod writes, "Too much complexity can appear to be total chaos. If you are using a strategy that appears random, then you also appear unresponsive to the other player. If you are unresponsive, then the other player has no incentive to cooperate with you. So being so complex as to be incomprehensible is very dangerous."

Programs that sought to exploit other players by cheating them through noncooperation made some short-term gains, but hurt themselves in the long run.

One significant insight provided by this experiment is that the strategies that did best for themselves did not do so by "defeating" other strategies that were submitted. TIT FOR TAT never scored higher than any of the strategies it was playing with, and sometimes scored a bit lower, but not by much. It did well by helping other strategies to do well for themselves at the same time, so that both strategies benefitted from cooperation. The more-aggressive strategies lost points by playing against each other, in mutually destructive games of excessive retaliation and noncooperation.

If the same four principles are applied to issues of defense and national security, they seem eminently sensible. They imply that

1. a country should never initiate war, but seek peaceful relations if at all possible;
2. it should not passively tolerate aggression, but defend itself vigorously if attacked, and only *after* it has been attacked;
3. it should not escalate a war by retaliating excessively, but constantly seek renewed cooperation and reward any sign of cooperation by immediate reciprocity; and
4. it should make its policies very clear and transparent, and not leave others in the dark as to its intentions.

With regard to nuclear weapons, these principles speak for an unambiguous policy of no first use. The only difference is that here we cannot afford to learn from repeated mistakes, as in a computer simulation. All nations must do it right, from the beginning, forever. Fortunately, the real world has available a much richer variety of forms of communication and cooperation than a simple choice between two alternatives.

# Bibliography

Axelrod, Robert. 1984. *The Evolution of Cooperation.* New York: Basic Books.

Barnet, Richard. 1972. *The Roots of War.* New York: Atheneum.

———. 1981. *Real Security.* New York: Simon & Schuster.

Baumol, William J. 1982. "Applied Fairness Theory and Rationing Policy." *American Economic Review* 72, no. 4 (September): 639–51.

Bay, Christian. 1982. "Hazards of Goliath in the Nuclear Age: Need for Rational Priorities in American Peace and Defense Policies." *Alternatives* 8, no. 4: 441–82.

Boulding, Kenneth E. 1962. *Conflict and Defense: A General Theory.* New York: Harper & Row.

———. 1978. *Stable Peace.* Austin: University of Texas Press.

Brams, Steven J., Morton D. Davis, and Philip D. Straffin. 1979. "The Geometry of the Arms Race." *International Studies Quarterly* 23, no. 4: 567–88.

Brams, Steven J., and Donald Wittman. 1981. "Nonmyopic Equilibria." *Conflict Management and Peace Science* 6, no. 1 (Fall): 39–62.

Bueno de Mesquita, Bruce. 1981. *The War Trap.* New Haven: Yale University Press.

Bundy, McGeorge. 1979. "Maintaining Stable Deterrence." *International Security* 3, no. 3: 5–16.

———. 1981. "America in the 80's: Reframing Our Relations with Our Friends and Among Our Allies." Address to the New York University Sesquicentennial Conference, October 16, 1981.

———. 1982. " 'No First Use' Needs Careful Study." *Bulletin of the Atomic Scientists.*

Bundy, McGeorge, George F. Kennan, Robert S. McNamara, and Gerard Smith. 1982. "Nuclear Weapons and the Atlantic Alliance." *Foreign Affairs* 60, no. 4: 753–68.

Calder, Nigel. 1979. *Nuclear Nightmares. An Investigation into Possible Wars.* New York: Viking Press.

Caldicott, Helen. 1981. "Introduction." In Ruth Adams and Susan Cullen, eds., *The Final Epidemic. Physicians and Scientists on Nuclear War.* Chicago: Educational Foundation for Nuclear Science.

Commoner, Barry. 1963. *Science and Survival.* New York: Viking Press.

———. 1976. *The Poverty of Power.* New York: Alfred A. Knopf.

Cox, Arthur. 1981. *Russian Roulette: The Superpower Game.* New York: Times Books.

Davis, Martin. 1970. *Game Theory: A Nontechnical Introduction.* New York: Basic Books.

De Grasse, Robert W. 1983. *Military Expansion, Economic Decline.* New York: Council on Economic Priorities.

Deutsch, Morton. 1983. "The Prevention of World War III: A Psychological Perspective." Presidential address given at the Fifth Annual Meeting of the Society of Political Psychology. *Political Psychology* 4, no. 1: 3–31.

Etzioni, Amitai. 1982. "Toward a Political Psychology of Economics." Address to the Fifth Annual Meeting of the International Society of Political Psychology.

Falk, Richard. 1982. *Normative Initiatives and Demilitarization: A Third System Approach.* Working Paper No. 13, World Order Models Project. New York: Institute for World Order.

Fallows, James. 1981.*National Defense.* New York: Random House.

Fischer, Dietrich. 1981. "Dynamics of an Arms Race with Offensive or Defensive Arms." Discussion Paper No. 81-06. Starr Center for Applied Economics, New York University.

————. 1982. "Invulnerability Without Threat: The Swiss Concept of General Defense." *Journal of Peace Research* 19, no. 3: 205–25. Reprinted in Burns H. Weston, ed., *Toward Nuclear Disarmament and Global Security. A Search for Alternatives.* Boulder, Colo: Westview Press, 1984.

Fischer, Philomena. 1984. "Effects of Self-confrontation Instruction on Students' Value Priorities and Attitude Toward War and Peace." Ph.d. dissertation, Fordham University.

Fisher, Roger. 1981. "Preventing Nuclear War." In Ruth Adams and Susan Cullen, eds., *The Final Epidemic. Physicians and Scientists on Nuclear War.* Chicago: Educational Foundation for Nuclear Science.

Fisher, Roger, and William Ury. 1981. *Getting to Yes: Negotiating Agreement Without Giving In.* Boston: Houghton Mifflin.

Galtung, Johan. 1967. "On the Effects of International Economic Sanctions: The Case of Rhodesia." *World Politics* 19, *no. 3.* Also in Johan Galtung, *Essays in Peace Research,* vol. 5. Copenhagen: Christian Ejlers, 1980. Pp. 117–46.

————. 1968. "On the Strategy of Nonmilitary Defense: Some Proposals and Problems." In Bartels, ed., *Peace and Justice: Unity or Dilemma.* Institute of Peace Research, Catholic University of Nijmegen. Also in Johan Galtung, *Essays in Peace Research,* vol. 2. Atlantic Highlands, N.J.: Humanities Press, 1976. Pp. 378–426.

————. 1975. "Violence, Peace and Peace Research." *Essays in Peace Research,* vol. 1. Atlantic Highlands, N.J.: Humanities Press. Pp. 109–34.

————. 1980. *The True Worlds: A Transitional Perspective.* New York: The Free Press.

————. 1984. *There Are Alternatives! Four Roads to Peace and Security.* Nottingham: Spokesman.

Galtung, Johan, Peter O'Brien, and Roy Preiswerk, eds. 1980. *Self-reliance: A Strategy for Development.* London: Bogle-l'Ouverture Publications Ltd.

General Defense. 1973. "Report of the Federal Council to the Federal Assembly on the Security Policy of Switzerland (Concept of general defense) (of June 27, 1973)." Bern: Zentralstelle für Gesamtverteidigung.

————. 1979. "Interim Report of the Federal Council to the Federal Assembly on the Security Policy of Switzerland (of December 3, 1979)." Bern: Zentralstelle für Gesamtverteidigung.

Grant, James P. 1982. *The State of the World's Children Report 1982/83.* New York: United Nations Children's Fund.

Gray, Colin S., and Keith Payne. 1980. "Victory Is Possible." *Foreign Policy* 39: 14–27.

Ground Zero. 1982. *Nuclear War: What's in It for You*. New York: Pocket Books.

Hofstadter, Douglas R. 1983. "Computer Tournaments of the Prisoner's Dilemma Suggest how Cooperation Evolves." *Scientific American* 248, no. 5 (May).

Hollins, Harry. 1982. "A Defensive Weapons System." *Bulletin of the Atomic Scientists*.

Independent Commission on Disarmament and Security Issues. 1982. *Common Security: A Blueprint for Survival*. New York: Simon & Schuster.

Johansen, Robert C. 1979. *Salt II: Illusion and Reality*. Working Paper No. 9, World Order Models Project. New York: Institute for World Order.

———. 1982. "Building a New International Security Order: Policy Guidelines and Recommendations." In Carolyn M. Stephenson, ed., *Alternative Methods for International Security*. Washington, D.C.: University Press of America. Pp. 47–67.

Kissinger, Henry A. 1979. "The Future of NATO." *Washington Quarterly*, 2, no. 4. Reprinted in Douglas J. Murray and Paul R. Viotti, eds., *The Defense Policies of Nations*. Baltimore: Johns Hopkins University Press, 1982. Pp. 121–25.

Köhler, Gernot, and Norman Alcock. 1976. "An Empirical Table of Structural Violence." *Journal of Peace Research* 12, no. 4: 343–56.

Leontief, Wassily, and Faye Duchin. 1983. *Military Spending: Facts and Figures, Worldwide Implications and Future Outlook*. New York: Oxford University Press.

Lifton, Robert J., and Richard Falk. 1982. *Indefensible Weapons: The Political and Psychological Case Against Nuclearism*. New York: Basic Books.

Lodal, Jan M. 1982. "Finishing START." *Foreign Policy* 48: 66–81.

Lutz, Dieter S. 1981. *Weltkrieg Wider Willen? Die Nuklearwaffen in und für Europa*. Hamburg: Rowohlt.

McNamara, Robert S. 1983. "The Military Role of Nuclear Weapons." *Foreign Affairs* (Fall).

Melman, Seymour. 1983. *Profits Without Production*. New York: Alfred A. Knopf.

Menger, Karl. 1934. *Moral, Wille und Weltgestaltung*. Vienna: Springer-Verlag. Translated as *Morality, Decision and Social Organization*, Dordrecht: D. Reidel, 1974.

Office of Technology Assessment of the U.S. Congress. 1979. *The Effects of Nuclear War*. Totowa, N.J.: Rowman & Allanheld, 1982.

Osgood, Charles E. 1962. *An Alternative to War or Surrender*. Urbana: University of Illinois Press.

Pipes, Richard. 1982. "Why the Soviet Union Thinks It Could Fight and Win a Nuclear War." In Douglas J. Murray and Paul R. Viotti, *The Defense Policies of Nations*. Baltimore: The Johns Hopkins University Press.

Quester, George H. 1977. *Offense and Defense in the International System*. New York: John Wiley & Sons.

Rauschensteiner, M. 1979. *Der Sonderfall — die Besatzungszeit in Oesterreich 1945–55*. Graz.

Richardson, Lewis F. 1960. *Arms and Insecurity: A Mathematical Study of the Causes and Origins of War*. Ed. Nicholas Rashevsky and Ernest Trucco. Chicago: Quadrangle Books.

Roberts, Adam. 1976. *Nations in Arms*. New York: Praeger Publishers.

Sagan, Carl. 1983. "Nuclear War and Climatic Catastrophe." *Foreign Affairs* 62, no. 2, pp. 257–92.

Scheer, Robert. 1982. *With Enough Shovels: Reagan, Bush and Nuclear War*. New York: Random House.

Schell, Jonathan. 1982. *The Fate of the Earth.* New York: Alfred A. Knopf.
Schwarz, Urs. 1980. *The Eye of the Hurricane: Switzerland in World War II.* Boulder, Colo.: Westview Press.
Sharp, Gene. 1973. *The Politics of Nonviolent Action.* Boston: Porter Sargent.
———. 1980. *Social Power and Political Freedom.* Boston: Porter Sargent.
———. 1981. *Making the Abolition of War a Realistic Goal.* Wallach Award Essay. New York: Institute for World Order.
SIPRI. 1982a. *World Armaments and Disarmament: SIPRI Yearbook 1982.* Stockholm International Peace Research Institute.
———. 1982b. *The Arms Race and Arms Control.* Stockholm International Peace Research Institute.
Sivard, Ruth Leger. 1981. *World Military and Social Expenditures.* Leesburg, Va: World Priorities.
Small, Melvin and J. David Singer. 1982. *Resort to Arms: International and Civil Wars, 1816–1980.* Beverly Hills, Calif.: Sage Publications.
Sommer, Mark. 1983. *Beating our Swords into Shields.* Miranda, Calif.: Center for a Preservative Defense.
Taylor, William J. 1982. "The Defense Policy of Sweden." In Douglas J. Murray and Paul R. Viotti, eds., *The Defense Policies of Nations.* Baltimore: Johns Hopkins University Press.
United Nations. 1978. *Economic and Social Consequences of the Arms Race and of Military Expenditures.* United Nations Publications, Sales No. E.78 IX.1.
———. 1980. *Interrelations: Resources, Environment, Population and Development.* United Nations Publication, Sales No. E.80. II.A.8.
U.S. Bureau of the Census. 1981. *Statistical Abstracts.* Washington, D.C.: U.S. Dept. of Commerce.
U.S. Conference of Catholic Bishops. 1983. "Pastoral Letter on War, Armaments and Peace." *Origins* 13, no. 1 (May 19).
U.S. Department of Defense. 1982. *Procurement Programs.* Washington, D.C.: U.S. Dept. of Defense.
Wilkes, Owen, and Nils Petter Gleditsch. 1979. *Technical Intelligence Stations in Norway.* Oslo: Rosenkrantz.
The World Bank. 1982. *World Development Report, 1982.* New York: Oxford University Press.
Zimmerman, Charles, and Milton Leitenberg. 1979. "Hiroshima Lives on." *Mazingira* 9. United Nations Environment Program.
Zuckerman, Solly. 1982. *Nuclear Illusion and Reality.* New York: Viking Press.

# Index